Ronald and Tim McCoy. This photograph was taken in July 1977, six months before Tim McCoy's death. Copyright © 1977 by Terrence Moore. Courtesy of Terrence Moore.

Tim McCoy Remembers the West

AN AUTOBIOGRAPHY

by Tim McCoy with Ronald McCoy

Preface to the Bison Book Edition by Ronald McCoy

University of Nebraska Press
Lincoln and London

Copyright © 1977 by Tim McCoy and Ronald McCoy
Preface to the Bison Book Edition © 1988
by the University of Nebraska Press
All rights reserved
Manufactured in the United States of America

First Bison Book printing: 1988
Most recent printing indicated by the first digit below:
1   2   3   4   5   6   7   8   9   10

Library of Congress Cataloging-in-Publication Data
McCoy, Tim.
    Tim McCoy remembers the West: an autobiography / by Tim McCoy
with Ronald McCoy; preface to the Bison book edition by Ronald
McCoy.
    p.   cm.
    "Bison."
    Reprint. Originally published: 1st ed. Garden City, N.Y.: Doubleday,
1977.
    Bibliography: p.
    ISBN 0-8032-3113-X.   ISBN 0-8032-8155-2 (pbk.)
    1. McCoy, Tim.   2. Pioneers—West (U.S.)—Biography.   3. West
(U.S.)—History—1848–1950.   I. McCoy, Ronald.   II. Title.
F595.M14 1988   CIP 87–30041
978'.03'0924—dc19
[B]

Reprinted by arrangement with Ronald McCoy

The buffalo-hunting warriors of the Great Plains, who fought a good fight for the way of life they loved and laid aside their weapons only to save the helpless ones about them;

The late Hugh Lenox Scott, Major General, West Point class of 1876, veteran of the Nez Percé, Spanish-American, and Philippine wars, Chief of Staff of the Army, soldier, scholar, linguist and historian, who taught me that the way to discover the answer to a question is to command sufficient information to ask the proper question;

And to Inga, who always thought it should have been called *Irish Tom's Canary.*

Contents

Preface to the Bison Book Edition by Ronald McCoy

This book is the autobiography of my father, Tim McCoy. Here, traveling along what he called the Old Trails, you will find recollections associated with his life as a man of the West: cowboy, rancher, intimate of oldtime Indian warriors, cavalry officer, silent and talkie movie star, consummate showman. It is a saga that crisscrosses geographic, temporal, and personal frontiers.

For my father, life's pleasure consisted largely of people encountered along Old Trails and the nurturing friendship of stalwart companions. Such memories were as important to him as the fulfillment of dreams.

Late in life my father was asked whether as the last of the illustrious Big Four of Hollywood's early Westerns—Tom Mix, Ken Maynard, Hoot Gibson, and Tim McCoy—he felt any sense of victory for outliving his contemporaries and qualifying as "a survivor in every aspect of that word."

"No, I have no sense of victory," he replied, "but there is a little bit of satisfaction in realizing that I am one of the few men that I know of who has done everything he ever wanted to in life. I have no unfulfilled ambitions. I have no frustrations. Any time an idea ever came to me I made it come true."[1]

Like anybody, my father experienced his share of disappointment. The collapse of "Colonel Tim McCoy's Real Wild West and Rough Riders of the World," which he took out on the road in 1938, was a crushing blow.[2] But his personal credo echoed that of another legend, baseball great Satchel Paige: "Never look back; something might be gaining on you."

The role that fate alloted Tim McCoy lay within that arena where dreams are formed and attained, a place inhabited by those who contribute to others' positive visions. That was the sort of magic he worked for an entire generation of children in the United States and everywhere else within the the reach of Hollywood's celluloid fantasies from 1928 to 1942 and beyond.[3]

Part of the allure of Western films has been explained by film historians George N. Fenin and William K. Everson, who point out that

> despite its indigenous American scenes, plots and characters, the Western is nevertheless a universal appeal to the universal imagination. It is the only aspect of the American cinema that is readily understood in Rome, Moscow, Tokyo, Bangkok, Sydney, Cairo, and Buenos Aires. It is an expression of the hopes and dreams of every man, as he struggles to assert his fundamental right to pursue peace and happiness, free from crooks on both sides of the law, and longing to look upon his fellow men as brothers.[4]

Just what were Tim McCoy, the other members of the Big Four, and those who followed in the trail they blazed trying to accomplish? This is a question that filmographer Jon Tuska has attempted to answer: "When you talk to men like Colonel Tim McCoy or John Ford, who straddled the silent and sound eras, . . . it wouldn't surprise you to learn that the concern has never been to depict the West as it once was, but rather to interpret its spirit and give it a new meaning. For such men, the Western has represented an enduring myth and they have been part of a living tradition bound up in the articulation of that myth."[5]

Yet recogniton of the fact that he was part of a mythology machine did not prevent my father from wishing for less repetitiveness in the film business. "Westerns became stereotyped," he once remarked to an interviewer about something he found himself powerless to control. "They looked as though they had been cut out with cookie cutters. The truth about the real West was twisted to conform to the writer's preconceptions, and when historical figures were used there was so much fiction they could have been anybody. However, you always have to remember motion pictures are not made to serve as documents of history. Movies are entertainment, but even so, I've always maintained you can give audiences authenticity with the entertainment."[6]

Many of the Tim McCoy films were visually different. After the mid-1930s his customary attire was basic black: black boots, black trousers, black shirt, black hat. Why? "Because everyone else was wearing white," he often responded, laughing. This daring quality of darkness cloaking a Western hero made an indelible impression on many viewers, including Fenin and Everson:

> McCoy's somber appearance in black made him seem like Nemesis in person, for outlaws in any case. He would walk slowly into a saloon, letting the swing doors flap behind him, and would stand there silently surveying the scene, glowering grimly at any obvous renegade, and flashing his eyes from side to side in a manner that became almost his trademark. Whether the outlaws accepted him as friend or foe, from that moment on, they knew they had met their master![7]

One fan, writer James Horwitz, a self-proclaimed Front Row Kid, attempted to track down his Western film idols in the mid-1970s. The result was *They Went Thataway,* an engaging book in which Horwitz touches on the effect Tim McCoy had on many young people. He was, Horwitz reflected, "a Cowboy hero with his own unique personality and image. Not to be mistaken for anybody else. If William S. Hart was the 'good badman.' And Tom Mix was the Rhinestone-and-Neon Cowboy. If Ken Maynard was the Daredevil. And Hoot Gibson the Ragtime Clown. Then Colonel Tim McCoy' s image would be the 'Man of Destiny.' In basic black. He wasn't every Front Row Kid's idea of a Cowboy-Hero. Only the smart ones'."[8] Horwitz remembered a man of style. It was "the military bearing and the air of an aristocrat" that helped create the Tim McCoy image, which Horwitz has characterized as "the straight and immaculate lightning-fast-on-the-draw Good Guy. The icy stare that froze the hearts and gun hands of the Bad Guys. The sideways glance, almost a twinkle in his eye, that told the Bad Guys they didn't have a chance and it would be wise to throw in their hands before he made them look foolish."[9]

Many of my father's hundred or so films were twentieth-century miracle plays, in which all that was right and good confronted and resoundingly defeated all that was evil and just plain wrong.[10] Tim McCoy never took those films seriously, at least not in the sense that he believed he was actually Lightning Bill Carson or any of the other characters he played on the screen. But it must also be said that in many ways he played himself, breathing life into his own vision of what a cowboy should be, of how a chivalric knight of the plains ought to behave. Thus, he never failed to pay attention to his status as a role model for impressionable youth.

The publication of *Tim McCoy Remembers the West* was set in motion by Paul Dyck, an artist and ethnologist who lives in Arizona's Verde River Valley. My father was impressed by the quality and extent of Paul's superb collection of Plains Indian artifacts from the nineteenth century and earlier. Eventually, this friend's dream of building a world-class museum to house that collection became a vision shared by my father. Appropriately enough, it was Dyck who in 1971 suggested that my father's life would make a good book.

In the beginning the process of putting the book together seemed simple enough: ask questions, preserve the answers on tape, transcribe those tapes, and work the transcriptions into a narrative. But my father was then eighty and spent ten or eleven months of each year making personal appearances in the U.S. and Canada. Each day he moved to a different town, and although Tim McCoy remained the gallant trouper he had been since the 1920s, it was a tough life for a man of his age.

Indeed, the book's completion lay another six years off and the bulk of the tapes were not recorded until after my father retired from the road in 1974. Only when he hung up his spurs did he begin living full-time in the beautiful Spanish Territorial home he had built in the early 1960s outside Nogales, a town on the Arizona-Sonora border. For the first time in his life, Tim McCoy found himself at loose ends with absolutely nothing to do. He desperately needed a project with which he could become involved. Thus, during 1975–76 we resumed our taping sessions.

My father searched through a voluminous collection of photographs, manuscripts, and notes.[11] This helped trigger recollections; many were taped, some written, most made just in passing. I then wrote a narrative based on those recollections. (My father was a raconteur of truly classic proportions, but early on we learned that what came across as a marvelous story when related orally did not necessarily translate well into the printed word.) Finally, he read, edited, and approved the manuscript.

Tim McCoy's was not only a good life but a relatively long one and a question that inevitably arose involved determining which episodes to include in the book and which to leave out. It may seem odd, for example, that this volume deals more with the real West than the reel West. My father is, after all, probably best remembered for the Western films in which he starred between 1928 and 1942. But he did not want this to be a book about his filmmaking days.

In fact, in some ways he did not even feel this needed to be a book about him. Notice, for example, that the existence of his children—two sons, Gerry and D'Arcy, and a daughter, Marguerite, from his first marriage and another two boys, myself and my brother Terry, from his second—a youthful singing career gone awry in New York, and more is either glossed over or not dealt with at all in *Tim McCoy Remembers the West* [12] The self-editing process began and ended, naturally enough, with my father and it will become clear to the reader that the aspects of life he felt warranted preservation concerned his memories of colorful people. Indeed, *Tim McCoy Remembers the West* is exactly the sort of book its title says it is: Tim McCoy's recollection of the West he knew so well.

Perhaps some things should be said about the life of Tim McCoy in his later years, at the time this book was written and in the months that followed.

He spent most of his time at home near Nogales. Almost all his contemporaries were gone, but he visited with friends when they came, especially Tom Wentworth, who ran a lumberyard in Nogales and with whom many happy times were shared between 1962 and 1978. He also passed countless hours at the Cavern, a restaurant across the line—as those of us from the border country say—in Mexico. The Cavern, chiseled out of a cave, had been a favorite haunt since the 1930s and the resident mariachi band specialized in singing a song called "Dos Horas de Balazos" ("Two Hours of Shooting"). It describes the visit of a young man to a movie theater where he watches cowboys on the screen shoot for two hours without reloading their pistols. The song's chorus consists of the names of cowboy greats: "Buck Jones, Tom Mix, Bill Boyd, Tim McCoy." The name of Tim McCoy came out as a sleek, elongated sound: "Tim McCooooooooooooooy!'" So Tim McCoy sat in the Cavern, listened to himself immortalized by a Mexican bard, sipped turtle soup, ate broiled sea bass, and felt utterly content.

He also read incessantly. My father's taste in literature ran toward narratives and novels rooted in history. He was interested in the Civil War, though the Revolutionary War and Napoleonic Europe also commanded attention. He could not pass up rereading one of Kenneth Roberts's fictionalized sagas of early America. Poetry held great attraction for him, and his own efforts along that line were obviously influenced by the work of Rudyard Kipling, a poet for whom he held particular esteem.

Tim McCoy was, at the beginning and up until the end, a dreamer for whom history revealed the elements of enjoyment. I can hear him yet, running me as a child through the paces of a serious but lightly administered history lesson. Each evening he covered a different topic. One night we talked of his old friend Emmett Dalton and the disastrous attempt he and his brothers and a couple of friends made to rob two banks simultaneously in Coffeyville, Kansas, back in 1892. Another night he helped me memorize the names of the tribes of the Iroquois Confederacy. Some evenings he played King, my mother assuming the role of Queen, to me as Sir Mud Face and my brother as Sir Pie Face in the glittering make-believe world of secret passwords and lurking dragons embodied by one of his better creations: the land of mystery and wonder his imagination bequeathed to those who qualified as Knights of the Mystic Circle.

Later, my father and I engaged in that special brand of verbal jousting and emotional combat which besets many fathers and their sons. But as I grew older we ceased assaulting one another for what we were not and then I began appreciating him for what he was, for the same qualities that so impressed Jon Tuska during interviews he had with my father in the early 1970s. As Tuska wrote:

> He has what few other men, younger or older, have been granted: he is a wise man. There is about him, about his person, his sharp memory, his straight posture and strong face, a magnificence that is only to be found among those who have lived both wisely and well. He looks upon life and the men he has known with a profundity, understanding, and sympathy that marks him as a very special person . . . . [Tim McCoy] carries with him the burden and the sagacity, most of all the freedom, of one who took a chance, did what his inner promptings told him to do, and who, as his reward, is both fortunate and assured that he has given to the world and to life as much as he has asked from them.[13]

One afternoon toward the end of 1977 a package arrived from Harold Kuebler, our amiable and relentlessly helpful editor at Doubleday. Inside was an advance copy of *Tim McCoy Remembers the West*.

"Well, here's to life," my father said softly that night, toasting the volume with a glass of champagne.

He examined the book's cover. The jacket illustration, inspired by his portrait at the Cowboy Hall of Fame in Oklahoma City, depicted my father in a series of frozen frames on a reel of film.

"See how the picture comes up into focus and then dims?" he asked. "Just like me: fading away."

Our last trip together was to Los Angeles in November 1977, where my father gave interviews in connection with the publication of *Tim McCoy Remembers the West*. Upon our return home he talked of plans for a journey to Wyoming the next year. He always retained his taste for travel: a journey to the Irish birthplace of his father, for example, or trekking up the Bozeman Trail in Wyoming and Montana. The summer of 1978, he hoped, would be the time for him to visit the site of Arapaho chief Goes in Lodge's grave in Wyoming and fulfill a vow he speaks of toward the end of his book.

But time was running out. Tim McCoy was eighty-six years old. His mind remained clear, but he was trapped inside an elderly man's body. "I just can't believe this is me," he said one night, undressing for bed.

"Inside here," he pointed to the side of his head, "I'm still a young man, still the fellow I've always been."

Early in January 1978 my father, suffering from congestive heart failure, entered the military hospital at Fort Huachuca, Arizona, an important cavalry post during the days of the western frontier. And there, on January 29, a beautiful though chilled Sunday, he died. He rests today with my mother, Inga, at Mount Olivet Cemetery in Saginaw, Michigan, beside the graves of his Irish immigrant parents.

.

The republication of *Tim McCoy Remembers the West* is a gratifying event because it allows Colonel Tim McCoy to make what his mentor Buffalo Bill Cody might have described as yet another final farewell tour. This reappearance was aided by the prompting of Aaron and Ruth Cohen of Guidon Books in Scottsdale, Arizona. Experiencing difficulty obtaining the out-of-print edition for clients, they approached the University of Nebraska Press. The result is the book you are now reading.

But the reappearance of *Tim McCoy Remembers the West* is also accompanied by a sad sense of a world left somewhat empty by my father's eternal absence. Yet I still feel able almost to talk to him, observing in my mind the ruddy, determined face of perhaps the finest gentleman, certainly the greatest romantic, I will ever know.

Tim McCoy was a man from a different time who outlived that time, survived into ours, and then traveled on. But he will forever permit us entry into his world through this book, in which it remains possible to revisit some of the highlights along the Old Trails of a life he lived so well and through which he enriched so many other lives. I shall always be grateful to him for taking the time to share those memories.

Anything more that might need to be said has, in fact, already been set forth: by Tim McCoy, in the pages that follow.

NOTES

1. Darryl Ponicsan, "High Eagle: The Many Lives of Colonel Tim McCoy," *American Heritage*, vol. 28, no. 4 (June 1977): 54.

2. For that last of the oldtime Wild West shows see Fred D. Pfening, Jr., *Col. Tim McCoy's Real Wild West and Rough Riders of the World* (Columbus, Ohio: Pfening and Snyder: 1955).

3. For Tim McCoy's movie career see Jon Tuska's four-part piece, "In Retrospect: Tim McCoy," *Views & Reviews Magazine*, vol. 2, nos. 1–4 (1970–71), and his *The Filming of the West* (Garden City, N.Y.: Doubleday, 1976).

4. George N. Fenin and William K. Everson, *The Western: From Silents to the Seventies* (New York: Grossman, 1973), p. 379.

5. Jon Tuska, "The American Western Cinema: 1903–Present," *Focus on the Western*, ed. Jack Nachbar (Englewood Cliffs, N.J.: Prentice-Hall, 1974), pp. 26–27.

6. Anthony Thomas, "Tim McCoy," *Films in Review*, vol. 19, no. 4 (April 1968): 221–22.

7. Fenin and Everson, p. 187.

8. James Horwitz, *They Went Thataway* (New York: E. P. Dutton, 1976), p. 97.

9. Ibid., p. 103.

10. For lists of Tim McCoy's films see Jack Spears, "Tim McCoy's Films," *Films in Review*, vol. 19, no. 4 (April 1968): 228–30 and Karl Thiede, "Tim McCoy Filmography," *Views & Reviews Magazine*, vol. 2, no. 4 (Spring 1971): 42–47, 96. Spear lists 96 films, Thiede 91. Setting aside *The Covered Wagon* (Famous Players-Lasky 1923), *The Thundering Herd* (FP-L1925) and *The Vanishing American* (FP-L 1926)—in none of which Tim McCoy starred—and including four films listed by Spear but not by Thiede leaves a total of 93 films in which he took a starring role. Two of these, *The Indians Are Coming* (Universal 1930) and *Heroes of the Flames* (Universal 1931), were twelve-part serials. So my father's standard answer of "about a hundred" accurately dealt with the question, "How many films did you make?"

11. The bulk of that material is in the Colonel Tim McCoy Collection, Western History Research Center, The University of Wyoming (Laramie). Indian-related documents and photographs are at the Paul Dyck Foundation-Research Institution of American Indian Culture, Rimrock, Arizona.

12. The brief singing career is mentioned in Agnes Wright Spring, "Colonel Tim McCoy: Thirty Years under Crossed Sabers," *Frontier Times*, vol. 46, no. 3, NS 77 (April–May 1972): 19.

13. Tuska, "In Retrospect: Tim McCoy," pt. 4, 40.

Preface

I have lately had cause to consider the words uttered by Augustus
Thomas, a turn-of-the-century New York playwright, who, when
asked for some helpful advice by an acquaintance preparing to
write an autobiography, replied: "Grow up quickly."

Most of us have after all had similarly prosaic experiences. And
while it is true that such experiences are a part of the making of
childhood and adolescent life, lengthy recitations of them are capable of congealing to such an extent that the reader may be confronted with an insurmountable palisade of boredom. So, in an attempt to heed the advice of Augustus Thomas, I have endeavored
here to grow up quickly while covering at reasonable length those
aspects of my youth, as well as of my later life, which, even in the
context of the times, were a little out of the ordinary: my association with veterans of the Civil War, my journey to the last frontier, cowboying days, encounters with desperadoes, contact with
the Indians, Hollywood during its Golden Age, the circus, and the
like.

I have also attempted to refrain from offering the reader too
much unsolicited advice, personal prescriptions or bits of my private cosmology. This is not, after all, a dissertation on the subject
of Time and Space. Instead, I hope it will be accepted with the
spirit in which it has been written and regarded simply as a narrative chronicling some of the colorful events in my life and some of
the individuals it has been my privilege to know through the
years.

It is my intention that as this narrative is passed along, you
might find a place within your heart for people who, at least on

paper, live yet. All of them, long-time resident and newly arrived, good guys and bad guys, cowboys and Indians, starlets and soldiers, had something to say and they said it as well as they could.

I hope that the relating of these experiences will give you, the reader, some pleasure, a little amusement and, perhaps, a certain insight; for those are the things I derived from the living of them.

Tim McCoy

Los Arcos
Nogales, Arizona
May 1977

Acknowledgments

As the secondary author, compiler and collator of this book, I am indebted to a number of people who illuminated certain aspects of my father's life for me. In various ways they helped make this book possible.

First, of course, is my father, Tim McCoy, whose life this book is about and who was most patient in giving me an education in topics not taught in schools. My respect for him has been immeasurably deepened.

Paul and Jean Dyck of Rimrock, Arizona, provided encouragement, inspiration and friendship in abundance. The initial impetus for this book came from them and they never wavered in their wholehearted support. Also, they gave me a free rein to explore the incomparable Plains Indian material contained within the Paul Dyck Research Foundation so that I might have a fuller appreciation of the significance of my father's life among the Arapahoes.

Dr. Arthur Woodward, formerly with the Heye Foundation Museum of the American Indian and past Curator of Ethnology and Anthropology at the Los Angeles County Museum; Michael Harrison, formerly with the United States Park Service; Kathryn Wright of the Billings *Gazette*; Robert McCraken of the Cheyenne (Wyoming) Newspapers, Inc.; Hugh Knoeffel of *Northern Wyoming Daily News*; Virginia Trenholm, author of *The Arapahoes—Our People*; Jon Tuska, author of *The Filming of the West*; Dick Frost of the Buffalo Bill Historical Center, Cody, Wyoming; Dean Krakel, Director of the National Cowboy Hall of Fame; Howard Strickling, former Director of Publicity at

Metro-Goldwyn-Mayer; Bill Barton of the Wyoming State Archives; Rep. Clarence Pierce of Vaiden, Mississippi; Pius and Mary Moss, Ethel Potter, Mike Goggles, Jr., Ike and Agnes Bell, Jess and Esther Miller, Will C'Hair, Suzanna Behan, Mike Brown, John Lee Whiteman, Billy Thunder and Father John J. Killoren, S.J., all of Wind River Reservation, were free with encouragement and advice.

Permission to photograph the elkhide the Wind River warriors painted for my father was graciously given by the Proctor family. The photographs themselves were provided by the Paul Dyck Research Foundation.

All other photographs, unless otherwise noted, are from my father's private collection.

The accounts of the Battle of the Little Big Horn given to my father by White Man Runs Him, Water Man and Left Hand first appeared in Colonel W. A. Graham's classic study, *The Custer Myth* (Stackpole, 1953). These accounts have been abbreviated for this book and are included through the courtesy of the publisher.

Harold Kuebler, our editor at Doubleday, has been a most constructive critic, helping to make this book a more readable work today than it was through its previous drafts and various incarnations.

Finally, there is my wife Elizabeth. For what she did and had to abide with during the process of putting this book together—reading, proofing, making suggestions and, among other things, thongs—there can be no earthly reward.

Ronald McCoy

Tim McCoy Remembers the West

Prologue

Yellow Calf, the widely respected Medicine Man of Wyoming's Wind River Arapahoes, rose from his sitting position, carefully adjusted the dark blue blanket around his 260-pound frame and began the first oration of the evening's council. The subject under discussion was whether any of my Arapaho friends would accompany me to England for the purpose of promoting *The Covered Wagon,* a silent-film Western epic, which was scheduled to open at London's Pavilion Theatre in September 1923, six weeks hence. The offer from Famous Players-Lasky, the film's production company, was clear: the Indians would board the White Star Line's S.S. *Cedric* at New York, sail to England, have their expenses covered and, for appearing in a prologue to the film, as they had done recently in Hollywood, receive eight dollars a day—money they could send to their families, who would otherwise have been dependent upon the government's niggardly dole. At the end of six months, they would be transported back to their reservation. That, the old warriors present in the council tipi agreed, was fine.

But, as Yellow Calf explained in signs as well as in English, for he was one of the few former buffalo hunters who could speak in the white man's tongue, there was a problem.

"It bothers me to go across the Big Water," he said, looking directly across the campfire to where I was sitting cross-legged on the ground with several of the old men, and giving me a penetrating stare. "I have talked with many Sioux who went over to this far country with Buffalo Bill. They tell me that when you take this big canoe it goes so far out onto the water that when you look back, there is no land and when you look ahead, there is no

land. They also tell me that the land you will be going to is a
small island."

Sighing, he spread his hands out in front of him as though be-
seeching me to answer, and asked, "What is to prevent the big
canoe from missing the tiny island and falling off the other side?"

He paused, as though waiting for my answer, which, as all present knew, could not be given in council until the elders who
chose to speak had done so. "No, High Eagle, you ask too much
of us."

So much for securing Yellow Calf's blessing.

Then another fellow stood, the antagonistic Broken Horn, and,
as usual, the stoop-shouldered, bowlegged, sour little man had a
detrimental story ready to spring from his lips. The fact that he
had long before made up his mind to stay put in Wyoming dis-
suaded him not one bit from lobbying against the proposal. If everybody stayed, then nobody would appear to be afraid.

"You know," he said with a scowl and in the high-pitched war-
ble used by the horseback Indians when giving a formal speech,
all the while gesturing graphically with signs, "you get in that big
canoe and pretty soon it goes up and down. You, also, go up and
down. You throw up so much that you die. Then the white man
throws you into the Big Water. How do you find the trail to the
Great Mystery when you are at the bottom of the Big Water?"

Prompted by the words of Yellow Calf and Broken Horn, most
of the old men were nodding their understanding and agreement.
I had not expected such strong opposition to my request.

As Wolf Moccasin prepared to stand up and further damn the
expedition, Goes In Lodge, whom I had known well for over a
decade, my closest friend among the Arapahoes and the man who
called me "brother," invited me to step outside with him.

Standing by the entrance in the cold night air, the eighty-year-
old former buffalo hunter, an eagle feather secured in his scalp
lock and an expression of quiet bemusement etched across his
lean and powerful face, pulled some paper from his soft leather
tobacco pouch and rolled a cigarette.

"Are you sure," he asked in signs, leaning toward me for a light,
"that this is a good thing?"

I nodded and replied, "If it were a bad thing, do you think I would ask you, my brother, to go?"

He puffed on his tobacco for a bit, smiled, fidgeted with a loose red ribbon on one of his long braids, tossed his cigarette aside and crushed the butt with the heel of his moccasin.

Back inside the tipi, we sat together and listened to Wolf Moccasin finish his speech. He had gone clear back to the time the Arapahoes were camped on White River, told everyone of the coups he had counted and the battles he had fought in his many years, the number of Crows he had dispatched to the Great Mystery and, when he finally found his way back to the announced subject of the council, cried, "I say, 'No'!"

As Wolf Moccasin sat down heavily and retreated into a private reverie, Goes In Lodge dropped his tattered red blanket and slowly got to his feet. Though he was not a chief, he was respected and his judgment was trusted by the members of the small group of surviving old-time warriors.

"You Arapahoes," he said in a reproachful tone while his hands, constantly in motion, made the signs for the spoken words, "are like small children. That which you do not understand frightens you. I have not been across the Big Water and, maybeso, I am scared, too." He paused, proudly raised himself to his full height and stared at me intently.

"It is as though the night is upon my eyes. I cannot see what lies ahead. But," he said, pointing a long, bony finger toward me and smiling confidently, "if my brother, High Eagle, will take me by the hand and lead me along, I will follow. For I know everything will be *ethiti*—good."

He sat down with an expression of satisfaction upon his face and allowed the message to sink into the assembly.

Then Red Pipe, a six-and-a-half-foot-tall warrior, whose face seemed chiseled from the most resistant stone, and who had been smoking his pipe, a long, wooden stem wrapped in colored porcupine quills leading to the holy catlinite bowl, stood up. As the light from the fire mingled with the dancing shadows in the council tipi, I could see quite clearly the craters in his stone mask, pockmarks from one of the white man's gifts to the old warriors:

the scourge of smallpox. Gazing at his fellow tribesmen he proclaimed in a gravelly voice, "*Nishkahai!* Let's go!"

As these words were echoed by the supportive murmurs of other Arapahoes, Goes In Lodge reached over and patted my hand.

Reminiscing about the decision my Arapaho friends took that evening well over half a century ago, I have often thought that their decision was as difficult to make as my own had been when I ran away from school in Chicago to try and become as one with my heroes of that time, the cowboys. Indeed, at that time my future prospects were probably even more in doubt than theirs.

But I am moving ahead of my story and as the King of Hearts explained to the questioning White Rabbit in one of my favorite childhood books, *Alice's Adventures in Wonderland*, "Begin at the beginning . . . and go on till you come to the end: then stop." And so I hope the reader will bear with me if I unfold my story at the beginning; for it is a good place to begin.

CHAPTER ONE

Beginnings

My first appearance in this world was on April 10, 1891, in the town of Saginaw, which is located on the lower peninsula of the state of Michigan a short distance from Lake Huron. I was the youngest of three brothers and three sisters. My parents were born in Ireland, Cathrin Fitzpatrick coming from Johnstown, County Kilkenny, and Timothy McCoy from Glyn, County Limerick.

I have seen the remnants of the place where my father was born. The site is on a lush slope which rolls down to the River Shannon and a long way from "Amerikay." In 1848, the English provided free passage for those Irish willing to emigrate during the time of the Great Hunger and it was from the banks of the River Shannon that he, then three years of age, and his family boarded a sailing ship bound for Canada.

After only a few months in Canada, the McCoy family slipped across the border into northern New York State, where there were few, if any, immigration officials, and settled among a community of immigrants who spoke only Gaelic.

When he was sixteen, my father enlisted in the Union Army to fight in the Civil War but did not see any action. However, as an active member of the Fenian Brotherhood, an underground Irish independence movement, he was one of two hundred men who, on July 1, 1866, invaded Canada through Buffalo, New York. Their banner was a green flag with a golden harp and their plan was to conquer that colony of Empire, open negotiations with the British and exchange possession of Canada for a free Erin.

They captured abandoned Fort Erie and whipped the Queen's

Own Rifles, a ragtag militia outfit. The Fenians rolled along somewhat spasmodically until the United States government, under heavy pressure from Great Britain, directed General Meade, the victor at Gettysburg and himself a Fenian sympathizer, to cut the Irish lines of supply. The invasion had lasted three days and, aside from my father's acquiring a bullet wound in the leg and making his way back to the States in a stolen rowboat (he was then twenty-one), all that ever came of this escapade was material for another Irish lament of defeat.

My mother made her way to America about 1870, when she was in her early twenties, and she and my father were married shortly afterward. At that time, he was attempting to become something of a lumberman, buying wholesale and selling retail. When his business interests collapsed and vanished, along with most everybody else's, during the Great Panic of 1873, she provided him with a steadying influence. Quietly but firmly she guided each of us, including my father, and desired only that her children be happy, if possible, and honest in all dealings and at all times. It seems strange that while she was a young woman when she came to America, and my father had actually been raised in this country, he always seemed more Irish to me, though I imagine that when she was young she must have been the typical colleen: dainty, pretty, with dark auburn hair, a rosy complexion and an ever present twinkle in her eye.

My father, to whom I was most closely attached, was the chief of Saginaw's police during the time I was growing up. Our house at 1008 McCoskrey Street was a large, rambling and comfortable two-story building. Our lights were lit by gas, our Christmas trees had burning candles attached to the branches and our plumbing consisted of an outhouse back by the barn where a team of horses, a carriage and a milk cow were kept.

On winter evenings I would lie on my stomach behind the nickel-trimmed wood-burning stove in the living room and listen to the stories of our neighbors, particularly Mrs. Murray, a local wag who talked about everything from leprechauns to Michigan's frontier days. She had lived in far-flung settlements deep in the timber country and remembered "wild" Chippewa Indians coming to her door for handouts of tobacco, coffee, molasses and sugar. Sometimes after listening to her stories I was afraid to go upstairs to bed. But when the time came, I went out to the kitchen, where glazed paving bricks were heated and waiting on the back of the stove. After wrapping the hot bricks in a woolen blanket, I carried them upstairs and laid them at the foot of my bed, where they remained throughout the night and kept me warm.

Ours was a home filled with warmth and affection, and my family orientation, as might be expected, was nationalistically Irish and devoutly Catholic. Over the years, I resigned myself to the former and thought my way out of the latter, though I remember with bitterness not being allowed to join the Young Men's Christian Association because of my religion. I also recall with equal parts of fear and amusement the American Protective Association —which we promptly nicknamed "Apes"—and their wild assertions that the cellar of our church was stocked with guns and ammunition in preparation for the day when the Pope, with a regal nod and a sly wink, would give the signal for a Roman rebellion.

In the days of the great timber barons, Saginaw was the hub of the Michigan lumber industry. The Saginaw River, with its tributaries, the Bad, Cass, Flint, Tittabawassee and Shiawassee, ran far up into the virgin timberlands and formed a natural, eight-hundred-mile-long highway over which logs were brought down to the sawmills in Saginaw. We were taught in school, and had no reason to doubt, that the Saginaw had more logs floated down it than any other river in the world.

In wintertime, when the snow was heavy and thick in the forests, tough lumberjacks went up into the timberlands and cut down the trees with axes and two-man saws. The logs were wrapped securely with heavy chains and attached to halters fastened onto horses or oxen and then dragged out to the riverbank. When the ice melted in spring, the lumberjacks rolled the logs into the river and the wood meandered its way down to the Saginaw mills.

The men who had been lumberjacks during wintertime became river hogs in spring, riding downstream atop the logs. They kept the wood from jamming the river by pushing with their peaveys

and cant hooks, which were, basically, pikes fashioned out of hick-
ory or ash with barbed steel tips mounted at the end.

Those lumberjacks were a picturesque bunch. Their trousers
were cut off at the knees and they wore calf-high boots with sharp
hobnails on the soles to keep from slipping off the logs. The most
colorful of the lot, by far, were the French Canadians, who wore
betasseled sashes across their bellies and red, green, blue or yellow
stocking caps cocked rakishly over one eye. They were the real-life
inspirations for the legendary Paul Bunyan as well as the French
Canadians' favorite, Pete Porou of Pea Soup Lake, another larger-
than-life, super he-man hero of the northern woods. "*I em,*" a
lumberjack looking for a laugh or a fight would challenge in a
gravelly voice, "*Pete Porou, en I cam frahm Pea Zoup Lak!*"

The French Canadians, whom I saw frequently in my youth,
served as the butt for innumerable jokes which played on their
struggle to master the English language and which, more often
than not, they had created and delighted in retelling. "*Wazz the
matta, Marie, you got no ears, you can't see?*" Or the story of the
French-Canadian fishermen in a boat which, during the night,
slips its anchor and drifts downriver: "*Hey, Lou-ee, wak up!
We're not here no more!*"

Living as they did for most of the year in the woods, their eating habits also came into question. "Do you mean to tell me," a
Saginaw cosmopolitan would ask, "that you actually *eat* porcupine? How do you prepare them?"

"*Wal,*" the lumberjack replies, "*first, you skin 'em. Then, you
stuff him with sour apples. Put 'em in the hoven, bakem brown.
By jingo! You know . . . I juss as soon have chicken.*"

The foregoing might not go down too well with today's
Quebecois, but no disrespect was intended. Indeed, there was
great respect for these men, who sometimes called out the same
rhythmic chant their courageous forebears, the *voyageur* trappers,
used when rowing their birchbark canoes along uncharted New
World rivers in the 1600s: "*Rolla-alon, mon bull, rolla-alon . . .*"

In late spring, the husky, bewhiskered river hogs came ashore.
They hit town with a roar and Saginaw was more than ready to
receive them properly.

Facing the river was Water Street, later renamed Tilden Street after a man who sought the presidency in 1876 and lost to Rutherford Hayes by a single, purchased electoral vote. At the top of Water Street were the saloons, which catered to most of the needs of the free-spending lumberjacks. Other requirements were filled at the end of the saloon section by The Line, a row of whorehouses stretching for five solid blocks. At the top of The Line was Ma Smith's prestigious seraglio for the elite. Farther down The Line, in what was definitely river hog territory, the price of the commodity dispensed diminished with the distance traveled until, at the end of Water Street, there were to be found one- and two-dollar establishments.

For the lumberjacks, who had been in timber country all winter, and ridden down the river with the logs for some time, money was for the spending. They spent it on their card games, women and drinking bouts, during which they attained phenomenal levels of drunkenness.

It didn't take much to get a brawl going in that town. If one river hog weaved into a smoky saloon and said to another, "They tell me you're a pretty good man; just step out here, I want to see how good you *really* are . . ." the ring would be formed and the fight was on. They didn't go in for knives or guns. They were simply fun-loving, rough-and-tumble lunatics.

There was one lumberjack, a famous character called Silver Jack Driscoll, who boasted he could whip any man that ever rode the river, which may very well have been the case. One night in a Saginaw bar, a river hog with either an unplumbed reservoir of courage or a corresponding quantity of stupidity challenged him. Silver Jack, growing bored with the preliminary sparring, finally knocked the fellow down, reached over, picked him up by the scruff of his neck and the seat of his pants and threw him out the front window. To add insult to injury, Jack latched onto an empty beer keg sitting at the end of the bar and hurled it out after his shattered opponent.

The etiquette of these hurly-burly festivals was such that it was not unusual for the loser's nemesis or an interested, eager bystander to take a running jump and land squarely upon the face of the fallen. The scars caused by those hobnailed caulk boots were glaringly apparent ever afterward and known throughout the state as "Saginaw smallpox."

But with the exception of their murderous forays into town, the lumberjacks were usually hard at work and it didn't take long for them to remove everything worth taking out of the forests. Where once there had been verdant slopes covered with virgin pine timber—by some estimates, five thousand feet of lumber per acre—by the time I was twelve years of age, nothing remained but stumps and slashings.

Then only a few logs, herded onto rafts with booms thrown around them and held together by iron chains, would float down the far from crowded waterway. As the rafts moved along, the former river hogs, now called boom men, guided them with their pike poles in an almost ghostly procession.

Kids, being then pretty much what they always have been, couldn't resist plunging into the river, paddling out and getting aboard those rafts. The boom men, recognizing the danger, would try to chase us off. We would, of course, pay no attention to them, as we ran along the logs and thumbed our noses. If they chased us, we'd dive into the river and swim ashore. But God help the poor guy who slipped between those logs and fell through, because there was not a chance of ever coming up again.

When I was growing up, the Grand Army of the Republic, or G.A.R., was a formidable force in this country. It was composed of Civil War veterans who had fought for the Union in that conflagration of division known in my time as "the war." With the possible exception of Grover Cleveland, who hired a man to do his fighting for him, there wasn't a man elected President of the United States, from Grant to McKinley, who wasn't a member of the G.A.R.

The great day for the veterans was Decoration Day, or Memorial Day as it was properly called. This observance originated when some women in a small town near an old battlefield decided to place flowers on the graves of Union soldiers who had fallen there. Making their way through the cemetery, they came upon a number of Confederate graves. Showing no partiality toward the dead, they decorated the graves of the Union soldiers and also those of the Confederates who were buried with them.

General John "Black Jack" Logan, national commander of the G.A.R., heard about this and, recognizing a good idea when he saw one, issued an order in 1868 establishing May 30 as Memorial Day, at which time the custom of honoring the dead by decorating their graves would be followed across the nation.

It was a big day for the veterans, who visited with one another and endlessly refought "the war." Ceremonies started in the morning, when firing squads from the National Guard went out to the cemeteries and fired volleys over the dead. In Saginaw, in the early afternoon, there was a parade, headed by my father riding a dancing black horse and leading a platoon of police which stretched across the street from curb to curb. The men were turned out in blue uniforms, bedecked with shiny brass buttons, high-crowned beige helmets, white gloves and, instead of the usual night sticks, special parade clubs made of two-foot-long rosewood with white cords and tassels at the hilts.

Following the police came a large, gleaming brass band, preceding the companies of the 33rd Michigan National Guard, the Naval Reserve and the Knights Templar wearing their white plumes and cocked hats. As in every parade, there followed a conglomeration of dignitaries in polished carriages, and bringing up the rear of the procession was the Fire Department in their shining red wagons drawn by teams of horses looking as well-groomed as the firemen's handlebar moustaches.

In the center of this ebullient throng was the G.A.R., dressed in Civil War-type uniforms, led by their fife and drum corps. To me, there is nothing in martial music, aside from a bagpipe band, that can compare to the trill of the fifes, the crash of the drums and the boom of the big bass drum. The kids of Saginaw would run alongside, so as not to miss a thunderous beat.

Those Decoration Day parades were cascades of color, music and noisy cheering. Flags and banners rippled and waved in the early summer breeze and the noise of the trumpets, drums and pipes, combined with the sound of marching feet, horses' hooves and wooden wheels clacking over the cobblestones, generated excitement in every breast, from the youngest citizen to the oldest statesman.

In making preparations for that parade, the Civil War veterans met before Decoration Day to tune up their drums by playing in their back yards at evening time. There was a man named Sawyer who lived about two doors down from us on McCoskrey Street and had been a thirteen-year-old drummer boy in the war. I suppose he was middle-aged then but when you're a kid they all seem like septuagenarians. Like any small boy, it didn't take me any time to start hanging around his place and be standing beside him where I could listen as he tuned his drum at sunset. Faced with the choice of either telling me to get lost or semi-adopting me, he took me under his wing and, in a short time, had those drumsticks in my hands. At first, he made me tap out rhythms on his kitchen table, where I practiced until I got so that he would let me play on the real thing.

The G.A.R. had formal sessions on Sunday afternoons and before going inside their lodge, the drum corps would be found outside, playing. I would be there, too, like an enchanted specter. And when I became adept with those sticks, the G.A.R. invited me to join their drum corps for the next Decoration Day parade. Did I feel proud!

My mother sewed a uniform for me which was blue with gold "frogs" across the chest. My mentor loaned me his Civil War drummer boy cap and when I came barreling down the street on Decoration Day, 1903, parading with the corps and feeling not an inch less than ten feet tall, all my chums were running alongside me, cheering and shouting encouragement because, after all, I was one of their gang.

Shortly afterward, the members of the G.A.R. decided to make me an honorary member of the drum corps and of the post, and began to lay plans for initiating me exactly as they would any veteran of the war. I was twelve years old.

I was nervous and excited that day. My father looked on proudly as the drum corps played me around in the lodge and escorted me to the adjutant, who entered my name upon the rolls, and then to the quartermaster, to whom I paid my dues of fifty cents. Finally, we marched to the center of the hall, where I faced the tall, white-moustached, barrel-chested, red-faced colonel, saluted and, after he handed me a cap, listened to my instructions. They were the most impressive words I had heard up to that time.

He talked to me as though I was one of the old veterans, and after almost three quarters of a century I can remember the opening lines of his oration: "Comrades, as you tread the declining path of life, the shadows lengthen and grow dark behind you. But we still keep step to the military music . . ."

After my initiation, I was allowed to join the G.A.R. in their reunions. Whenever there was a reunion within about a hundred miles from Saginaw, the fife and drum corps would board the train, travel to the site, march in the obligatory parade, enter the hall of the hosts and, in general, visit most grandly.

Those reunions afforded me an early insight into the human side of history and nothing I have learned since has told me there is any more interesting or significant aspect to the study of that subject. I encountered the Civil War through the men who had fought in such holocausts as Shiloh, the Wilderness, Cedar Creek, Malvern Hill and Gettysburg. Some of them were shattered remnants.

On a hot and muggy July afternoon in 1904, my father and I were waiting at the station for the train to take us to a G.A.R. reunion. On the corner of the station platform stood a tall, pale and skeletal-looking white-haired old man. He was wearing a woolen overcoat with the cape thrown over his shoulders and a broad-brimmed hat pulled down almost to his ears. There was something more than a little odd about being dressed like that on a hot day. I asked my father if he knew him.

"That man," he whispered, nodding toward the strange, almost transparent figure twenty feet away, "is a good deal younger than he appears. He spent time at Andersonville prison camp during the war. It took away his health and he wears that coat, always. He says it keeps away the chill."

Here was a touch of reality amid those moments of pomp and pageantry.

When a Civil War veteran died, his G.A.R. comrades sent a firing squad to the cemetery with him and myself as a drummer to play the Long Roll. It was played on a muffled drum and in such a manner that, as the casket began its descent into the grave, the roll would sound lower and lower until, by the time the coffin had reached the bottom of the grave, the beat, like that to which the man had marched, was finished.

After the graveside farewell, the remaining veterans would return to the G.A.R. hall, clean and oil their rifles, placing a cork in the barrel to keep out moisture, and put their weapons away in the racks. One day, when I was putting my drum back where it belonged, I happened to notice an old, battered bugle on the shelf above the gun rack. A member of the firing squad, seeing my fascination with the instrument, said, "Take it along home, son, and learn to play the thing. It isn't doing anybody any good sitting up there."

Since I didn't have an instructor, I had to fight that damned bugle day and night for weeks and it was a minor miracle some public-spirited soul didn't make off with it for the good of the neighborhood. Eventually I learned the service calls and then I had two jobs. When I went to a veteran's funeral I would play the Long Roll, walk some distance behind the firing squad, unhook the bugle from my belt and blow taps.

One evening, as I was sounding out my bugle in our back yard, a neighbor who belonged to the Naval Reserve came along. There were four divisions of the Reserve in Michigan; two in Detroit, one over at Benton Harbor and the fourth in Saginaw. In those days, all the states bordering the Great Lakes had a division or so of Naval Reserve and each state had its own training ship.

This reservist said, "Timmy, we don't have a bugler at the present time. How would you like to belong to our outfit?"

"That would be great," I answered, "but how could I? I'm only a kid."

"Let me see what I can do about it," he replied.

A couple of days later, he took me down to talk with the commander, who got in touch with the authorities, who contacted the governor, who in turn granted special permission for my enlistment in the Naval Reserve on April 4, 1905. I was just fourteen years old.

A uniform was cut down for me and I attended the night drills which were held every week and where I learned everything the sailors did by going through their paces with them. If they were practicing bayonet exercise, I was doing bayonet exercise. If they were slashing through cutlass drill—for the military, as always, was engaged in its time-honored custom of fighting the last war— I learned how to handle a cutlass. I also went on their cruises. The main cruise was in summer and lasted for four days. Over Fourth of July we'd do a two- or three-day cruise and during Labor Day there was yet another cruise. The ship we sailed on was the U.S.S. *Yantic*. She had been commissioned during the Civil War and in my time was used only as a training ship. Though powered by steam, she was bark-rigged, which meant that the fore- and mainm'st were square-rigged and her mizm'st was fore- and aft-rigged. I had a ball on those cruises, swinging up into the shrouds, whipping up the ratlins, climbing into the perch and keeping the lookout company in the crow's-nest.

With those heavy masts on her, how the old *Yantic* could pitch and roll! I was seasick on the night of my first cruise. The next morning, half-asleep and wishing I was fully dead in my swaying, canvas hammock, I wondered what stupidity had caused me to join that outfit. I thought I should have hitched onto something more land-oriented. Such reveries of liberation ended abruptly when the heavily muscled Bos'n came by and caught my attention by whacking me across the behind with his belaying pin to awaken me in proper sailor fashion.

I stayed with the Naval Reserve and the *Yantic*'s whiskered, flat-hatted, bell-bottomed old salts until I went away to school in 1908.

My father was an inveterate reader and had a comprehensive library. He read history and historical fiction, mostly, and I cannot even begin to speculate how many times he plowed through *The Decline and Fall of the Roman Empire*.

He started me reading history at a very tender age by taking dime novels away from me, saying, "If you want to read some really thrilling adventures, go into my library and find the works of Alexandre Dumas. Read *Viscount Bragelonne*, *Twenty Years After* and *The Three Musketeers*. You'll be entertained and, if you're lucky, you might even learn something."

It was one of my father's convictions, to which he adhered as though it was Holy Writ, that aside from a knowledge of history a fluency in the language was essential, and that the effort to speak and understand English properly was futile unless one had a command of Latin. So it came about that at the end of summer 1908, when I was seventeen, my father packed me off to St. Ignatius, a Jesuit college in Chicago, where a good many students were trained for the priesthood and where I was exposed to Latin morning, noon and night.

While in Chicago I lived with my mother's two bachelor brothers and three spinster sisters in a two-story graystone house on Shields Avenue and Fifty-fifth Street. And while I enjoyed the company of my aunts and uncles and reveled in their Irish stories, songs and food, I was certainly not intent on becoming a priest, for my Irish Catholicism was even then on the verge of collapse.

I studied hard at St. Ignatius but still found time to enjoy the pastime my father had steered me onto, namely, reading for pleasure. However, I was no longer poring over Alexandre Dumas. Instead, I became immersed in such books as Owen Wister's *The Virginian*, with its tales of the cowboys and its dreams of the frontier.

One of my most memorable childhood experiences, and my initial exposure to the West and its exciting life-style, had come a few years before, on July 16, 1898, to be precise. That was the day I first met Colonel William F. "Buffalo Bill" Cody, the famous hunter, guide, Indian fighter, showman and hero of all stories he related. Without any doubt, he was a courageous figure in the West and the proportions of his image were a good deal larger than life.

My first encounter with Buffalo Bill came about because his Wild West Show had come to Saginaw. It was a fantastic spectacle, consisting of six hundred and fifty cowboys, Indians, Cossacks and Bengal lancers, to name but a few, all performing unbelievable stunts and uniformly showing grace, agility and expertise in horsemanship. The shouts of the riders, the bright colors of their costumes and the stirring music paled into insignificance when the star of the show, Colonel W. F. "Buffalo Bill" Cody, rode into the open-air arena sitting majestically atop a prancing white stallion. At that moment I joined his legion of fans across America and throughout Europe. And although at this late date I cannot separate the shooting tricks he performed on that day from those he is known to have performed on other days, I have never forgotten the excitement which welled up inside me when I saw this living legend make his spectacular circuit of the arena.

Since my father was chief of police, he was able to take me back to the famous man's dressing tent. What a thrill that was! Cody was the most impressive man I had ever seen, unmatched either before or since. As someone once said, he was the "greatest one-man tableau that ever lived."

He sat in his tent, holding court in a dark cutaway coat. His shirt was trimmed with the kind of long collar worn today, only he was wearing them then. Around his neck was a four-in-hand tie, half a size larger than is fashionable now, and in that tie was a stickpin with the three feathers of the Prince of Wales, given to him as a token by the Prince when he was touring England, probably around 1890.

As to what was said, I remember not a word. I stood motionless, staring at the man towering above me, awed into speechless fascination by the face into which were etched deep lines of varied experience. It was probably one of those, "Well, hello, young lad," "Oh, yes sir!" types of conversation that pass between the idol and a young supplicant.

Years later, I would have the opportunity of renewing my acquaintance with that remarkable gentleman, but for the time being I and my friends had to be content imitating Buffalo Bill and the Indians, by riding wooden broomsticks across the front yards and through the back streets of Saginaw.

As I became older, and while still a young man, we all rode horses, for the automobile was far from being established as a mode of transportation. If you could afford it, you had a Western saddle.

Wild horses still ran loose on the ranges out West and there was a railroad freight agent in Saginaw who imported these critters, broke them and sold them to peddlers. Naturally, the kids of Saginaw were down at those corrals beside the freight yard at every opportunity, where the main attraction was the cowboys. These men were as exotic and colorful to us then as they are to the children of today, who, regretfully, are only exposed to this way of life through television and films.

I would perch on the top corral rail and watch the cowboys in action and it wasn't long before one of the cowboys, whom I knew only as Bob, handed me a rope, outside of the corral of course. By example he showed me how to handle it and make it do, more or less, what I wanted it to do. Before Bob left Saginaw he showed his fellow cowboys what a good teacher he was by allowing me to step inside the corral and throw the coil so as to loop it over the neck of a bronco. My experience inside that corral made me acquire a certain respect for the cowboys who daily stood in the midst of rearing, galloping, half-wild horses. And while it was clear to me that a cowboy's life was fraught with danger, I still thought it would be a most exciting profession.

In 1908, while I was at St. Ignatius, I became excited when my uncles told me the Miller Brothers 101 show was coming to town. It was formed from a wild bunch of cowboys who had been gathered together in Oklahoma and molded into a wild West show.

I haunted the coliseum where they were playing. Every day I would go and watch the Westerners perform and by the time I came home to Saginaw for Christmas vacation that year, I had already made the decision to head West and become a cowboy. I did not tell my family and for all my parents knew, I would be finishing the school year at St. Ignatius.

Several months after arriving back in Chicago, I slipped away from my relations' house with a pauper's purse of a few dollars squirreled away in my pocket, a toothbrush and a change of clothes in a small satchel, and bought a ticket on the railroad. When the ticket seller at the station asked me my destination, I was at a loss for an answer. Would it be Nebraska, Arizona, Oklahoma, Montana or Wyoming? I decided on Omaha, Nebraska, feeling that before I actually got there, something would occur to influence my direction.

It was late spring 1909, and I was eighteen years of age. I felt some qualms about my lies of omission to my parents, but if I had told them of my plans, they would certainly not have approved. In the years to come, I always kept in touch with them by letter, occasionally by a visit, and their attitude can best be illustrated by a passage from one of my father's letters to me: "Well, son, it's your own grave you're digging. I just hope you aren't going to be a horse's ass all your life . . ."

CHAPTER TWO

To the Last Frontier

When I entered the day coach of the train which would take me from Chicago to Omaha, there was a single seat vacant, next to which sat a tall, handsome man. He had an auburn moustache and was wearing a black Stetson hat, dark frock coat, string tie and polished leather boots.

"Anybody sitting here?" I asked him.

"Nope," he replied, without looking up from the newspaper he was reading.

He was obviously a western man and meeting him thrilled me. After I had made a few comments about the weather he laid his paper aside and we were soon in earnest conversation. Bit by bit he dragged my story out of me and finally asked, "What part of the West you gonna hit first?"

"I don't know," I replied.

"What about Wyoming?"

"Why not?" I shrugged. It sounded about as good as anyplace else.

After revealing that his name was Jim Aminette and that he came from a town in Wyoming called Lander, he explained his business was rounding up wild horses in the Red Desert, breaking the broncs and shipping them East for sale.

As the train traveled farther West, he said, "I'll tell you, I'm gonna stop off at Grand Island in Nebraska. When we get to Omaha, you buy a ticket as far as Grand Island and come along with me. The biggest damn horse and mule market in the United States is at Grand Island and you'll get a chance to see plenty of the wild West there, if that's what you're hankerin' for."

Well, that sounded about right. So when we rolled into the station at Omaha, I went to the ticket office and bought a ticket for Grand Island, though I had never heard of the place.

Our first morning in Grand Island, Jim took me to the stockyards, where there were enormous corrals for the horses and mules. As I leaned over the fence I saw a man come walking down an alley between the corrals, leading a skittish, half-broke bronc. He was a tall, gaunt, western man, dressed in black, and he had a long, drooping red moustache that practically covered his chin.

"See that fellow there?" Jim asked.

I nodded.

"Well, sir, he killed two men in one day up at Lander."

Of course, I didn't believe a word he'd said and started popping off right away. "Now, look here, Mr. Aminette, I know I'm a newcomer to the West but you don't have to feed me that dime-novel stuff."

"No," he laughed, "it's true! As a matter of fact, he's just been released from the penitentiary and he's here breaking horses instead of stones. C'mon over, I'll introduce you to him."

The man's name was Jim Dollard and Aminette apparently knew him pretty well because he said, "I'm gonna be around here for a few days. This kid's traveling with me and he's got nothin' to do. Can you use him? He tells me he can handle a rope."

Dollard looked me up and down with his sharp green eyes, the coldest eyes I had ever seen. If a look alone could kill, Dollard was capable of disposing of considerably more than two men in a single day. "Well," he drawled, "if this squirt can be of any help to me I can use him. Maybe he'd do to footrope a bronc or two."

During my brief stay at Grand Island, I worked in the corrals with Jim Dollard for a dollar a day. I had roped some half-broke broncs back in Saginaw, but to be corralled with this wild bunch right off the range was an entirely different matter. It was also my introduction to the real West, which could sometimes be hectic, to say the least.

Trainloads of horses fresh from the wild life arrived hourly at the stockyards, where the cars were unloaded and the horses turned loose in the corrals recently vacated by their half-broke predecessors. "Half-broke" usually meant they'd been in the corral for a couple of days and had calmed down somewhat.

The horses which had previously occupied the welcoming corral were driven, roped or dragged to another enclosure, where, one by one, they were placed into a confining chute, saddled and bridled with a rope, mounted by the daring bronc riders and turned loose into the breaking corral, a space about twenty-five yards on each side. As long as there was daylight, the stockyards reverberated with the sound of creaking saddle leather, jingling spurs, loud curses, impatient snorts and, occasionally, the grunt and thud of a cowboy falling from a bucking bronco.

My job was to help rope the horses by their feet, preparatory to the cowboys' crawling aboard. Now, a bronc is not gentle, to say nothing of tame, and footroping one of them was usually dangerous and always frightening. If the two or three men performing the task didn't coordinate their actions, one or more of the ropers might catch a sharp, strongly put hoof alongside the head, flush against the shoulder or deep into the stomach or groin. During the three days I was at Grand Island and working for Jim Dollard, I spent a considerable amount of my time running in frantic circles around panicked and perturbed horses.

At the end of my day's labors, which were considerable for me but well within the normal routine of the tough, lean cowboys, I slept the sleep of the dead in a livery barn on the same bed of hay as the tamer horses.

Three days later, as we were preparing to leave for Lander, Jim Aminette said, "Don't think about a ticket, son. You see, whenever they ship livestock into these markets they're allowed one man to come along free for every two cars of stock. Later, the cowboy gets a pass from the railroad so's he can get back to his stompin' grounds.

"And you know," he added with a look composed of equal parts mock-naïveté and slyness coming over his face, "I wouldn't be a damn bit surprised if, since some of those fellers never go back, they might have a few extra passes lying around in the office at the yard. If a man was to get hold of one he'd have to travel under an assumed name, of course. But, what the hell, that's one way to get to Wyoming!"

Later that night, Jim Aminette and "Jake Larabee" boarded the train out of Grand Island and were off for Lander.

In those days, the wooden seats in the coaches were constructed much like a reclining barber's chair so you could sleep in comfort. When I woke up early the next morning, I lifted the green window shade, looked out and saw a vast expanse of plain stretching toward rolling hills on the horizon. The sun was just rising and beginning to break across the seemingly limitless sky, casting an expanding orange glow over the entire landscape. In the near distance, I could see red buttes jutting upward like gigantic chessmen randomly dropped by a passing primeval god.

As I looked at this scene that neither painter nor photographer could ever completely capture, I took a deep breath and sighed. Then I took a small notebook out of my coat pocket and continued with a pastime I had grown to enjoy back in Saginaw: the writing of verse. The realization that I was finally out West propelled me excitedly to write the following lines, which express my wonder and awe of the West as well today as they did on that long-ago morning in 1909.

> These are the Mountains of the West,
> Where the Sun God seeks his slumber;
> Where the West Wind goes a-whooing,
> And Evil Spirits lurk . . .

I saw my first real-life, non-wild-West-show Indians face to face when we stopped at a place in Nebraska called Gordon where a couple of hawk-nosed, broad-shouldered, thick-chested Indians boarded the train. Somehow, a lot of people have the idea that the Indians of the plains looked like squat gnomes. But that isn't so. Many of them, particularly the northern tribes like the Sioux, Cheyenne, Arapaho, Crow, and Blackfoot, are a good deal larger than most whites, and stand over six feet tall.

The two Indians who got on at Gordon were dressed in fashionable dark blue woolen suits with matching vests, white shirts, somber ties and wide-brimmed black hats. They had plaited their hair in long braids wrapped with red and yellow trade cloth, and on their feet were moccasins beaded in colorful, geometric patterns.

"Couple of Oglala Sioux from Pine Ridge," Aminette said after one disinterested look at them. "Probably goin' over to visit with some of their Arapaho relatives on the Wind River Reservation," he mumbled before turning his attention back to his nap.

Since the reservation in Wyoming was still some distance away, I decided to throw caution along the tracks and see if I could get into a conversation with these distinguished-looking men. Naturally, I expected them to speak English as I was not exactly fluent in their lingo, Lakota. While I sat staring at them, making no attempt to hide my curiosity, they came over to where Aminette and I were and sat down quietly across from us. This did not help to reduce the intensity of my wonder.

In the course of my paralysis, one of the Indians looked at me and nodded. Sensing an opening, I asked him if he was, truly, a Sioux.

"Yeah," he replied, with the expansive exuberance of tone I was to encounter so many times among the Plains Indians. "Yeah," he grinned, "me Lakota. Ride with Buffalo Bill!"

He paused and looked at his moccasins for a moment before his face broke into an immense and genuinely pleased and pleasing smile. Thumping his chest several times, he announced proudly, "Me helluva dancer, too!"

The question I asked had been answered and our conversation ended. I soon learned that among the Indians there was a widespread reticence to offer information freely, for they were a private people, especially among strangers.

Later that night we arrived at the southern end of the reservation and pulled into Arapaho, a town about twenty-five miles from Lander. The only buildings to be seen were a store, the local agency building and the railroad station. If there was ever a one-horse town, this was it; there wasn't even a dog in the street.

As I got off the train to stretch my legs and get some fresh air, I saw fifteen or twenty cowboys lining the station platform and lounging on the wooden benches. They were dressed to the nines in tall hats, bandanas, silk shirts, heavy chaps covered with natural white or chocolate-colored Angora wool, and boots polished to a fine shine.

Standing to one side, and conspicuously apart from the cowboys, a delegation of long-haired Arapahoes wrapped in red and blue blankets had assembled to greet the two big Sioux. Although my first brush and conversation with the Indians had been brief, I found the experience thrilling, and my interest had been aroused and my appetite whetted. I could not help but wonder: Where had these people, so different from anyone I had ever known, come from? Who were they? Clearly, they were a world apart from my previous conception of them as, basically, wooden.

At about eight o'clock that night the train pulled into Lander, Wyoming, the end of the line. Years before, some ambitious planners for the Northwestern Railroad had attempted to lay a transcontinental track. When they hit Lander, they found themselves up against the foothills of the Rocky Mountains and that's as far as they ever got. The slogan of the town was, "Where rails end and trails begin." And that was surely true.

Jim escorted me along the main street to a rooming house where I got a small, barren room that didn't cost too much. Since I had only about five dollars left in my pocket, I greatly appreciated the favor. Then he went on home and I took my first look at Lander.

I felt an overpowering rush of excitement as I stepped out of the rooming house onto the wooden sidewalk and began wandering up the main street. With its unpaved streets, cowboys sauntering in and out of saloons from which came gay dance hall music and flickering light, which illuminated the hitchracks where horses were tied, patiently waiting, and a few Indians making restrained tours of inspection, this western town was an adventure.

Standing in front of one saloon was a group of four or five cowboys who were having a grand time and feeling no pain. They were the most picturesque bunch of Westerners I had seen up to that time and I was particularly impressed by one of them, a tall, weathered, lean man with a long black moustache. He was wearing a high-crowned, auburn-colored beaver Stetson hat tilted back on his head, a yellow silk bandana tied rakishly around his neck, an emerald green shirt and a pair of puffy, white Angora chaps which exploded from his legs, setting off elaborately tooled leather boots.

I looked down at my own attire and realized that since I had left Chicago dressed in ankle-high boots, slacks and a checkered shirt, my Saginaw version of a western outfit, I looked a bit of a freak. That night I decided that if I was to be a cowboy I would someday be a well-dressed one, Angora chaps and the works.

On the opposite side of the street from my rooming house was the town's one real hotel, the Freemont. It had stood there, as the cowboys put it, since Christ was a horse wrangler. In winter, the only heat in the place came from a large, wood-burning stove in the lobby, and according to the theory embraced by the management, the heat put off by that stove was supposed to go up to ceiling registers and warm the rooms above. This theory, however, never seemed to work in practice, and one night, when the thermometer stood at about forty degrees below zero, a wool-buyer named Billy McCoy, who later became a friend of mine, fought the cold as long as he could. At about four o'clock in the morning he began to become concerned about freezing to death and, when he couldn't stand it any longer, got up, dressed and came downstairs to the lobby to try and keep warm by the stove.

Just about that time, a dairy owner who supplied milk to Lander's restaurants, bars and the hotel came in the door. He had been driving into town in an open sled, making deliveries, and was wrapped in a bearskin coat, sealskin cap and otter gauntlets.

As this glacial figure stepped in the door, with frost across the front of his bearskin coat, the sealskin cap steaming, his beard filled with icicles and layers of frost obscuring his eyebrows, Billy McCoy turned around, looked at him and cried, "Jesus! What room did *you* have?"

My first night in Lander was thrilling. The noise of the colorful throng milling along the sidewalk, the music and the unmistakable sense of excitement in the air were even more than all the things I had ever hoped the West would be.

As I went back to the rooming house and climbed into my bed, I could hear the wooden sidewalks clumping with the reverberations of high-heeled cowboy boots and, occasionally, the jingle of a spur. Frequently, from the saloons across the street I heard the cowboys' raucous shouting.

"What's the biggest river in the world?" a single man would call out.

"Powder River!" came the communal, roaring response.

"Why?"

"Because she's an inch deep, a mile wide and God only knows how long!"

But the favorite rally cry seemed to be one bellowed by cowboys galloping their horses up and down the street: "Whoo-eee! Cowboys in town! Trouble expected!"

I was a long way from Saginaw.

After that first night in Lander, I was left to my fate. My friend Jim Aminette, upon arriving at his home, found a telegram calling him East on business. He was outward bound by five the next morning and I never saw him again.

Many years later, when I was making films in Hollywood, I received a letter from him with the return address of General Delivery, Red Rock, Arizona. I wrote to him immediately but my letter was returned. I put it into another envelope and sent it off again. It also came back and I was never able to tell him what I owed him, which was a pity because he had been a great influence upon my life. It was because of Jim Aminette that I went to Lander. From there I became a cowboy and it was through cowboying that my association with the Indians began, an association which proved to be my entry to Hollywood. I was indebted to that man in the most fundamental of ways and I profoundly regretted never having the opportunity of telling him so.

After my friend disappeared, I kicked around town a few days and discovered it was one thing to want to be a cowboy and another to get a job as one, unless you'd paid your dues and learned the tricks of the trade. The serving of an apprenticeship was required. And while one could eat in a restaurant and for only fifty cents be served a succulent T-bone steak, baked beans, garden-fresh peas, aromatic coffee and hot apple pie with vanilla ice cream, my few dollars had been considerably eaten into and work's compelling beacon arose and began projecting a message of dire emergency. I decided, though it was more a matter of no choice than of choice, to take the first job I could find.

It was summer, the ranches were putting up hay and I was offered a job going up into the hayfields of the Double Diamond, a huge cattle outfit on Wind River, about sixty miles, or two days' ride, north of Lander. Their operation was typical of many of the ranches in Wyoming which raised cattle. The ranch's herds grazed on the open range in spring and summer while the fallow portion of the grazing land was used for the growing of hay to feed the animals in winter when the weather often made it hazardous to keep the stock out in the boondocks. Then, as it got cooler, the cattle were brought in to graze in the previous summer's hayfields. Out West, the alfalfa was grown in immense irrigated meadows, for acreage meant nothing to them. The hay would be cut twice in summer. The six- or eight-inch stalks which grew after the second cutting were caught by early fall frost but did not go to waste because cattle would soon be brought in from the open range and could eat them during the winter months. In short, the plains ranches were both efficient and self-sufficient.

My first job in the summer of 1909 was running a sulky rake, something I had been introduced to back in Saginaw, where on weekends I'd go out and visit my pals from school who lived on farms not far from town. Usually I'd be planning on a marathon session in a swimming hole but, invariably, upon arrival the father would put me to work alongside his sons and one of the things I learned more about than I wanted to was sulky rakes.

Farming then was a far cry from what it is today. In those days we had no bailers, and horse-drawn mowers went through the fields two abreast, cutting a wide swath. Afterwards, the hay lay a couple of days until the sun burned out the moisture. Then I came careening along with my sulky rake. As the teeth of the rake became flush with the ground, I tripped the mechanism and the rake jerked the hay into windrows. Later I went down the line and pushed the windrows into stacks about five feet high, which we called haycocks.

I knew about the job but there was an added dimension here in Wyoming I hadn't counted upon. Instead of having the pulling power of a nice, steady horse as would have been the case in Saginaw, my sulky rake was hitched to a team of broncs, hardly less wild than the ones I had encountered in Grand Island. Each time I attempted to maneuver them into a turn, the pole of the rake goosed one and started him bucking. This antagonized the other bronc, who then commenced his routine of trying to break free from captivity. Thus, I spent much of my time dodging from one side of the seat to the other to keep from getting my head kicked off.

After the hay had been put into haycocks, it was the bull rake's turn to come along. This awesome contraption, with a horse at either end, had long teeth which skimmed the ground, scooped up the haycocks and took them to the stacker.

The stacker, operated by a single horse, hurled the hay to the top of a pile where a couple of men with long pitchforks built an oblong stack twenty feet wide, fifteen feet high and about thirty feet long.

After I'd worked the sulky rake and we got along to the business of constructing stacks, they promoted me and I, being a novice and not knowing any better, found myself looking groundward from the top of a stack. It was without doubt the toughest job in that part of the world and none of the small number of cowboys who had been called in from the range to help with the haying, and with whom I shared the bunkhouse, wanted anything to do with it. As I have said, there were two men atop a stack and my partner was a brawny blond, perfectly described by his nickname: the Strong-Backed Swede.

It was rough going out in the hot sun. As soon as the rolled-up and hard-to-handle load came up, it was dumped on top of us. We then spread it quickly by building up the corners and working on the sides. I had to work like a maniac to keep up with the Strong-Backed Swede because at about the time we got the first load scattered and put into shape, up came another. If we slowed our feverish pace for even a few moments, we found ourselves up to our necks in hay, for we were already waist-deep.

The final coda in this grand symphony of sweat was topping off the stack in such a way as to make it look like the gables on a roof so it would shed water. Though I saw no indication of it at the time, the rain in Wyoming, like the sun, is almost beyond belief.

After I had sweated, slaved and burned for about a month and a half the haying season came to an end. And since I had served my apprenticeship, which seemed, more than anything else, to be a testing of what the Mexicans call *macho,* I finally achieved my ambition of becoming a cowboy, joining the Double Diamond's fall 1909 roundup as a horse wrangler.

It was the responsibility of each cowhand to provide himself with a hat, bandana, chaps, spurs, rope, bedroll and saddle. Fortunately, I had saved some money from my turn with the sulky rake and was able to pick up much of this equipment in Lander. The all-important boots were, by custom, either Hyer or Justin, available in town for $9.50. The only brand of hat allowed was Stetson, named after John B. Stetson, who made the first western hat. Pants were durable denim, manufactured by Levi Strauss and Company, and cost a dollar a pair, about the same as they had when old Levi himself sewed canvas britches for gold miners. The only drawback to "Levi's" was that the hip pockets were trimmed with brass studs, which had to be pounded down so as not to destroy the cowboy's most prized possession, his saddle. It was often said about a man that he was riding on a $40 saddle atop a $20 horse.

With my hard-earned money I bought my gear in several of Lander's shops and though the saddle was a wreck I picked up at a livery barn for $5 I was finally dressed as a working cowboy. Thus, I was ready for the Double Diamond roundup, although lacking the one essential component: my own horse.

CHAPTER THREE

Irish Tom's Canary

"C'mon, sonny, let's see what's in the corral," Mat Brown, the husky Double Diamond foreman bellowed soon after we had made the two-day trip by buckboard from Lander to the ranch not far from Wind River. It was morning and the cowboys were sauntering, though some emerged stiffly, from their log bunkhouse near the foreman's rambling and slightly dilapidated headquarters.

"This way to the cavvy," Mat Brown roared, slapping me on the back and knocking me forward several quick steps. I tried to concentrate on the things I had learned from the foreman during our journey. A cavvy, I had discovered, was a herd of horses, a bastardization of the Spanish word *caballada*. Indeed, much of the terminology used by the cowboys was derived from Spanish, having been brought up to the northern Plains by those far-riding cowpunchers who had come up the trail from Texas. Thus, one's rope (*la reata*) was a lariat; your saddle had taps, or *tapaderas*, covering the stirrups; to protect himself from sticker-bushes the cowboy wore chaps, *chaparreras*; the bronc he sometimes had to ride was certainly *bronco*, crazy or wild; and he worked for a ranch, or *rancho*.

The Double Diamond outfit was part of a conglomerate known as the Mill Iron Cattle Company, composed of the M-Bar, the Circle and the Double Diamond ranches. From its bases along Wind River and Owl Creek, the Mill Iron Cattle Company monopolized the surrounding Wyoming country by throwing cattle all over the territory and running ten thousand or more animals loose for miles and miles across the vast, unfenced range land. It was owned by Jake Price and Colonel Torrey, a Spanish-American War veteran who at the outbreak of that war had organized and led an outfit similar to Roosevelt's Rough Riders called Torrey's Terriers.

"You just keep luggin' that cack of yours"—Westerners called a worn-out, weather-beaten saddle such as the one I was burdened with a cack because it was deemed about as comfortable a ride as sitting on a cactus—"and I'll find you a horse, don't worry." I nodded at Mat Brown's words and shyly looked around at the cowboys going about their early morning chores. Some were saddle-soaping their "bat wing" chaps, while others were saddling their mounts.

It was customary for a cowboy joining an outfit about to go on roundup to accompany the foreman to the corrals at the ranch, where the foreman roped out the newcomer's string of six or eight mounts. It then became the cowboy's business to recognize his horses by their appearance, which could be a subtle thing to say the least.

The last horse Mat Brown caught for me was a beautiful, blue-colored Appaloosie, a very different animal from the others he had already given, all of which looked like Don Quixote's rejects. I wondered why such a fine horse was being given to me, a greenhorn from Michigan, and my suspicions were roused to a fine peak because I figured there had to be a catch.

As soon as he had turned the Appaloosie over to me, Mat Brown said, "Son, this is a greatly misunderstood horse. He's really a fine animal, you just have to watch him. When you get ready to mount, do it gentle and do it quick. Pick his head up firmly and, if he jumps, keep your heel irons away from him and you'll be able to calm him down. But once he starts to buckin' with you, he's the kind of critter that'll keep at it all day. Just treat him easy, don't try to fight him and you'll have a fine ride."

Then, patting me on the back and half-snickering, he added, "Good luck, *cowboy!*"

As I've already said, I had started to write light verse back in Saginaw and planned to continue doing it out West. Later, after I had several poems completed, I had them printed up in a little paperbound book. Sometimes I would ride over to Jackson Hole and sell them for a few cents apiece to the dudes, though I found they were bought and appreciated as much or more so by the cowboys. Appaloosie, as it turned out, was the inspiration for my first Wyoming cowboy poem.

You're the orn-yest, meanest cayuse ever born
this side o' hell.
Why there's meanness just a-oozin' through your hide,
    When your temper starts to bubble
    You're a ring-tailed source o' trouble
And you sure can make a boy sit up and ride.

In the chill of early mornin', when we're
saddlin' up to go
And I'm trying to make connections with my cack,
    It's a prayerful sort o' minute
    'Cause before I'm halfway in it
You bog down your head and try to break my back.

If I loosen up a minute fer to ease my tired joints
Then you grab your tail and pitch to beat the deuce
    And the cause of this sun fishin'
    Is your ingrown disposition
Oh! you wall-eyed streak o' meanness, Appaloose!

But fer all your darn fool actions, you're the top horse
of my string
And I like your grit, you paint-splashed little scamp.
    Why, you'll jolt me till I'm purple
    On the long end of a circle
Then fer cussedness come pitchin' into camp.

When the herd is hard to handle and they're cuttin'
forty ways
Then my other knot-head broncs hain't any use
    But let the critters come a-tearin'
    If it's you and me off bearin'
'Cause the cow hain't born can outguess Appaloose!

If the gang rides into dinner with their quirts
a-swingin' free
And we race to see who'll be first into camp
   You sure settle to your knittin'
   When you hear the old boy yippin'
And we quit 'em like a pay-car would a tramp.

When I'm called to join the roundup out across
the Big Divide
I'll ride o'er that skyline trail without remorse
   But if spirits have the savvy
   I'll go through St. Peter's cavvy
Till I find my little Appaloosie horse.

Until roundup time, the cattle were generally ignored and allowed pretty much to fend for themselves, except during serious
storms or other natural disasters. Because of the enormous size of
the unfenced spreads, daily supervision of the far-flung herds was
impossible, and due to this lack of supervision, cattle could sometimes stray into the wilderness or mire in a sinkhole and be lost
forever. Though we lost some cattle in this way, our greatest losses
came from rustling.

There were two roundups during the course of a year, fall and
spring. The beef roundup in the fall was when the critters bound
for eastern meat markets, usually fat yearlings, were collected and
driven to the railheads. The spring roundup was the occasion on
which the lately born calves were given the owner's mark by appli-
cation of a hot branding iron.

The roundup was conducted by a self-sufficient band of
mounted men who fanned out over the country, located lone and
grouped cattle and managed them as a herd during the drive to
the shipping pens. It was a well-organized operation, rarely veer-
ing from an established procedure that was much the same in
both spring and fall. The number of men employed in this task
naturally depended upon the size of the herd. On my first
roundup, I was one of about a dozen cowboys.

In return for my labor, I received forty dollars a month, the use
of my horses, food and the ground upon which I slept. I was also
expected to abide by trail law and the first rule that had been

adopted by the Wyoming Cattlemen's Association was that anyone riding with the roundup was not, contrary to popular myth,
permitted to carry a pistol. For some reason a Winchester rifle
packed snugly into a sheath and attached to a saddle did not fall
under this rule and you could, and most of us did, throw a six-
shooter in your bedroll. This practice was allowed as long as you
kept the weapon there. But putting one on the hip was definitely
out and the breaking of this rule was sufficient cause for immediate dismissal. This restriction came about because of many painful
experiences wherein cowboys grated against each other's nerves,
got jumpy and felt the need to throw a few shots at their compadres. It was a rule that saved everybody from many complicated
and potentially fatal situations and, besides, allowed the ranch not
to lose any time, money or personnel.

The outfit traveled with two wagons. First came the mess
wagon, which was similar to a covered wagon with a canvas
stretched over the top to protect its contents. The grub was stored
in this wagon, and attached at the back was a mess board that let
down to make a table on which the cook could work. Among the
accouterments of the cooking end were Dutch ovens, which were
put on coals to cook everything a cowboy needed: steaks, fried potatoes, baking powder biscuits and coffee.

The second vehicle was the bed wagon, which carried the roundup's sleeping rolls and was driven by a man who handled the
horses at evening time, the nighthawk. Having held every job possible during my eight years of roundups, including cook—a position I occupied for less than a week when, by popular demand, I
was put back on a horse—I can testify from personal experience of
seemingly endless duration that between caring for each cowboy's
string of horses and driving the bed wagon, a nighthawk enjoyed a
state of almost total sleeplessness. It was an odd position to be in
and uniquely capable of giving the cowboy a feeling of loneliness,
which I tried to capture in a poem I wrote shortly after my first
roundup.

> Yellow moon a-risin'
> Stars a-shinin' bright
> Night guard's song comes driftin' down across the night.

Night air's gettin' chilly
Heavy with the dew
Boys are in their blankets—wish that I was, too.

Horse bells softly tollin'
Sure a lonesome sound
Spooky kind o' shadders a-dancin' on the ground.
Cavvy holdin' easy
Mostly layin' down
All except the Pitchfork string, they're rampsin' all around.

Noddin' in the saddle
Waitin' for the dawn
Tryin' to keep from dozin' off, gosh! this night is long.
Horses up an' grazin'
Scatterin' 'cross the flat
Over in the coulee a coyote starts to yap.

Mornin' star a-shinin'
Gee! the air is damp
Time to start the cavvy a-trailin' into camp.
Cook's announcin' breakfast
Sure a welcome sound
Lord, I'd like to hit the bunk and sleep the clock around.

When morning came, and it came mighty early on roundup, I'd pack up my bedroll and throw it into the bed wagon. After shaking out my boots thoroughly to be rid of any visiting creatures with no legs or more than four that might have crawled in during the night, I took my saddle, which doubled as a pillow, picked out the first of the three horses I would ride that day and got to work immediately after breakfast.

As camp broke and the two wagons rolled out in slow pursuit of the moving herd, the horse wrangler, who handled the horses in the daytime, strung out his cavvy of perhaps as many as a hundred and fifty head and herded them some distance from the wagons until we got to wherever the camp was going to be made for noon. It was then his job to turn the cavvy loose on the prairie so they would get a good feed. Of course, he had to keep a watchful eye over his charges. There were enough problems to worry about on roundup without having the horses take off in all directions, which is precisely what happened once when old Jack Utterback was wrangling.

Jack, who never ceased reminding us that he had "come up the trail from Texas, boys," walked with a limp because one of his ankles had been crushed years before when a horse he was riding slipped and rolled over on top of him. To my mind, he was the image of Hopalong Cassidy. I don't mean the handsome hero portrayed by Bill Boyd in the movies, but the fictional character created by Clarence Mulford: a small, wizened cowboy with a long moustache and walking along with a gimp.

One day, around noontime, when those of us who'd ridden in from the herd were grabbing a quick dinner, Jack went off into the brush. Suddenly, we heard a yell and his pistol roar off with three shots. The entire horse herd picked up their ears and, snorting wildly, took off in disarray across the prairie. As Jack came out of the brush, proudly holding the offending rattlesnake in one hand and a smoking six-shooter in the other, the look of triumph on his face was replaced by one of astonishment as he watched the horses galloping off into the distance. It was only fair that Jack was sent out alone to retrieve the cavvy.

Early the next morning, as we sat beside the dying campfire, muttering, we heard the horses returning and, above the noise of their hooves pounding against the hard ground, Utterback joyously hollering, "I got 'em, boys, I got 'em!"

When we broke camp and mounted our freshly caught horses, I asked Jack how he had managed to round up the entire herd, as they had probably scattered far and wide.

" 'Twer'n't nothin', boy," he said, jawing on a plug of tobacco. " 'Twer'n't nothin', really. After all, they was a-foot and I was ridin' a-horseback!"

We were a self-sufficient outfit with no need for a line of supply. What we hadn't brought with us in the mess wagon we took from the herd, cutting out an overgrown calf or a short yearling and butchering at sundown. The meat was hung on the tongue of the mess wagon and the pole was driven into the ground so the night air could cool off the beef. It would then be cut up, put into canvas sacks and thrown into the bottom of the bed wagon, where the sleeping rolls were piled on top so the sun wouldn't spoil the meat. After the nighthawk had finished driving the wagon during the day, the meat was taken out, removed from the sacks and hung up again on the wagon tongue where the night air allowed it to become neither too fresh nor outrageously gamy.

After the butchering and curing processes were completed, we'd have a breakfast of liver and bacon, which was a treat. Otherwise, we lived on solid beef all the time.

When the roundup outfit stopped to eat shortly after midday, it was my job as the new man aboard to construct a corral out of iron stakes about three feet high, linked together by a single rope. It was more of a hint than a formidable barrier to the horses because the cavvy, being pretty well broke, would usually, unless provoked, stay put once they were inside.

After that minor feat of engineering, a wrangler had to anticipate the arrival of the cowboys from the herd for what we then called dinner and now refer to as lunch, because when the cowboys had finished eating those horses had to be ready to go.

The hands galloped in hell-bent for leather, stepped from their mounts, pulled saddles off, turned horses loose and started kicking lids from Dutch ovens, spearing steaks, pouring coffee and wolfing food. They couldn't take an hour or two over their meal because they were supposed to get there, fill up, return at a run to the herd and relieve some other hungry cowboy who was waiting patiently to come in and eat, too. So as soon as the cowboy finished his meal, he grabbed his saddle, took down his rope, went over to the edge of that single-strand corral, picked out the horse he was going to ride that afternoon, hopped on and got back to the herd, pronto.

We often vied with each other in contest to see who could get there and back first. Sometimes we would neglect our meals to beat somebody else out there, not even stopping to gather our ropes properly but coiling up as we roared off into the distance. Staying in the vicinity of the mess wagon, staring contemplatively into a cup of hot coffee and waiting until it cooled down, qualified one for the derisive title of "coffee-cooler."

Easily bored with the routine of a job, youth doesn't like to stick around one place too long, and while the next working place may not actually offer golden promise, it is at least in another part of the world. The key to the cipher of youthful movement, that wanderlust familiar to observers throughout the ages, would seem to be a combination of boredom, a yen for variety and the eruptions of an individual's hormones.

This business of wandering can be either a progressive or a cyclical thing. One may move across life's broad plateau toward the mountains lying on the distant horizon or continually find respite at the familiar touchstones and watering spots. To me, it has always been a matter of how far you have to go to find your particular poison; and some cowpunchers, in the role of saddle tramps, went what they called a "fer piece," riding toward jobs in northeastern Wyoming's Powder River country, where they worked on various ranches. Others rode what amounted to a regular circuit, working down on Owl Creek for the Padlock or the M-Bar, crossing the river and cowboying for Irish Tom, moving over to the Pitchfork or traveling up through the Big Horn Basin; then they'd drop down onto Wind River after crossing the Owl Creek Mountains and work for the JK, head on toward the Double Diamond, down to the Circle, and pretty soon they'd be back at the M-Bar. There were no hard feelings between the range bosses and their men over this continual migration. It was just a part of the cowboy's life-style and, as we used to say about roundup, bronc breaking and fence mending, "came with the territory."

The thing that put the bee in my britches and got me moving from the Double Diamond was that I had spent the long, cold and boring Wyoming winter of 1909–10 in the confines of the ranch's bunkhouse, with only occasional, dreary forays outside. I remember vividly at some point during the seemingly endless frost reading a poem in a magazine which extolled the virtues of lush Wyoming. Somehow, it didn't jibe with what I saw outside the window and, between furtive glances at the bunkhouse thermometer, which outside frequently registered a teeth-shattering forty degrees below zero, I wrote an answering piece.

> There's a poem some guy's written
> 'bout Wyoming's azure skys,

'Bout the rattlesnakes and wood ticks,
    porcupines and bottle flies,
'Bout the purple snow-capped mountains
    and the zephyrs in the air,
'Bout the wolves and bobcat kittens,
    coyote, skunk and grizzly bear.

He goes on to tell of punchers
    with their chaps and cartridge belts
And their silver-mounted saddles,
    Hyer boots and Stetson felts.
How they'll work from dawn till evenin'
    if you'll keep their tummies full;
How they rope and tie a critter;
    how they love to throw the bull.

Oh, he sure gives some description
    of this healthy, wealthy state,
And he longs to travel back here
    (so he says, at any rate)
Once again to ride the ranges
    after cattle that are fat,
And to see the reckless cowboy
    come a-lopin' cross the flat.

But of one thing I am certain:
    it's apparent in his rhyme,
This guy must of hit Wyoming
    in the good old summertime,
When the range grass starts a-wavin'
    and the young calves romp about
And that funny springtime feelin'
    makes a fellow want to shout.

'Course the things he's writ are true enough,
    as near as I recall,
But there's sides to old Wyoming
    he hain't never seen at all.
He hain't never stood a night guard
    when the rain's a-peltin' down,

Nor slept out with just one blanket
    when there's snow upon the ground.

'Cause when winter shuts down on us
    and the blizzards start to rage
And the cowboys start a-figurin'
    where they've spent their summer's wage,
When the springs are all froze solid
    and the valley's filled with snow
Deep enough to strike the breechclout
    of a long-geared 'Rapaho;

When the range cows stand and shiver,
    too plumb weak to even grave,
And the hump that's in their middle
    cheats a camel forty ways;
When the whole darned landscape's covered
    with a blanket soft and white—
That's the time to hit Wyoming
    if you want to hit her right.

That's one side of this here country
    that our poet's never seen.
Why! It would freeze the golden romance
    out of any poet's dream.
I'm no pessimist, nor cynic,
    poet friend, I'd have you know,
But who the hell can dream of romance
    when it's twenty-eight below?

I've a tip to give you, pardner,
    if you'll mind it not the least:
That's to spend the whole darned winter
    in some swell hotel back East,
And keep right on a-writin'
    with your clean descriptive pen,
But don't hit old Wyoming
    till the summer's here again.

Immediately after my first Wyoming winter I used part of my savings and bought a horse from the ranch for $40, linked up with a cowboy about six years older than me, Stanley Harris, and, to celebrate the arrival of spring 1910, left the Double Diamond. It was our intention to ride over to Johnson County in northeastern Wyoming. The attraction of that particular part of the country was that at the time there was a war going on between the cattlemen and the sheepherders.

Over on our side of the Big Horns some of the outfits ran both cattle and sheep, but on the other side of the mountains it was not quite that simple. The cattlemen had experienced their troubles for years with sheep, it had boiled over into a bloody mess a generation before and now they had defiantly drawn what they called the Dead Line through the open grazing land, declaring no sheep were to cross into cattle country.

The sheepmen, naturally, took a dim view of such an arbitrary rule, since the range was unfenced and owned by the United States government. They felt they had as much right to use it as the cattlemen. Imbued with a sense of righteousness, some sheepherders decided to cross Blue Springs and move into fine pasture country. The result was that one night their herd was jumped by some cowboys. The unfortunate sheepherders were tied to trees and beaten to within an inch of their lives. The sheep fared worse, being stampeded by the cowboys over the rim of a canyon.

But the really big news concerned an event known as the Ten Sleep Raid. Two sheepmen, in defiance of the Dead Line, moved into cattle country. All was quiet for a couple of days but late one evening a band of riders came crashing into their camp, shooting wildly. The herders were killed, their wagons were burned and all their sheep were either scattered or shot.

Like most young fellows, Stanley Harris and I just couldn't wait to be headed toward the action, which, obviously, was in Johnson County. So, having saddled up and thrown our bedrolls and camping gear onto a packhorse Stanley owned, we set about crossing the Owl Creek Mountains. We traveled at a leisurely pace for about a week, following indistinct cow paths and trying to keep our distance from the chilly, craggy and precipitous high-timber country. Each morning we rose early, ate a hearty breakfast of bacon, eggs, potatoes and coffee, mounted and rode along while talking and admiring the phenomenally and magnificently verdant territory. Mountains, water, cool air, blooming wild flowers, elk, antelope and deer were in abundance. The only people we encountered were Indians.

The reason for this was that one of the situations enjoyed by the big cattle outfits on the eastern side of the Big Horns was the leasing by the ranchers of reservation land from the Indians. This arrangement suited the interests of both parties as it gave the cattlemen a considerable piece of additional grazing land and provided the tribes with a paltry income, for range land was plentiful and rent cheap.

Indeed, much of the land the Indians had was generally not used by them. Their individual allotments for farming were small, usually not running over 160 acres; besides which, most of them, as a result of having been rounded up and penned on the reservation a mere thirty years previously, were immersed in a depression of such stupefying depth that they viewed any attempt at picking up a plow as an effort ordained to fail. At the very least, the government's sparse rations could be supplemented by food purchased with the rent money either at Moore's trading post at Fort Washakie or Pony Hayes's place over at Arapaho.

The Indians we encountered along the trails were a little off their usual beaten path, but as I was to learn, they liked to visit relatives in other tribes and usually thought nothing of riding for a couple of weeks to do so. They belonged to one of two tribes: the Arapaho, who were generally tall and lean, or the Shoshoni, who tended to be shorter in height and more heavy-set.

They rode bareback, with a blanket thrown across the withers of their horse, and because they were in a state of transition, their clothing was an odd and colorful mixture of two cultures, the old and the new. Usually they wore tall, dark, reservation-style hats with a conical crown and a broad, flat brim. Held in the beaded hatband would be a single eagle feather or a white breathfeather plume from the eagle's tail, sometimes dyed orange or red. I noticed immediately that the old-timers of both tribes invariably wore moccasins, while the younger men preferred to wear boots.

After a couple of days I was able to recognize to which of the tribes a rider belonged. The Shoshonis were, on the surface, more colorful. Their shirts were usually made of red or green silk and around their necks they wore a yellow or blue silk muffler. Their pants had foxing along the cuffs, about a foot wide and decorated with flowered beadwork. But the Arapahoes, because they were poorer, would often be more simply dressed in a gray muslin shirt, vest, trousers and moccasins.

It was also possible to differentiate between the tribes by the dressing of their hair. The Arapahoes, like their friends the Sioux and Cheyenne, usually parted their hair in the middle and brought it down in two braids wrapped in red strouding or otter skin. The Shoshoni, on the other hand, was a pompadour Indian and, like the Crow, greased the front of his hair into a stiff roach, leaving the rest hanging loose. The old men of both tribes still wore their scalp locks. Looking much like a Chinese queue, it was formed by gathering the hair at the crown of the skull and letting it fall toward the back of the neck in a single, thick braid invitingly decorated with feathers and beads.

Another distinction between the two tribes was found in their beadwork. The Arapaho designs tended to be geometrical while those of the Shoshonis were more floral in arrangement.

There existed between the two tribes, however, differences of a nature less superficial and quite a bit more substantial than their hair dressing and style of beadwork. In fact, the Arapahoes and Shoshonis detested one another.

In 1868 the Shoshonis had been rewarded for their service as scouts for the United States Army by being awarded a 3-million-acre reservation in Wyoming known as the Wind River Agency. Thus, in 1874 they gladly provided the sixty-three soldiers of Company B of the 2nd United States Cavalry with 167 of their warriors under the leadership of their chief, Washakie, for the express purpose of knocking hell out of their ancestral enemies, the Arapahoes. The goal was achieved by attacking unwary villages, running off pony herds and shooting inhabitants, regardless of age or sex.

Then, in 1878, either through bureaucratic blunder or the exercise of a sense of humor of the driest sort, the government moved 938 Arapahoes and their two thousand ponies to one of the Wind River Agency's choicest areas. To say that the relationship between the two tribes was chilly would be grossly to understate the situation.

And while the Indians may have been aware of the differences between them, it was a matter about which most cowboys were woefully ignorant. To a cowboy riding the range in search of stray cattle or horses, every Indian he encountered was "John."

The first thing cowboys like my traveling partner, Stanley Harris, said when they hailed an Indian on the open range was, "Hello, John, how the hell are you?"

The Arapaho or Shoshoni, offended by familiarity of a sort they equated with rudeness, would usually respond with "Ugh" or "Me no savvy." Even if they spoke English, which most of them did not, they could not be bothered by trafficking with these crude white men.

The Indians sometimes exacted vengeance for this treatment and the standard line of the time concerned the cowboy who asked an Indian if he'd seen a stray horse.

"This horse, he's brown?" the Indian replies.

The cowboy nods.

"Brown with white spots?"

"Yeah, John, that's him," says the cowboy, eagerly awaiting word of where the runaway can be found.

"This brown and white horse havem Double Diamond brand?" asks the Indian.

"Right," says the cowboy, becoming increasingly impatient. "Now, where the hell is he?"

"Me no see him!" the Indian laughs as he pulls away and gallops off.

My curiosity about the Indians came early. Though they were no longer as free, wide-ranging or boisterous as they had once been they continued to cling tenaciously to their roots and, in so doing, personified a quality which the white man calls a "primitive" outlook and perspective. By doing this they could not help but strike me as exotic and interesting. Being at heart a romantic, I was intrigued by the possibility that, having come from an unencumbered, natural state, the Indians were able to look upon the world as we must all have seen it before the influence of "civilization," before that time when we forever lost a firm grasp upon our own, probably common, roots. Somehow, I felt sympathy for these people and thought this "Hello, John, how the hell are you" business was an improper, disrespectful way to treat them.

So when I'd see an Indian coming along on his pony, I didn't say, "Hello, John." I'd stop and say, "*Hou.*" He would say, "*Hou,*" and wouldn't utter another word. Then I might ask him something in English and he'd respond with "Me no savvy."

With all of this "Hello, John" and "Me no savvy" I was faced with a dilemma. If I did not speak their language and they did not understand mine, how was I ever to communicate with the Indians?

After about a week or ten days, Stanley Harris and I had crossed the mountains and dropped down to a stream rushing hard with newly melted snow. We followed it along some gulches and by aligning ourselves with the Big Horn River set a meandering course for the little town of Thermopolis, which we figured would be a good place to stop over before the last leg of our journey to Buffalo, in Johnson County.

I learned one important fact from the journey Stanley and I made: when a couple of fellows are thrown together too much, one gets on the other's nerves, and vice versa. It was called "cabin fever" and happened most often if you were stuck out in a line shack, a little log cabin built in the middle of nowhere and from which a couple of cowboys periodically rode to check up on widely scattered herds. You get to the point where you don't like the way the other guy does this and you can't stand the way he does that. If there were three cowboys in that shack, the heavy weight of monotony was lifted and things were different. But with two men, the first thing you know you're practically ready to kill one another. The same thing could happen in camp and we called it "camp fever": you've seen quite enough of each other and just wish to God the same old face would melt away. By the time Stanley Harris and I reached the outskirts of Thermopolis we'd been riding the river with each other too long and each of us was suffering from an acute case of the malady.

We had forgotten all about the war in Johnson County, which was probably just as well, and were intent on getting jobs wherever we could. We had also reached a mutual, unspoken agreement to part company as soon as possible, which we did immediately upon commencing our ride down the main street.

"Well, Tim, I'll be seein' you," Stanley Harris mumbled, turning his horse to one side. The last time I saw him he had tied his riding horse and his packhorse to a hitching rack and disappeared into the dark recesses of a saloon. I was still in awe of the West and decided to take a look at the town.

Thermopolis, aptly named after the area's hot springs, was founded in the late 1890s, near the northern entrance of Wind River Canyon, on the banks of the Big Horn. The country surrounding the natural bowl in which the town nestles is composed of sharply cut red rock hills on which grow short, scrubby pines, brown grass, green-gray sagebrush and, in spring and summer, softly dark mustard-colored wild flowers.

When I arrived in 1910, the streets were of dirt and the sidewalks and all but one of the buildings were constructed from wood. Each day the nearby thermal springs pumped over 20 million gallons of 135-degree sulphurous mineral water which bubbled forth from the earth and cascaded into the Big Horn, leaving sulphur deposits on the canyon walls, turning some from red to yellow and green. Today, some 50 million gallons gush forth every twenty-four hours, and the terms of the treaty by which the Shoshoni chief Washakie ceded the Medicine Waters to the white man remain in force: one quarter of the water belongs to the public and cannot be bartered or sold by or to anyone.

By the time I arrived Thermopolis had become, more or less, a fairly respectable place. Yet, even in my day some strange characters continued to move in and out of the town. They tended to remain anonymous by using as camouflage the town's 3,500 inhabitants and the numerous visiting cowboys who were looking for a good time and a long weekend.

Thermopolis boasted two churches, one Catholic and the other Protestant, which, aside from providing religion, sponsored quilting bees and teas for the women of the town. There was a Masonic lodge which, along with the abundant fishing and hunting grounds throughout the Basin country, provided the men with their social activities. The cowboys, however, invariably headed for the saloons and honky-tonks. Thermopolis had arrived at the point where there was actually some semblance of law and order, chiefly because incoming riders were required to deposit their guns with the bartender immediately upon entering a saloon.

If the churches and lodges were the social clubs of the tamer inhabitants of the region, the saloons were the private haunts of the cowboys and sheepherders, some of whom had been out on the range for months and arrived in town with their pockets bulging with unspent pay. There was, however, one saloon just off the main street where the diverse elements of that part of Wyoming intermingled, Skinner's.

Tom Skinner had built his establishment out of brick and for many years it was the only solid building in town. Above the saloon was a hall where the "respectable" people gathered for weekly dances. In the years to come I would be numbered among those cowboys who, wanting to join in the festivities and dance with a girl instead of tossing calves, had to make certain concessions such as wearing a clean shirt and bandana. The cowboys would ride into town straight from the range, looking as though soap and water had gone out of fashion and smelling pungently of cows, calves, horses and the bunkhouse. The cowpuncher's joy was to jump quickly from his horse, rush to the nearest hotel and hire a room with a bath. Within the space of thirty minutes, he would reappear, bound for the nearest bar. With his hair clean and brushed, his fingernails white, and wearing shiny boots onto which were strapped gleaming spurs, he sought to strike a pose that would make any modern Grenadier Guard envious.

Everybody tried to be on his best behavior during these social evenings, and as long as things stayed that way, all was fine. Once in a while some cowboy might shoot up a place, but that was the exception rather than the rule. Yet, while Thermopolis was on the verge of becoming a "respectable burg," it retained the freewheeling, rough-and-tumble qualities of a western cowtown, for it was a place in which bank robberies were planned, rustlers prospered and gunslingers made occasional appearances.

After tying my horse to a hitching post that morning of my arrival in town, I went into the shoemaker's shop on the main street to have my boot heels repaired. Shortly afterward, the town marshal, a heavy-set old boy, sauntered in, just to see if this newcomer was a "bad 'un." He asked me what I was doing in town, which, I later learned, was his standard question. If a visitor was too scruffy-looking for his taste he would inform him that the afternoon train should be arriving shortly and he didn't want to see him in Thermopolis after it had departed. When I told him I was looking for a job he volunteered, "Irish Tom is going to be starting day after tomorrow. You contact Irish Tom, sonny."

Irish Tom was a cattleman who lived in Thermopolis because he didn't actually have a ranch. However, he and his partner, the town banker, owned a large number of homesteads which were scattered all over hell and gone, and controlled most of the area's springs. As a result, they ran a far-flung cattle outfit.

Irish Tom's name at baptism had been Thomas Walsh and he was raised, much as my father had been, in an American Gaelic-speaking community; as a result he had a brogue which could have been rent with a cleaver. He was about fifty years of age and of lean build although he walked stooped over, almost hunch-backed. He had another nickname, which came into being when a cowboy staring at him one day from across the herd asked nobody in particular, "What's that goddamned thing over there?"

The reply was, "Why, that's Irish Tom."

"The hell it is!" the cowpuncher roared. "That critter looks to me to be a big boar ape!"

The name stuck and from then on, Thomas Walsh was known throughout the Big Horn Basin as Irish Tom, the Boar Ape.

After a short talk with Irish Tom, I hooked up with his outfit in time for the spring roundup of 1910. On the day I arrived in Thermopolis the mess wagon was in town being loaded up with the possibles, and Tom took me out that afternoon to a line camp he had at the head of Buffalo Creek. Two cowboys lived in the one-room house, which was fashioned from the local sandstone. To the side of the house was a small corral where the saddle horses were kept.

I was there to outfit myself with a string of horses and also to act as the third man, the one who would take the edge off any impending attacks of cabin fever. One of the cowboys was Wicks Duncan, a husky, quarter-breed Shoshoni, and a hell of a good cowboy who could ride almost anything with four legs. The other was Henry Rothwell, son of the owner of the Padlock Ranch and a cool, practical cowboy who had just returned from college in the East.

Wicks and Henry slept in the cabin while I had my bedroll laid out on the ground opposite the door. The first morning I was there, I was jarred awake by a yell. As I turned my head toward the hollering, I saw Wicks standing outside the cabin door he had just opened, whispering hoarsely, *"Henry, don't come out!"*

Henry appeared in the doorway and drawled in a voice thick with sleep, "Why not, Wicks?"

And that's when he heard the buzz. Coiled in front of the door was a rattlesnake, the biggest one I'd seen up to that time. It was damn near five feet long.

Wicks stepped deliberately over the top of the serpent, though how he kept from being struck I will never know, walked into the cabin, past a frozen and now wide-awake Henry Rothwell, got his pistol, came back and shot the critter.

My bedroll had been laid out not over fifteen feet from the snake and why he didn't crawl into my bed with me to keep warm, as rattlers are prone to do, is something I never figured out. My luck was holding.

Several days after I arrived at the line shack, Irish Tom had recruited the seven men required for him to mount his roundup. It was a smaller operation than the one I participated in during my baptism as a cowboy for the Double Diamond. Still, certain elements remained the same no matter how many cowboys worked the range, for each roundup involved the same cast of characters: horses, cattle and cowboys.

On roundup, the beef herd, after being collected in scattered groups during the day, was bunched together at night and added to on the next day. As the herd grew larger and larger it had to be handled right and held tight at night so the beeves didn't drift away or stampede. This procedure involved the use of two-man guard teams. One man rode clockwise around the herd while the other moved counterclockwise, marking out an imaginary fence. It was this night guarding which served as the inspiration for the idea of the singing cowboy.

It didn't take much to spook the cattle, which were about half-wild anyway. If a man rode up quickly to the herd at night and stopped to light a cigarette, the flash of the match might spark them and they'd be off and gone. Or if a horse shook himself, the sound of the saddle leather at night practically jarred your teeth loose, and that, too, would spook the beef. In order to keep the beeves from getting edgy, we'd sing as we rode the night circle. The cattle heard our voices, got to know them, started becoming accustomed to the singing and any further, unusual sound would hopefully not cause them undue concern. Cattle, besides being spookable, are also pretty dumb. Let them eat, don't cause them any bother and they're fine.

I had a better than average tenor voice in those days and sometimes, if I was on an early guard, the cowboys would stay awake and listen to me sing. Mostly I sang the soft, lilting melodies I had heard my parents and their Irish friends singing when I was growing up. My fellow cowboys enjoyed such songs, for it was unusual for them to have anybody around who knew anything other than "Texas songs," like "Chisholm Trail":

> C'mon boys, and listen to my tale
> and I'll tell ya 'bout my troubles
> on the old Chisholm Trail,
> Come a ky-yi, yippi-yippi-ay, yippi-ay
> Come a ky-yi, yippi-yippi-ay.

The words to yet another "Texas song," this one about a real-life gunslinger and notorious murderer named Sam Bass, started out this way:

> Sam Bass came from Indiany,
> that was his native home,
> And at the age of seventeen,
> young Sam begin to roam.
> He came out here to Texas,
> a cowboy fer to be,
> And a kinder-hearted feller,
> you'd seldom ever see.

The popularity of such songs, which may have been real enough down in Texas, was vastly overrated elsewhere. It eventually got to the point where if anyone sang "Sam Bass," or broke into a single chorus of "ky-yi, yippi-yippi-ay," the cowpunchers would beat him half to death by "chapping"; in other words, taking off their heavy leather chaps and whaling hell out of the poor bastard.

I was sitting around the fire one night at suppertime when somebody asked who was on second guard.

"Oh, Ted Price and the Canary," came the reply from Irish Tom.

I looked up and said, "Wait a minute, I'm on guard with Ted Price."

Frank James, kind of a half-outlaw type, looked at me and said, "Hain't ya heerd yer name yet, young feller? *You're* Irish Tom's Canary."

CHAPTER FOUR

Big Guns and Dangerous Men

About two years later, after having left Irish Tom's outfit and experienced several changes of scene by working for the M-Bar, Padlock and, again, the Double Diamond, I was back with Irish Tom. It was while we were preparing to make the spring roundup that I met a cowpuncher unlike any other I had seen before. His name was George Shakespear.

George was a thirty-year-old, long-haired Arapaho, who was known to his own people as Buffalo Lodge. Aside from being a nearly delicately featured Indian who wore his hair in long braids wrapped in otter skin, George was also an expert cowboy. It should be clear by now that I tended to be drawn toward the Indians and so it was natural I would try to pull the night guard with George. When he had satisfied himself that my questions were not part of an elaborate practical joke, George was very forthcoming with information.

He told me he had gone off to white man school as a boy. The first thing that happened to him was that the white men cut his braids off. "How did that make you feel?" I asked him one afternoon as we rode together at the back of the drive.

"It made me cry," he replied sadly.

The next event in George's life at the school was the bestowing on him of a "proper" name. This happened to all the Indian children whether they were sent to Dr. Roberts' Episcopal St. Michael's Mission or the Jesuit St. Stephen's, run by the Blackrobes. It also happened to adults when they were first moved to the reservation.

One of my friends, Yellow Calf, a Buffalo Caller in the gone days and a man with strong Medicine, had his name altered to George Caldwell. He never used the name and whenever it was mentioned, he would mutter with disgust, "Become like a white man, believe in Jesus Christ and everything will be fine."

Red Turtle, George's brother, became William Shakespear; White Antelope's son was known as Faustinus White Antelope; Drives Down Hill was transformed into Mr. D. D. Hill; White Bull became Charles W. Bell; and Lone Bear, last of the Arapahoes' great council chiefs, was known to the government as Lon Brown. Red Pipe was carried on the agency rolls as Ralph Piper; Row Of Lodges was altered to Mr. Rowlodge; Wolf Elk became Wolf Elkins; Runs Behind was renamed Behan; and Ice Man inexplicably became C'Hair. And on and on.

Although many of the surnames came from buffalo times, others bore a more distinctly white tone, Cornelius Vanderbilt being a fairly typical example. It is therefore quite understandable that a George Shakespear should have been created up on Wind River.

From George, I learned that what existed within the Arapaho tribe in 1912 were three distinct groups of people. The first, of which George's father was a member, was composed of the older tribesmen who had fought the white man and lost. They had outlived their ways and, to their unending sadness, knew it. The second group, into which George fell, had been born just before the reservation period or shortly after its beginnings. They were born in tipis and reared in a buffalo culture which had no buffalo to hunt. It was the grandchildren of the old-timers, some of whom live yet, who were the third part of this depressing jigsaw: still Indians, all they knew of the bygone days was picked up secondhand and epitomized by the broken remnants surrounding them.

George Shakespear and his brother, William, had turned to cowboying as a way of earning a living. But the rampant prejudice of the whites sometimes made it a rough go. Many of the other cowpunchers thought they were being clever fellows by threatening him: "George, goddamnit, one of these days we're gonna rope ya, tie ya down and roach that hair." So George, like many of his people, and for the same reasons, became a stoic and silently endured the humiliation.

There were times, however, when the tables could be turned. Once, William Shakespear came to pay George a visit. It wasn't long before the cowboys noticed that he was missing the first joint of his left thumb. As George explained later, it had been torn loose some years before when William inadvertently allowed it to slip between a rope he'd looped over a charging calf and his saddle horn.

"Hey, John!" one of the grizzled cowboys shouted across the campfire at William, who was engrossed in conversation with his brother.

William looked up and gave the man a stare that would have chilled anyone even slightly more sensitive than this particular saddle tramp.

"How'd ya lose that finger?" the cowboy asked.

"You mean this?" William asked, holding his mangled thumb up for all to see.

The cowboy nodded.

"Well, a long time ago I used to interpret up at Fort Washakie. And whenever the white man wanted to make a new treaty with my people I had to tell them what the white man was saying. Of course, all the white man wanted was to take away some more land. But, you know, after the treaties were made they always asked me to put my thumbprint on the paper to make it legal. And damned if there weren't so many treaties that, after a while, my thumb just wore away."

Sometimes, after a day of rounding up cattle, George and I would sit together by the campfire at night. I would ask him about the Arapahoes and particularly about a peculiarity I had noticed for some time: they always seemed to be talking with their hands.

"Oh, that's the sign language," he replied, putting down his coffee mug. "That's how the old-timers talk. You know, 'Rapaho speaks 'Rapaho. Sioux fella speaks Sioux. Cheyenne, he speaks Cheyenne. How anybody gonna learn all those languages? Each language, he's completely different."

George continued, his hands in motion. "So, sometime, somewhere, Injun comes up with sign language. That way, all of us can understand each other. So, all over the Plains, everybody can speak the same way."

He paused, took a sip of his coffee, thought a moment and added, "Yeah, it's a pretty good idea."

"When these fellows meet, they hold that open right hand out in front of them. What's that mean?" I asked.

"If you got no weapon in your hand," he answered, "your hand, he's empty. So, when you do that you're showing the other fella you're not gonna kill him."

I started asking questions about things that would be of common interest on the range and learned that the sign for a cow, the critters I'd have to ask the Arapahoes about, was made by holding one crooked finger to either side of the head.

"Same as buffalo sign," George explained, "but smaller horns."

He also told me that if I said, "*Whoaha*," the old-timers would understand I was speaking about cattle. This was because when the warriors used to perch atop hills and watch the white men bringing cattle and oxen with the wagon trains the only consistent words they could make out were "whoa" and "ha." So they figured that the name for the white man's buffalo just had to be *whoaha*.

I found that the sign for white man was made by drawing a finger across the forehead because they were the first people the Indians had seen wearing hats.

George didn't particularly like talking about the Shoshonis, or *Sussoni* as they called themselves, but he did tell me they were Snake Indians. The sign for them was made by showing, with the index finger of the right hand, the path a snake makes wriggling across the ground. The Arapahoes, he explained, were referred to by tapping the fingers of the right hand against the left breast, in a gesture the meaning of which will ever be in dispute. Perhaps they were the mother people, from whom all other tribes descended, an explanation which jibes pretty well with each tribe's notion of its being the Tribe. It may, however, have gone back to the days when the Arapahoes tattooed themselves with coal rubbed onto the ends of sharp porcupine quills.

I wanted to know from George how to go about asking a question, such as "Did you see a black horse?", since sign language had developed along lines quite different from English, in that the noun precedes the adjective and the intent precedes everything. To illustrate: question sign-you-see-horse-black-day-this? I found that the questioning attitude was signified by holding the right hand straight out in front of the body and shifting it, without moving the arm, left, right, left, right, as in: this way-that way.

So George Shakespear became my teacher and I his willing and eager pupil. When I felt I would not be making a complete fool of myself, I set out to give it a whirl.

Riding along the trail I would meet an Arapaho and, just to break the ice, ask him in signs if he was of the *Hanunahaiee*, which is what they called themselves. (Aside from being an almost unpronounceable word for an English speaker, it's one with an obscure meaning. Some say it means "Our People"; and while I have no quarrel with that interpretation, the one the old men gave me over the years was positively mystifying: "Wrong Root Diggers.")

I learned later that these old men were fascinated that a young, green cowboy had not come galloping up in a cloud of dust and insulted them. The respectful attitude made them curious, for they seldom encountered it from a white man. And even though they hadn't dropped along the trail in a state of shock, they were surprised and pleased.

Soon the melt would begin.

Irish Tom's outfit was what we cowboys termed a "pool wagon." The ranchers with small homesteads on the other side of the Big Horn, at places like Alkalai, Kirby, Buffalo and Bridger creeks, had maybe one, two or three hundred head of cattle. For them to run a big "wagon," or roundup, at their own expense was out of the question. They didn't need it and they couldn't afford it. So what they would do was send a "rep" to the Boar Ape's spring and fall roundups. This rep would bring along his own string of horses and look after his boss's interests.

During the spring roundup, the rep saw to it that the calves belonging to his employer were branded; during fall roundup, he made sure the proper beef was cut, thrown into the herd and shipped East to market with Irish Tom's cattle, thereby guaranteeing full trainloads. It was the only way the small operators could stay in business, and in return, Irish Tom received a portion of their profit for services rendered.

It was a satisfactory arrangement and suited everybody's needs. There were, however, certain drawbacks inherent in the pool wagon business at that time. These drawbacks are best explained by the story about an impoverished cowboy who was planning on going into the cattle business.

"You got money?" he was asked.

"Nope."

"You got cattle?"

"Nope."

"Well, just what the hell *do* you have?"

"A long rope, a fast horse and an idea."

In other words, there were a devil of a lot of rustlers among those fellows. So many, in fact, that the Boar Ape's outfit was known throughout the Big Horn Basin as the Outlaw Wagon.

I have seen motion pictures and television programs where rustlers brazenly run off with several square miles of stampeding cattle. This makes for exciting film footage but it is not how the rustlers plied their trade.

Some of the ranchers with small homesteads in the Basin rode with the pool wagon as it traveled through their part of the country. If they were on the circle in the morning, and charged with bringing in cattle for the day's roundup, a couple of them might get together and, with their eyes peeled like a ferret's, ride slowly down a gulch. When they came across a cow with an unbranded calf, the calf being the primary object of attention, they'd drive them into the brush and leave them there. This routine would be repeated, with the rustlers taking enough head to make the risk worthwhile but not such an amount as might strain the credulity of the other members of the pool wagon beyond the bounds of reason and common sense.

There weren't many riders around the country, except cowboys looking after their stock, and it was impossible for them to cover everything. There were, however, rare occasions when rustlers were observed in action. I recall one afternoon on the spring 1912

1. My debut as a fourteen-year-old, flat-hatted, homesick bugler aboard the U.S.S. *Yantic*. Summer 1905.

2. The embryonic cowboy in Saginaw during the summer of 1908. One year later I went West.

3. Colonel William F. "Buffalo Bill" Cody. From the time I first met him in 1898 he became and has remained an inspiration to me. When I was a young cowboy in Wyoming he was gracious enough to offer me his company.

4. The real thing: Irish Tom's Canary, about 1912.

5. Goes In Lodge, the former buffalo-hunting Arapaho warrior who became my brother. The gorget at his neck is made from shell and his breastplate is constructed from hair-pipe bone, a popular trade item in the old days. His buckskin shirt is early reservation period and pale in comparison with the few pre-white-man-contact examples that survive. He was the epitome of the proud, long-haired old-timers.

6. About four months before I met them, these Arapahoes gathered at the dedication of their dance hall near Ethiti, Wyoming, on February 2, 1912. From left to right: Red Pipe, Painted Bear, Wolf Elk, Ben Warren, Button, Goes In Lodge, Paul Sleeping Bear, and Chester Armstrong. The white man names some of them bore attested to the influence of the government and the missionaries. Both the old dance hall and the old men have long since vanished.

7. Goes In Lodge and I talking in sign language. This picture was taken after we had known one another for about ten years. His fully beaded moccasins and my pressed shirt and tooled boots indicate we were probably in Cheyenne, Wyoming, for a Frontier Days Celebration.

8. Yellow Calf, the head Medicine Man among the Wind River Arapahoes, conductor of sweat lodge ritual and a Buffalo Caller in pre-reservation days. This is how he appeared in 1922, when he worked his Turtle Medicine during the filming of *The Covered Wagon*.

9. Washakie, head chief of the Shoshonis, with his subchiefs. His son, Dick "All-Injun Celebration" Washakie, is to his immediate right. About 1881.

10. Sharp Nose, war chief of the Arapahoes and Washakie's longtime antagonist. His blouse was standard U. S. Army issue and recalls his service as chief of General Crook's Arapaho scouts in 1878, two years before this picture was taken.

11. Washakie in 1898. This photograph was taken by Captain W. C. Brown. Two years later, the old Shoshoni would "lose the way" and call upon a white man friend for assistance.

12. Learning to be a cavalryman during "forty miles a day on beans and hay" maneuvers at Fort Snelling in 1917.

13. The adjutant general of Wyoming, 1919.

14. General Hugh L. Scott, Custer's Crow scout White Man Runs Him and I at the Crow's Nest during our inspection of the Little Big Horn battlefield in 1919.

roundup seeing two men I happened to like driving several calves belonging to a man of whom I was not particularly fond down the dry wash below me.

One of my friends looked up, saw me, reined in his horse, pulled his Winchester rifle from its scabbard, laid the weapon across the pommel of his saddle and stared at me.

"Well, Tim, I guess you've got an idea what's goin' on here," he said, nervously.

"A pretty good idea," I replied.

"Well, whatcha gonna do?" the second cowboy asked.

"I may've read the brand wrong," I answered, "but if you boys are doing what I think you're doing, I'd suggest you don't do it again while I'm around. And if I were you, I sure as hell wouldn't let anybody else see you with those calves. We all know some fellows who'd drop you on the spot, don't we?"

They nodded. Then the first cowboy suggested I take a cut of the meat when they'd finished butchering. I shook my head and rode off. The next morning, when the camp awoke, the two men were gone and never returned to Irish Tom's outfit.

They'd probably gone off to do what most rustlers did. After the roundup had passed through, and working with the law of averages, these entrepreneurs retrieved their catch and moved their little herd to a corral up at the head of a creek or off in the timber. The calves remained in the boondocks until they were old enough to wean, at which point the rustlers shooed the cows off and put their brand on the babies.

And, lo and behold, without money or land, but having a long rope, a fast horse and an idea, their herds grew and they prospered. Then they started to get greedy and began making moves which, more often than not, proved to be fatal. No longer content with picking off calves, rustlers earmarked a fat yearling or even a two-year-old, butchering in the brush.

At the dark of the moon, the meat was loaded into a buckboard and brought into town, where the rustlers would have a fence, a butcher who didn't ask inconvenient questions. After all, he was getting his beef mighty cheap. And even though there was a law requiring that all locally bought beef be accompanied by a fresh, branded hide as proof of legitimate ownership, some shopkeepers swore they never noticed that the hide was getting old, dusty and stiff.

I recall once in Thermopolis when a couple of rustlers were arrested during the town's semi-annual "cleanup" campaign. These jaspers had been caught with a T-W, Thomas Walsh or Irish Tom, brand on the freshly skinned hide of a steer they didn't happen to own. The rustlers were locked inside the jail and the hide was taken by the sheriff, who folded and placed it in a strongbox and sealed the metal container within the vise-like grip of several chains and padlocks.

A week later there was a trial and during his dramatic summation to the jury the prosecutor had the chains and locks hacked away. Not bothering to examine the evidence carefully, he reached into the box and, with a flourish, held the offending object before the eyes of the jury, who guffawed derisively at the obviously old and moth-eaten skin they beheld. Case dismissed.

Particularly bold rustlers would sometimes work over the beef's existing brand with a hot running iron, and many cattlemen and range bosses spent some sweaty hours attempting to come up with foolproof brands that would stymie even the most artistic and creative rustlers. I have seen many explanations for the famous XIT brand found down in Texas. Some say it utilized the Roman numeral X and stood for "Ten in Texas," meaning the ranch, sprawled over ten counties. The simple fact, however, was that the brand could be applied with a single straight-iron and was damned hard to alter.

A story circulating in my time concerned the legendary IC brand. Rustlers picked up a yearling and altered the markings to read ICU. Shortly afterward, their catch disappeared and when they recovered the critter, its markings had again been changed, to ICU2. The story is apocryphal; nevertheless, certain brands were eminently alterable. For instance, HE easily became ⊞, the Window Sash. CY, the brand of my friends the Careys, could, without too much effort, be worked into ⊗, Coffee Pot. oo must have been hit particularly hard: ∞, Dumbbell, and 88, Eighty-Eight.

Shortly before I arrived in Wyoming, any cowboys who were found with a fire, a running iron and a flimsy story near cattle belonging to someone else usually disappeared quietly and permanently. As civilization made its encroachments upon the West, the forces of progress appealed for adherence to the rule of law, but as the story of the sealed box at the Thermopolis trial demonstrates, the rule of law was sometimes not exactly an effective deterrent to rustling. In the first decade of the present century, and spilling over into the second, at the time I was riding for the Double Diamond and Irish Tom, the slow-to-rile big operators, growing impatient with the courts, and angry at the continued ripping off of their herds, turned to older, tested and proven means to discourage rustling. Then big guns, in the hands of dangerous men, were brought into the country and enterprising cowboys began to fall.

When I first arrived in the Big Horn Basin, there was an upheaval going on in the long-rope-fast-horse-and-an-idea business. The big-time ranchers, convinced that the costly losses they had been suffering at the hands of cattle thieves could not be reduced by resorting to the time-consuming twists and turns of the legal system, had turned to illegal, more direct and indisputably effective means. They began to import hired guns to "discourage" rustlers.

The men the ranchers employed were called "regulators" by some, "bushwhackers" by many and certainly kept at arm's length by most. When one of them rode into Thermopolis, or word arrived that such a character had been seen in the vicinity, the atmosphere throughout the Big Horn Basin thickened. Pressure built and tension grew until, one day in a deserted place, the sound of a single shot from a .30-.30 Winchester rifle echoed along the red hills and a lone cowboy, shot from behind and already dead, tumbled from his horse and fell in a crumpled heap upon the ground. Then the dealer in death reported to his employers and, mission accomplished, contract fulfilled, collected his blood money and departed from the area as quickly and as quietly as he had arrived. And while the frequency of such episodes, reminiscent of the truly wild West, was declining in my time, they had by no means come to an end.

It was about noontime on a pleasant spring day in 1912. Wicks Duncan, the quarter-breed Shoshoni cowboy, and I had ridden into Thermopolis from Irish Tom's line camp to pick up some supplies. Cowboys were sauntering down the street and into saloons, looking for a few drinks and perhaps a game of Blackjack or Six Card Draw, probably biding their time until the whorehouses opened for business. At about the same time Wicks and I arrived on the scene, and from the other end of the dusty street, Sam Barry, a dark-moustached man of small stature and a large reputation, made his appearance. He was riding his black horse at a walk down the main street. And though he was known by sight to many of us, there were few cowboys who had ever exchanged words with him. Sam Barry was not a talkative man.

His arrival in town had its usual effect. There were furtive glances and sharp whisperings among the hands gathered along the sidewalks. Some of them mounted their horses and galloped into the hills or out onto the open range to spread the word. The general reaction could best be described as fear bordering on terror, though Sam Barry was the most mild-mannered of men, caused no offense, raised no arguments and never got into a fight. But Sam was far from his usual haunt near Cody, about three days' ride to the north, and since he was a professional it was assumed he was in Thermopolis on business. Sam Barry's business was man-killing.

He did not kill indiscriminately and shot only those cowboys who were widely known as rustlers. For this he was paid $600 per head. To prove that the deed had been done, it was his custom to remove one of his victim's ears and deliver it to his employer upon completion of each job. Nothing about Sam Barry indicated he was anything but a slow-moving character. Nothing, that is, but his stare, which, as I could observe and as Irish Tom often remarked, was "just like a rattlesnake's."

Wicks had just gone off to leave our horses at the livery barn when the barn's owner, Ben Ivy, came up the street and asked me to join him in Happy Jack's saloon for a drink. We walked through the short, swinging green doors together and stood at the bar rail. Sam Barry came in immediately behind us, having tied his horse to the hitching rack, slowly looked around and, after carefully surveying the town, decided it would be safe to do so.

"Why doesn't somebody kill that sonofabitch?" one cowboy at the bar muttered to a friend.

"Why don't you kill him?" his pal rasped in sharp reply.

"'Cause I hain't no rustler."

"You better hope to hell *he* knows that!"

Sam Barry smiled the thinnest of smiles and for the next few minutes sat like a rock in his chair, sipping his beer quietly, talking to no one and looking at nothing in particular. Nobody joined him at his table and Happy Jack's, usually a gay, boisterous place, took on the ambience of a funeral parlor.

I noticed that when Barry entered Happy Jack's, Ben Ivy had immediately turned his back to the barman and faced toward the new arrival. After Sam Barry left and the saloon began to lighten up a bit I turned to look at Ben and saw beads of sweat across his brow.

Ben Ivy was considered a mite peculiar, even in those parts. He was a heavy-set, dark-haired man who wore his hair down to his shoulders and, with his full beard, bib overalls and loose denim jacket, cut a figure "mighty weird," as Irish Tom used to say. He had a penchant for keeping his back to walls, corners, trees, anything that might afford protection from an incoming rifle round. The reason for this was never ascertained, nor was it asked. You didn't ask questions of the Westerners. It was just that whenever Ben came to join us out at the line shack and we'd offer him a seat by the window, he'd drawl in his southern accent, "If you don' mind, brutha, I'd just as soon sit over there by the wall."

"Do you know Sam Barry?" I asked him, which was about as direct a question as one would dream of asking in the Big Horn Basin in 1912.

Ben ran a thick hand through his tangled sideburns and I could not help but think of Irish Tom's remark about Ben having recently visited a barber. According to Tom, the barber had unearthed a chipmunk and three nests of field mice.

"Well, brutha, I don' zackly know the man. But I seen him round here enough to know what it is he does."

After ordering another double shot of whiskey, Ben continued, "See, there's a chance he's here to blow somebody's brains all across the rocks. Then again, he might be here just to put a little scare into some of our less law-abiding folks. You never really know with Sam Barry. But all he has to do is show his face and rustlin' goes a-way down."

As he turned to the barman and said, "I'll have the same again, brutha," I looked at his denim overcoat, trying to see if I could answer the cowboy's usual question about Ben: "Just how many six-shooters does he carry?" The answer, so far as I could see, was two, one tucked into either side of his belt buckle. They were old and big and fashioned from gleaming blue steel, but I only got a quick glimpse, for in a moment, he had turned around, shot glass in hand and ready to resume his story.

"I was in here the morning Sam Barry arrived about four or five years ago," he said, downing the glass and shoving it across the bar. It was soon filled again, but Ben Ivy had apparently decided it was time for a rest.

"Yes, brutha. And do you know who was in here at the same time? Why, just some of the most flagrant rustlers this side of God's green gate. Bob McCoy, Kis Eads and Frank James." The same Frank James who had given me my nickname of Irish Tom's Canary. I had often wondered why the closed-mouthed Frank James was so jumpy. One time when I was with him and we were belly-down, drinking some water from a creek, a rock tumbled down the bank. Frank quickly whipped out his pistol and before I could begin to think about what was happening, drilled six shots into a sapling behind us. Most of us carried five shots in our revolvers, keeping the first chamber empty to prevent any accidents. But Frank always kept his fully loaded. Besides, he had sawn off the trigger and created a fast-fanning machine. As I say, jumpy.

"Well, I'll tell you, brutha," Ben continued, "those boys was mighty scared. Yes sir. Kis Eads hightailed it for his father's place a few miles east of town. Frank James moved into the Emery Hotel, where he had his food and drink catered while keeping the curtains tightly drawn, his window locked and that quick-barkin' pistol of his cocked. And ol' Bob McCoy, he picked up some provisions to last him and his wife a week or so and rode at a gallop out of Thermopolis."

Ben gave me a look which indicated that if the story was to continue I would be buying the next round. In those days, I drank no alcohol but, still, found some of the most engaging conversation in the saloons. Ivy knew his mark, for I immediately plunked down the fifteen cents the bartender needed to refill Ben's glass.

"Thank ya, brutha, thank ya," Ivy murmured, sipping on his drink. He placed the glass down carefully on the bar and pushed his gray Stetson back on his head.

"Bob McCoy lived 'bout five mile out of town," he continued. "And once he'd crossed the bridge over the Big Horn and turned right he figured he was safe as safe could be. But Sam Barry was just a little smarter than Bob McCoy."

As Ben Ivy related it, Sam Barry arrived at the Big Horn ahead of his prey. He knew the people he was after and he knew their routes, having come into the Basin surreptitously a week beforehand and spending his time studying the situation. Upon reaching the Big Horn, Sam Barry climbed into a rowboat he had stashed, rowed to the opposite bank and ran up the hill to hide in an abandoned shack along Bob McCoy's route home. As Bob passed by, Sam Barry let him have it with two rifle shots. In my time, the rotting screen over one of the shack's windows still bore the holes created by the bullets as they tore though the screen and into Bob McCoy's back.

The job done, Sam Barry caught Bob McCoy's horse, removed the saddle, which he threw into the brush, and then let the horse loose. The animal lost no time in making for his corral at Bob's home, where his arrival caused Bob's wife no end of consternation.

Several days later, Bob McCoy's body was fished out of the Big Horn River by some passing cowboys who observed a pale hand stiffly protruding at the river's edge. It was weighted down around the neck by a horse's nose bag filled with rocks. His left ear was missing.

Many, many years later, when I was in Hollywood, I discussed the killing with a man I had worked for, the range boss of a big cattle outfit.

"Do you think Sam Barry did it?" I asked him.

"I am certain," the man, who will remain anonymous, replied.

"But how can you be so sure?"

"Because," he answered, "I'm the fellow who paid Sam Barry off."

Ben Ivy was staring into his empty glass. His face registered the expression I would come to know as that of a man whose story is done but who is still capable of furnishing further tidbits of information from an inexhaustible repertoire.

"And what happened to the others?" I asked, handing the bartender another fifteen cents.

"A thousand thanks, brutha," Ivy intoned, still quite lucid. "Well, Kis Eads did not wait around to take a tour of the scene of the crime. No sir. Before the corpse was dredged out of the waters, Kis came into town driving a buckboard. Beside him on the front seat sat his pretty little wife and a Winchester rifle. They visited the dressmaker's, where Kis bought her a gingham dress. They entered the shoemaker's, where he bought her a pair of fancy shoes. They appeared, brutha, to be just another young couple enjoying a day on the town. But eventually, they sauntered into the same meat market where Kis had wholesaled some of the beef he and his partners had run off from the large herds. While his wife inspected the cuts in the meat case, Kis kept right on going. He walked by the butcher to the rear of the store, turned once to glance nervously over his shoulder, opened the door and dashed for the horse he had arranged to be tied in the alley waiting for him.

"The last of the local people to see Kis was 'Doc' Gillam, a friend of mine, who happened to be a passenger on the southbound stage coming into Thermopolis from Cody.

" 'There, less than a hundred yards away and on a hill about five miles out of town,' Doc told me, 'was a lone rider. He was riding hard but when he saw the stage he pulled up and sat his saddle, a rifle thrown across his lap. I leaned out the window as we went past, thinking I recognized him, and shouted, "Kis!" He sat bolt-upright, hesitated a moment, waved and galloped off.' "

It was the last anybody in the Big Horn Basin ever saw or heard of Kis Eads.

"And what about Frank James?" I asked Ben Ivy.

"Well, you ride with him. Why don't you ask him?" he replied merrily. "All I'll tell you is two weeks after the killing of Bob McCoy, Frank emerged from the Emery Hotel and beheld the light of day. His eyes were bloodshot and he was a thinner, older-looking man than when he checked in the day Sam Barry hit town."

Since the statute of limitations for whatever activities Frank James had been engaged in had not yet run its course, the only answer he would give to my carefully phrased questions about the event was a grunt. One evening, over coffee at Irish Tom's line shack he mumbled, "If you wanna know, ask Walt Putney, the sonofabitch."

I knew Walt Putney, a short, bowlegged cowboy and small-time homesteader. He had gray eyes, a black moustache flecked with gray, and a quick smile. In the Basin country, he passed for downright gregarious. I did not know that he had, not too many years before, served a term in the Wyoming State Penitentiary, and while I no longer remember whether he did his time for bank robbery or horse stealing, both were sidelines he had been known to have worked.

"Frank James, eh?" Putney said after he and I had dined alone one evening in Irish Tom's line shack. It was the custom in those days that if anybody showed up at a line shack, cabin or rancher's house, he was fed, given a place to sleep and made to feel as comfortable as possible. Walt had happened to come by late in the afternoon, and, remembering Frank James's words, I invited him to spend the night, hoping we would get around to discussing the wild and woolly aspect of Thermopolis' history.

Putney smiled. "So he called me a sonofabitch? You know, when I think about that jumpy bastard I can't help but recall a scene that took place in Thermopolis a few years back. The sheriff, Virgil Rice, was playing a game of poker with some of the boys in a saloon. He was studying his cards carefully and a lot of time had passed when a newcomer to town snapped at him, 'Well, are you in or out, you sonofabitch?' Rice gave him a mighty chilly stare and hissed, 'When you call me that again, pardner, *smile*.' Did you know that when that eastern feller, Owen . . . Owen . . . now, what was his name?"

"Owen Wister?" I volunteered.

"Yep, that's him. Owen Wister. When he was here, he heard that story and they tell me he used it in some book he wrote."

I had known Wister visited the area while doing research for *The Virginian*. Walt Putney was just one of many cowhands who remembered the quiet man who, upon hearing a new expression or a colorful story, whipped out his notebook and started writing. Trampas, I'd been told, was a real cowboy named Trampas. Shorty was a character who was still alive in my time, Shorty Holland. And, by common agreement among the cowboys, the Virginian was a composite.

Walt Putney chuckled and poured himself another cup of coffee after stacking our dishes by the wash tub in a corner of the shack. "Did you ever see Frank's shooting machine?"

"You mean that pistol without a trigger, Walt?"

"That's the one. Isn't that something?" Walt shook his head slowly. "You just know that anybody who packs something like that has got some powerful worries on his mind. Now, I ain't sayin' nothin' agin Frank, but I remember a time that pistol damn near killed a good friend of mine."

One day, Walt Putney recalled, and for reasons he was never able to ascertain, some desperadoes in Thermopolis decided to do in one of their former compadres, a rustler, sometime bank robber and friend of Putney's named Tom O'Day. By lot, a sinister-looking local named Bagby was selected to do the job. Lacking a weapon, Bagby borrowed Frank James's pistol.

When Tom O'Day rode into Thermopolis on a pleasant summer day shortly after noon, he was asked by the town marshal to turn in his revolver for "the good of the town," which he did with some reluctance.

Tom O'Day was not exactly a naïve customer and he decided to move around town as quietly and inconspicuously as possible. Instead of heading for his normal watering spot, Happy Jack's saloon, Tom went into an adjacent coffee shop-restaurant, which consisted of a tiny room with four or five tables and twice as many spindly chairs.

Bagby, who had been watching O'Day's movements from behind a mannequin in the window of a haberdasher's, slinked across the street, braced himself against the door and came flying into the restaurant, bellowing, "You're in for it now, Tom!"

O'Day froze in his seat and stared, wide-eyed, as Bagby raised James's pistol and prepared to fire. But the unfortunate Bagby had never fired a pistol without a trigger and the result was that as Bagby instinctively raised the pistol, cocked the hammer back with his thumb into what had always been the locked position and let go of the hammer, the weapon discharged immediately, throwing a .45-caliber slug into the ceiling, the shock practically knocking Bagby off his feet.

O'Day, unfrozen by the noise and the realization that this was actually happening to *him*, jumped from his chair, knocking his table halfway across the room, and dashed behind the cook's counter, where a tray of porcelain coffee mugs was placed. Grabbing the tray, he began hurling the mugs at Bagby and, to the accompanying sound of erratic, out-of-control shooting, hoots, howls and shattering porcelain, drove his assailant into the street.

Bagby, realizing he had failed, ran down the main street of town and disappeared around a corner. Tossing the tray to the ground as he stepped out onto the sidewalk and jumping on his horse, Tom O'Day whipped his mount at a gallop toward Wind River Canyon. He was never again seen in Thermopolis.

"And that was too bad," Walt Putney said sadly, shaking his head slowly from side to side, "because Tom O'Day was a good man to ride the river with and a hell of a more interesting character than Frank James." He paused, sipped some coffee, glanced at me a couple of times and then stared into his cup, obviously deep in thought.

"Well," he continued, "I don't suppose there's any harm talking about it now. It happened a few years back. See, there was a time Tom, a couple of other fellows and I robbed a bank."

Walt then told of the day he and his friends were engaged in a conversation outside Happy Jack's, talking quietly among themselves. Suddenly they mounted their horses and rode out of town together. Such a scene, even in my time, usually meant a "job" had been planned. And the upshot of that particular discussion was that they would ride to Belle Fourche, South Dakota, and rob a bank.

But somewhere between Thermopolis and Belle Fourche, the conspirators calculated the projected take from the bank was not sufficient to meet their needs and, concluding they needed additional cash flow, made hasty plans to rob the saloon, in which a massive steel safe harbored the house's share of the considerable gambling revenues. Upon arrival in Belle Fourche, Tom O'Day tied his horse outside the saloon while Walt and the others entered the bank. Apparently they had failed to agree on a schedule, because as Tom was leaning against the walnut bar, sipping from a shot of whiskey, all hell broke loose down the street, in the direction of the bank.

O'Day, cursing, ran outside upon hearing the shots. He was just in time to see Putney, a sack of silver coins thrown over his shoulder, and his other friends leap onto their horses, throw some shots at a gathering, angry mob of the town's citizens and make their break from Belle Fourche, pursued by numerous rifle shots and threats from the locals.

"I'll get 'em, I'll get 'em!" O'Day shouted, running for his horse. But just as he mounted, a stray shell crashed into the animal's hoof. His horse reared and O'Day tumbled to the ground. Getting up and dusting himself off, he immediately knew that time was of the essence. Latching onto a mule which had also been tethered to the hitchrack, he jumped aboard. Trotting past the bank, he was heard to yell, "I'll pursue the varmits, boys, I'll get 'em!"

As he passed the bank, futilely kicking the mule to try and pick up some speed, somebody shouted, "He's one of *them!*" Before Tom O'Day knew what was happening, a shell from a Winchester buried itself in his shoulder and he flew out of the saddle and lay on the ground, dazed.

In the meantime, Walt Putney was faring a little, but not much, better. Several miles out of town, the posse of about twenty irate citizens closed in on him. Suddenly a rifle shot caught him just below the right shoulder blade, blowing him off his horse and into a muddy irrigation ditch, where he lay motionless.

"It was the sack," Walt said. "Damn! When that shell hit, it crashed into that sack of silver. The impact was terrific, and I'm sure it saved my life because the posse rode by, thinking I was deader 'n hell."

Everybody except Tom O'Day made a safe getaway. And since the jail in Belle Fourche had recently burned down during an escape attempt, he was incarcerated for three weeks in the iron cell which rose like a bear cage above the charred rubble, and in which he was exposed to the elements and the jeers of contemptuous passers-by.

"What ever happened to the money in that sack?" I asked.

"Oh yeah, the money," Walt grinned. "Well, the sack was pretty well torn, as you can imagine. And some of the silver was scattered all over that ditch and across the trail. It was a mess. Now, I ain't makin' no confessions, understand? But you must agree, Tim, that I've got myself a right nice little homestead."

Guthrie Nicholson was British, and very much so. He owned a half interest in the M-Bar Ranch and was a partner in a conglomeration of ranches which formed an empire known as the Rocky Mountain Cattle Company. Guthrie called the dogies "calves," with a broad *a*, supervised roundup and sipped afternoon tea. He was a kind man and over the years I came to know him well. And while he did not relate the following story to me until we met one evening in 1920 in the bar of Cheyenne's Plains Hotel, it took place during the time of my life about which I am now writing, namely, 1912. It is about his association with a man very much unlike himself, Sam Barry.

Both men happened to be in Happy Jack's one afternoon in 1910. Perhaps Barry was in Thermopolis on business, which is likely, or maybe for a holiday, which is not so likely. Nicholson was a rarity in that part of the country and he and Sam began to chat. Nicholson bought Sam a drink, Sam bought him a drink and after this had gone on for an hour or so, Nicholson lost count of who was supposed to pay for the current round.

"Sam," Nicholson recalled saying, still steady with a pint of whiskey in his belly, "tell you what: let's twist for the drinks."

Barry smiled and the two men dug their elbows into the bar, locked hands and pushed and pulled, beads of sweat forming on their brows, until Nicholson brought Sam's arm down with a dull thud.

"Okay, Nick," Barry grinned, "this round is mine."

When the time came to serve up the next two shot glasses, Sam Barry challenged Nicholson. "Let's twist for the drinks!"

Again, Nicholson won the contest. And after several hours the unbeaten Guthrie Nicholson left Happy Jack's and his convivial companion.

Two years later, in the spring of 1912, one of Nicholson's friends came riding in hard from the range. He had been whipping his horse for most of the thirty-mile westward trip from Thermopolis to Nicholson's house at the M-Bar. Upon arrival, he practically threw himself from his horse and rushed into Nicholson's palatial log house.

"Nick!" he shouted, running frantically through the rooms in search of his friend. "For chrissakes, Nick, where are you?"

"I'm right here," Guthrie said, emerging from his library, carrying an open, leather-bound book in one hand and wearing a velvet smoking jacket. "What's the problem?"

"The problem is that Sam Barry is on his way over here."

"No problem. Nice chap. We know each other."

"Nick, he hain't comin' for a social call. He's gonna kill you!"

After finishing his cigar and downing his brandy, Nicholson, at the urging of his nervous friend, dressed, saddled a horse and rode away from his ranch. His friend, satisfied, took off in the opposite direction. But Nicholson was not riding away from Sam Barry. Instead, he decided to head toward Meteetsie, where he knew Barry would probably make a stop before hitting the trail for the Big Horn Basin.

Meteetsie was so small it was just barely a village. There was a livery barn, a general store, a post office, a hotel and, naturally, a saloon. The first stop Nicholson made was the saloon, and it was there he found his man.

Barry must have been feeling confident of himself because for once his back was to the door. He was standing at the bar rail having a drink when Nicholson walked up behind him and said quietly, "Sam, how about twisting for the drinks?"

Sam wheeled around, faced Guthrie and gave him a stare which Nicholson described to me as being "not in the slightest bit friendly."

"Whataya wan'?" Sam Barry snarled.

"I'll twist you for the drinks," Nicholson coolly countered.

Sam Barry shrugged and the two men twisted and drank,

twisted and drank into the small hours of the morning. As dawn approached, the man from Britain placed a hand gently upon the arm of the man from Cody.

"I heard you wanted to see me, Sam," Nicholson said softly.

"That's right," Barry nodded. "I was comin' to see you, Nick. But I hain't no more."

"Who sent you?"

"Let's just say a former business associate of yours, and leave it at that."

"And how much was he going to pay you?"

"The usual. Six hundred dollars for your ear. But I hain't gonna do it now, Nick."

Nicholson smiled, put on his sheepskin coat and started walking toward the door.

"Nick," Sam called after him.

"Yes?" Nicholson said, turning to face Barry.

"You know, there may come a day when I'll be needing that six hundred dollars. When that happens, I'll send you a telegram, telling you I'm on my way to Owl Creek. That okay?"

"That'll be fine, Sam, just fine," Nicholson said, leaving the saloon in Meteetsie, alive.

"And did he ever send that telegram?" I asked Nicholson, when we talked about the encounter eight years later.

"No, as a matter of fact, he didn't, Tim. But you can be sure that Sam Barry's credit is good with me. He can draw on me for that six hundred anytime he wants, just so long as he lets me keep my ear."

A man much like Sam Barry but more widely known and therefore less successful in maintaining the first and most essential part of an enforcer's credo—silence and anonymity—was Tom Horn.

Since Horn was hanged in 1903, I never knew him and what I was told about the man indicated I wouldn't have really wanted to. Several of my friends had drunk and been associated with him, one was nearly shot by him and another finally put the hood over his head preparatory to the drop that threw him into the Long Swing.

Tom Horn stood over six feet tall and weighed well above two hundred pounds. Photographs of him show a face which, in a simple sort of way, was handsome but a shade on the cold-looking side. He had been, or so he said, in the Spanish-American War and had even spent time in Arizona as an Army scout tracking down renegade Apaches. By the late 1890s, he was employed by the Wyoming Cattlemen's Association as a range detective. In theory, it was his job to ride the open country, specifically in the vicinity of Cheyenne in southern Wyoming, and reduce the frequency with which rustlers struck the widespread and unsupervised herds of cattle. In practice, Horn did the same job Sam Barry performed, the difference between the two men being that Tom Horn was on a retainer from the Association. Indeed, the fee per job was identical, and must have been the going rate: six hundred dollars a head.

Like Sam Barry, Horn planned his escapades thoroughly, did his business quickly and made a speedy departure from the scene of the crime. Instead of taking an ear, it was Horn's trademark to, whenever possible, place a small rock under the head of his victim.

One of Horn's first known marks I heard about was a cowboy known variously as Isham Dart, Nigger Isham and the Calico Cowboy. Isham was supposed to be about the best bronc rider in southern Wyoming but because of segregation barriers was not able to compete officially in any rodeos. He was apparently thought of as a personable man and almost universally well liked. He also happened to be a rustler, and in October 1900, as he and two of his friends left his cabin and walked toward the corral to saddle their horses, there was the report of a single rifle shot and the Calico Cowboy dropped to the ground, dead.

"I am certain," Bob Hubler, one of the men I rode with for Irish Tom, told me, "that the man who killed Isham Dart was the man whose horse I was riding soon afterward. You see, that morning my father had given me some peculiar instructions. I was to take one of our best horses to a spot down in a draw by a creek, tie it up and walk away about a quarter mile and wait. When I heard a shot I was to go back to where the horse was tied, though none too quickly, and retrieve it.

"Damnedest thing," Hubler chuckled, "I was waiting just as I'd been told and then, after about ten minutes, there was a single shot. I walked down to the creek and what I found was a different horse, short of breath and heavily lathered. I always figured that it was Horn had taken ours and left his as he made his way toward an alibi."

In Horn's time there was a saloon in Cheyenne owned by Harry Hinds. Harry was not tall but as big through his shoulders and chest as almost any two other men. He had started out in Wyoming as a blacksmith for the Deadwood–Cheyenne stage, opened the saloon and when I came to know him during occasional forays to Cheyenne, was proprietor of what was then the finest eating, drinking, gambling and sleeping establishment in southern Wyoming, the Plains Hotel.

"Did you ever know Tom Horn?" I asked him one evening as we sat together in the lounge of his hotel, where I had decided to take a short vacation after Irish Tom's spring roundup.

"Know him?" Hinds roared. "Why, that miserable sonofabitch almost killed me one time. Sure I knew him, and I was never so relieved as on the day he was hanged."

It was, as Harry related the episode, about 1901. The gambling tables were busy, the saloon crowded and business good. Above the saloon were a couple of rooms Harry sometimes let out and, peering from the window of one of them, Harry could see above the curtain line and into the window of a haberdasher's store across the street. The store was owned by two men with whom Hinds had experienced some unsatisfactory business dealings. And there, in the store, were the two partners, gesturing toward Harry's saloon. The man to whom they were talking was Tom Horn.

Feeling "a mite uneasy," Hinds left his post beside the upstairs window when he observed Horn exit from the haberdasher's and walk across the street to his saloon. When he reached the bar, he noticed Tom Horn lolling at the opposite end of the railing, a whiskey in his hand and a scowl across his face. As Hinds suspected, Horn was not as drunk as he appeared and was, in fact, cold sober. The feigned drunkenness was a ruse and its purpose became clear momentarily.

Beside Horn stood an elderly, bewhiskered prospector, whom

Horn without warning seized by the back of the neck. With two rapid motions, Tom Horn brushed the prospector's shot glass across the bar and onto the floor, picked up the old man, smashed the cigar he had been smoking into his face, threw him onto the bar and, with a mighty effort, slid him its length to a shattering crash on the floor at the other end of the room. The saloon became quiet as the patrons waited to see what was coming next. Harry Hinds started to make a beeline for Horn, but stopped, realizing that was probably just what Horn expected him to do.

"Horn causes a ruckus," Harry explained, "I grab Horn, and he blows the roof clean off my head and walks away by pleading he thought it was self-defense because he was 'drunk' and didn't know any better. But instead of falling into that trap, I decided to lay one of my one."

When Harry reached Horn, he stood in front of him and said, "Now, Tom, why did you go and do a thing like that?"

"Wanna make somethin' outta it?" Horn snarled.

"Of course not, Tom, but you can't go knocking people around for no reason."

"Is that so? And who says I can't?" Horn said menacingly.

"Well, Tom," Hinds replied in a soothing voice, as he checked his balance, braced his feet, distributed his weight, calculated his distance from Horn and edged a little closer, "if it means that much to you . . ."

And that is when Harry Hinds lowered the boom by bringing his right fist up and, with a single, shattering blow square in Horn's face, sent the bushwhacker to his knees. Then, picking up a beer mug, he cracked it alongside Horn's head, jumped on top of him and delivered several hammerings into the man's slack jaw.

"When I was satisfied that bastard wasn't going to be getting to his feet at any point in the near future," Harry said to me grimly, "I unbuttoned his coat and found, just as I thought I would, a revolver tucked into his belt. Now, Tim, wouldn't you say I am normally a mild-mannered gentleman?"

I nodded.

"But, you see, Tom had managed to get me riled. So I pulled his gun out and beat the living hell out of him with it. There was a space of several minutes there when I thought I might've killed him."

"What happened next?" I asked, hanging on Harry's every word.

"When Tom Horn regained consciousness," he replied, an icy look in his eyes, "he was lying, bound hand and foot, spread-eagle, on a brass bed in one of the upstairs rooms. And the first thing he saw was me, sitting beside him, and pointing the cocked revolver at his head."

"Please don't kill me, Harry," Horn pleaded.

"I ain't gonna kill you, you miserable sonofabitch," Hinds spat, "but I know damn well I ought to. Now, when I untie you, I want you to get your ass out of my saloon and never come back again. Because if you do, I'll throw a .45 slug into your brain case the minute you darken my door. Is that clear?"

Horn nodded painfully and, untied, bloody and bruised, made his way downstairs and staggered out the door.

"Weren't you afraid of him after that?" I asked Harry.

"Afraid? 'Course I was afraid! I did, however, take out some insurance. See, Tim, I immediately developed the peculiar habit of sleeping beside a double-barreled, sawed-off shotgun. And even then, I don't think I got much sleep until after the morning of November 20, 1903, which is the day they hanged that nasty bastard."

On the second evening of my break from the Outlaw Wagon, Harry Hinds invited me to join him for supper. We passed an enjoyable evening, talking about the old days, and then, as coffee was served, Joe Cahill, the husky former deputy sheriff of Cheyenne in Horn's day, joined us.

"Joe!" Hinds said expansively, waving to a waiter to bring him a bottle of the brandy he kept for himself locked away in an oak cabinet behind the bar of the Plains. "Sit down, join us for some talk. This young fellow here wants to know something about Tom Horn."

"Is that so?" Cahill said, smiling to Hinds and eying me carefully. "And what would you be wanting to know?"

"Well, what sort of a man was he?" I asked.

Hinds grimaced and Cahill laughed. "Nice guy, hell of a nice guy. But twisted. And not too damn bright, either. But if you talked to him, like I did, when he was behind several feet of brick wall and separated from the civilized world by an iron gate, you'd never have guessed what a cold-blooded killer he really was."

The conversation shifted to the cause of Horn's downfall, his killing of an unarmed fourteen-year-old boy. Cahill knew the case well.

"What happened," he explained, "was that Horn had been hired to kill the boy's father. But on this particular morning, in July of '01, the boy arrived at the entrance to his family's ranch wearing his father's hat and riding his father's horse. Horn was about three hundred yards away when he fired the shots, so it's understandable that it wasn't until he inspected the body and placed the little stone under the boy's head that he realized a mistake had been made. It was the biggest mistake Tom Horn ever made. Rustlers were one thing. They were fair game. But taking pot shots at their kids, well, that was just out of bounds."

Joe Cahill sniffed the brandy the waiter had poured for him and grinned. "Nice, Harry. Very nice. I wonder what the enlisted men are having tonight."

Hinds snorted and then Cahill explained how Horn had been apprehended. "Joe La Fors did that, and he made a right fine job of it, too. Joe was a range detective who had suspected Horn's involvement in the boy's killing. So in January of '02, he invited Horn to join him in a room at the Inter-Ocean Hotel, told him he wanted to discuss a possible job for Horn outside of Wyoming. 'Course, Horn found that attractive because after the boy's killing he had become what you might call a hot property."

"Horn was stupid," Hinds interjected.

"No doubt about it," Cahill agreed. "See, son, in order to establish his credentials, Horn shot off his mouth about what a professional and reliable killer he was, ticking off names, dates, places, prices, distances of shots and other items a connoisseur of the trade might find of interest. What he didn't know was that La Fors had arranged for the sheriff and Charlie Ohnhouse, the court reporter, to be in the adjoining room. Charlie took down every damning word. The next day, we placed him under arrest and charged him with the boy's killing."

After a long trial, during which Horn was defended by a battery of lawyers that, it was rumored, set the Wyoming Cattlemen's Association back about half a million dollars, the jury reached its verdict. Tom Horn was found guilty and sentenced by the judge to the mandatory penalty, death by hanging.

"He tried to escape one time," Cahill said. "But he screwed that up pretty good. A guard he'd cornered gave him a Belgian revolver with the safety catch on and poor Tom couldn't figure out what to do with it. After that, I had a Gatling gun placed at the jail's entrance to discourage further such attempts. You have to realize there were a lot of ranchers and cowboys who were upset about Horn being convicted for something they'd been condoning for years."

Cahill explained how on the morning of November 20, 1903, three months after his escape attempt, Horn was taken from his cell and escorted into the prison yard, where a gallows had been erected. This was no ordinary hanging, the gallows having been constructed in such a way that when the doomed man stepped on the trap door, a complicated hydraulic mechanism was set into motion, emptying water from a tank. When the water level reached a state of imbalance in relation to the weight of the man, the trap was automatically released. Then, the man above, with a heavy coil of hemp looped around his neck, fell into eternity.

"Horn had expressed great interest in the construction of that infernal machine," Cahill said, leaning back in his chair. "I remember one morning when a sandbag was placed on the trap he called out something from his cell window. I couldn't hear him too well so I yelled for him to repeat it. 'How much weight you got in that bag?' he asked. 'About two hundred pounds,' I hollered back. 'Well, Joe, that's just about right.'"

As deputy sheriff, it was Joe Cahill's job to place a hood over Horn's head and adjust the rope so the massive hangman's knot rested near the prisoner's left ear. That done, Joe stepped back from the trap and waited. The small crowd of witnesses stood, staring in silence, listening to the eerie sound of splashing water.

"You nervous, Joe?" Horn asked in a muffled voice.

"A little, Tom, a little," the deputy replied.

"Joe?" Horn whispered.

"Yeah, Tom?"

"Don't be."

And that was the end of Tom Horn.

Tom Horn was hanged three years into the present century. Somehow, that seems significant, for it is a very different period from that which preceded it. The frontier was closing down and people were being subjected to new pressures. As the years passed, the tenuous camaraderie which existed between the pursued and their pursuers would evaporate and there would come the dawn of the day of the homicidal maniac.

Perhaps the best epitaph to those former days was uttered by Judge Knight of Lander at the time he sentenced Tom O'Day for horse stealing. Walt Putney was present in the courtroom when the sentence was read and related it to me as best he could remember it.

"Tom," the judge said imperiously, "if I were to send you to the penitentiary for all the crimes I know you've committed, you'd be rotting in the deepest hole for the lifetimes of ten men. But I'm not going to do that. I'm going to impose a light sentence and hope that by the time you've had a chance to think things over you'll be willing to go straight when they let you out."

O'Day, relieved, broke into a grin. Judge Knight sighed and then resumed. "Damnit, Tom, don't you realize that you fellows are behind the times? Did you ever hear of a thing called the telegraph? Or the automobile? Ever run up against an automatic rifle? You see, Tom, there's no place for your breed any more. It's over. And if you don't stop living in the past, I'm afraid something's liable to happen to you."

There was another breed for whom there appeared to be scant place on the closing frontier. But if anybody had warned them to stop living in the past because otherwise something might happen to them, the old-time Indians would almost certainly have given the bearer of the warning a look of disdain, turned on their moccasin heels and trudged back to their tipis.

CHAPTER FIVE

The Feel of the Drum

It was 1912 and one of those insufferable July days when the sun
fills the bowl of the Wyoming sky with such a bright white glare
that to look over, under, sideways or through is to invite a shot of
solar lightning that penetrates to the core of one's brain. George
Shakespear and I were riding our horses at a walk along the
southern edge of the reservation on a cross-country search for
strays. We rocked listlessly in our saddles, for the two of us were
as tired, thirsty and caked with prairie dust as our mounts. The
only sounds to reach our ears were the creak of saddle leather, the
clomp of hooves and an occasional snort.

Suddenly, George squinted through the glare of rising heat rip-
ples, reined his horse in, held his right hand high and shouted,
"*Whoahai!*" Trying to focus, I peered ahead and saw a lone horse-
man riding bareback. At George's cry, he dug his heels into his
pony's ribs and trotted toward us. As he pulled up alongside us, I
could see he was a tall, wiry old Arapaho, dressed in a cream-
colored muslin shirt, black vest and dark, threadbare trousers. On
his head he wore a high-crowned brown Stetson with a red-tipped
eagle feather which stood straight up from the left side of the
beaded hatband. His moccasins were soft from wear and una-
dorned by decoration.

I looked closely at the old man sitting so upright on his pinto
pony. He had fine features, quick, penetrating eyes and a broad,
thin mouth which gave an impression of steady resolve coupled
with a sense of detached bemusement.

Silky brown otter skins were carefully wound round his two

black braids. Delicate golden crucifixes dangled from his ears.
When he turned his head slightly I could see a tightly wrapped
leather pouch, about the size and shape of a smooth, well-worn
stone that might fit snugly into the palm of a man's hand, swaying from the hair behind his left ear.

"Now you got a good chance to use the signs," George said.
"Chiatee—Goes In Lodge—speaks no English."

Slowly, not wanting to make a fool of myself and trying
desperately to cover my nervousness, I embarked upon my repertoire of signs.

"You Arapaho?"

"*Ahh-h!*" he said, making the sign of affirmation. "*Hanunahaiee,*" he grinned, tapping his chest and unraveling more signs in
rapid-fire succession.

He stared at me, saw my look of incomprehension, threw back
his head and laughed long and deep.

"Goes In Lodge says, 'You come to dance, three suns from
now,'" George interpreted, adding, "You gotta go, Tim, very bad
manners if you say no."

Nodding acceptance, I followed George's lead and the three of
us shook hands in parting.

I had met the man who would become my brother.

Three days after Goes In Lodge had issued his invitation, I rode
across the narrow flat of a valley, forded the shallow Little Wind
River and headed toward the distant smoke of the Arapaho cooking fires, which hung in the sky like wispy blue-gray clouds.

The encampment was partially obscured by some trees but a
few canvas tipis were quite distinct. I say canvas, because those of
the hide variety had gone out of style owing to the near-extinction
of the buffalo. More than anything else, the presence of these
tipis signified the continued existence of the old horseback Indians, described by the white man's agents as "non-progressives."

Not appreciating the tipi for the properly ventilated habitation
that it is, the pushers and shovers who hailed the White Man's
Road had moved as many Indians as would leave their time-tested
lodges into unventilated Army-style walled tents. In winter, squat
cast-iron wood-burning stoves heated those tents to a degree just
this side of an inferno. When the sweating Indians stepped out

The Feel of the Drum

83

into the cold for a breath of fresh air, the result was pneumonia. The next move had been to log cabins. Still, to the government's consternation, the use of tipis persisted.

From the outskirts, the village, a mixture of small, run-down log cabins, walled tents and canvas tipis, seemed to be a man-made monument to random selection and confusion. A mangy black and white dog skulked along the perimeter of a pile of cracked bones while another feigned an attack upon my horse. Half-naked children playing tag ran between the tents and cabins, laughing and squealing with delight. The women were busy with their usual household chores, hauling wood on their backs and hanging strips of meat to dry on outdoor racks.

The aroma which permeated the village was something pungently new to me. For one thing, the musky odor of cooking fires, which used burning twigs for combustion, dung for body and sweet grass for scent, was all-pervasive. And for another, there was an acrid, sick-sweet smell which indicated some mighty fresh butchering had recently taken place in the vicinity. The smell was a little gamy for my taste and right off I could tell it was one of those things for which appreciation requires a lifetime association or the slow acquisition of an appetite.

As I rode by one tipi, I noticed several long-haired old men sitting cross-legged upon the ground at the entrance. They were stripped to their breechcloths and spoke quietly among themselves, punctuating their words with sweeps of three-foot-long, auburn-hued eagle wing fans.

Before I reached the fifth tipi, the routine of the Arapaho camp abruptly changed, for the arrival of a white man was something totally unexpected, not particularly welcomed and potentially ominous.

The old men stood up and shot sharp glances in my direction. The women flocked into huddled groups and called the children to their sides. Even the dogs snarled. I was beginning to wish George Shakespear had prepared me better for the reaction of the Indians, though he had warned me about the dogs, saying, "They don't know you. Besides, you don't smell same as 'Rapaho."

In time, I discovered that the absence of a warm welcome was a surface matter and as unrelated to the inner feelings and true nature of the Arapaho as the white man's grin is to his hidden motivations.

Searching for a friendly face, and almost simultaneously abandoning all hope of finding one, I asked an ancient, gray-haired fellow, who looked as though a gust of wind might blow him over, where Goes In Lodge's tipi was located. I had used sign language, which caused him to squint at me suspiciously. Without saying a word, he pointed a gnarled finger to a tipi a short distance away, its canvas yellowed by exposure to the sun.

Dismounting, I tied my horse's reins to a small tree and, drawing myself up to my full height, walked, with mock confidence, to the tipi. A wooden lance about six feet high had been driven into the ground beside the entrance. Attached to the staff, and rippling in the mild breeze of late afternoon, was a wide strip of bright red cloth to which was affixed about twenty-five black-tipped eagle tail feathers, the battle honors of a warrior of the Plains.

From within the tipi came the sound of a drum beating and a man singing softly in a high-pitched voice. I scratched my fingers across the entrance flap of the tipi, as George had instructed me to do, and was answered by a hearty, "*Whoahai!*"

Pulling the flap aside and bending low, I entered. Inside, to my surprise, the tipi was bright and airy, the canvas walls to the rear having been rolled up from the gound about two feet to provide for extra ventilation. Goes In Lodge was sitting directly opposite the entrance, reclining on a lazy board, a back rest made of many hard willow reeds held together by thin leather supports. Laying his small shield drum aside, and smiling in greeting, he motioned me to take a seat on the ground beside him.

After I had presented him with a package of tobacco and a jar of honey—"Bad 'Rapaho manners not to bring a gift," George Shakespear had explained earlier—Goes In Lodge pulled a brightly quilled and elaborately fringed pipe bag from behind his lazy board and removed the long calumet. From his leather tobacco pouch, he scraped some kinnikinnick, a strong mixture of birch bark, dung and bear grease with just a hint of tobacco. Having loaded the red bowl, he raised the pipe, made his prayers while pointing it to the four directions, lit the contents of the bowl from the embers of the small central fire pit, puffed and passed it to me.

Putting the wooden stem to my mouth, I puffed the bittersweet smoke and then returned it to him. I was beginning to feel welcome.

Goes In Lodge then produced the not quite dry bladder of a steer and from it scooped the goldarnedest mess I have ever seen. The palm of his hand was covered with a dripping, quivering lump resembling headcheese. I gave it a suspicious glance and shrugged my shoulders, for to refuse an offering of food was unthinkable. Goes In Lodge stretched out his hand and said, "*Ah-sayna*. Beef."

"*Ha-ho*. Thank you," I replied, demonstrating that I knew at least a little Arapaho, though I was beginning to discover that compared to the spoken word, sign language was a cakewalk.

The mixture was pemmican, a conglomeration of powdered beef jerky, crushed berries and fresh bone marrow. Warily, I took the sloshy offering in my hand, nodded my not altogether sincere appreciation and began to eat. It was awful.

After our little feast, Goes In Lodge again filled his pipe and we passed some relaxed time smoking. "You know," he said in signs, slowly, in deference to my halting acquaintance with them, "sometimes things happen to let me know I am an old man."

"What things?" I asked.

"My chest gets sore."

I started in as to how all old men probably get that sort of thing. "*Ahh-h*," he replied, "there is more to it than that."

He puffed on his pipe, very, very slowly. Time meant nothing to the old-timers. "*Natchakaw*, a long time ago," he continued, making the sign, a pantomime of pulling back the string of a bow, "when I was a young man, I went out with five of my comrades to find some horses. We traveled for a moon toward the Yellowstone country and walked the whole time. That way, we would not be likely to forget what we were doing and return to our people with empty hands. The hungry man will quicken his step if he smells buffalo scent from the other side of a hill. And, my friend, Goes In Lodge was horse-hungry."

The old man explained that the little party traveled by night and hid during the day so the Crows would not know they were coming. "Crows, mean people," he said, chuckling. "Not like Arapaho."

Eventually, when they were a long way from their usual stomping grounds, the Arapahoes found a village of about thirty lodges with a large pony herd, and late that night made their approach.

"I was the Wolf," Goes In Lodge said, "so I went ahead of my friends to see if the pony herd was guarded. I crept into the village to make sure everyone was asleep. The dogs did not bark at me like they did at you today. No, those dogs could not tell Crow from Arapaho. Then I returned to my friends and told them it was safe to go over to the herd.

"I was a young man then," he said, pulling his shoulders back, "and my heart ached for brave deeds. So I went back into the village where I had seen a pretty horse tied beside the lodge of a Crow chief. It was a pinto. They were useful horses to have in those days."

I made the question sign to indicate that I did not quite understand what he meant. Goes In Lodge smiled and nodded slowly, as if thinking to himself how ignorant the young bucks were becoming. He then explained that during raids or when out scouting, any Indian in a position to make a choice of mounts would invariably choose a pinto: from a distance, the white spots were guaranteed to seem invisible while the brown spots would merge with the brush and trees. He challenged me to name another type of horse similarly endowed with natural camouflage and, when I could not, grinned triumphantly.

"I was starting to carefully untie that pony," he continued, "when I heard a yell. I turned and saw my friends coming on the run from the other side of the village. They were riding fast on their new horses, moving the rest of the herd with them, crashing into tipis and throwing fire sticks into the lodges. And all the time, they're hollering: 'You stupid Crows! Wake up! Some brave Arapahoes are stealing your horses!'

"Wolf Elk was the last of my friends coming through and he saw me. 'Come on!' he shouts. 'Nishkahai! Whip up!' But Goes In Lodge has nothing to whip up because that pony outside the Crow chief's lodge gets frightened. That Crow chief is awake now, for sure. And Goes In Lodge thinks, maybeso, the time has come to leave.

"I ran through the village and behind me I hear the Crows yelling and shouting. Their hearts are bad and Goes In Lodge knows if those Crows catch him, they'll cut him up real good. I ran so fast it was as though I had eagles under my feet. I ran through the night and never stopped. My heart pounded until I thought it would tear from my chest. My lungs ached and blood came from my nose. And still I ran on.

"The next day, I stopped by some large rocks where I hid. My Medicine was good," he said, gently rubbing the leather pouch behind his ear, "because a bunch of Crows rode past that day and never saw me.

"Since then, I sometimes get these pains in my chest," he concluded, tapping in the region of his heart, "and I know it is because of that long run."

Suddenly there was a scratching at the tipi entrance.

"*Whoahai!*" Goes In Lodge called out.

A stocky old man entered. His dark hair, lightly sprinkled with gray, hung loose and he had a red blanket wrapped around his waist, skirt-style. I scooted aside to make room for the newcomer. As he and Goes In Lodge, obviously old friends, exchanged greetings, I surveyed my surroundings.

The furnishings of the tipi were undoubtedly sparser than in buffalo days; still, I was sitting on a buffalo robe similar to the ones we had encased ourselves in during winter sleigh rides through Saginaw. And buffalo robes constituted the two beds behind the lazy board. The canvas liner of the tipi, basically a dew cloth, was decorated with colorful but faded warrior drawings detailing Goes In Lodge's exploits. A long and circular war bonnet container made of resistant and hardened leather, called a parfleche, was richly painted in green, red and blue designs. It stood beside the lazy board, while several square parfleches, used for storing clothes, food and other articles were stacked to the right of the entrance. The contents of the tipi, while old, used or faded, bespoke the style of life this man had once enjoyed. The point that stuck in my mind was that, even then, he was still living in the old days and ways.

The visitor was introduced by Goes In Lodge. "This is my *ba*, friend, Wolf Elk."

The old warrior stared at me and said, "*Haba*, greetings."

Just then, the dance drum started to beat in the distance. I looked toward the entrance of Goes In Lodge's tipi and saw darkness beginning to fall. "What were you singing about when I came?" I asked my host.

"Good times," he replied.

"And the words?"

"No words. Song is sound. Don't need words," he smiled. "Whenever I feel good and sometimes when I do not feel good, I sing. All of our people sing. Life is for hunting, fighting, feasting, loving, dancing, smoking and singing."

"But those days are gone," Wolf Elk interjected, with bitterness in his voice.

"*Hainawa*, I know," Goes In Lodge replied softly.

"When we were young men," Wolf Elk continued, "there were many buffalo, elk and antelope. We hunted for our food, we lived a good life."

"*Iyahuh*. It is all gone now, Wolf Elk," the old man said with sadness in his voice.

"And then, *Niatha*, the Spider, came and took everything away. Even the buffalo!"

"*Nahinan!* Stop!" Goes In Lodge said gruffly, his face turning hard. "Sometimes, my friend, you are like the child who does not remember his manners. Perhaps water poured down your nose will stop your crying!" Then, his eyes glistening, Goes In Lodge turned to me and, smiling with half his heart, laid a hand on my shoulder and said, "*Maybeso*, we go to the dance now?"

After the three of us had left the tipi and were walking through the village in the pleasant coolness of early evening I asked Goes In Lodge if the Shoshonis came to the Arapaho dances. Wolf Elk stopped in his tracks, his face registering shock, as though I had spoken a forbidden word and broken a taboo of particularly long standing.

"No," Goes In Lodge laughingly replied, touching Wolf Elk's arm, "and if the Snake People came, this man would eat them!"

We all laughed. I did not know then that Goes In Lodge himself had, figuratively speaking, eaten his share of the Snake People.

"*Ahuna!* There it is!" Goes In Lodge said, pointing to the top of a small rise where a building the size of twenty tipis stood. It was the dance hall. Made of square logs, and with a conical, corrugated-iron roof, it had been dedicated five months before, in February 1912.

Indian girls, some dressed in red flannel dresses decorated with innumerable elk teeth, were milling about in clusters, whispering and giggling about the young men mounted on their ponies or standing apart from the group and parading in their celebration best. Some of the young bucks carried heirloom war clubs and a few wore the brightly painted and quilled buckskin war shirts which were fringed with scalp locks or horsehair and undoubtedly belonged to their fathers or grandfathers.

As we came to the open doorway I could see crowds of brightly dressed people and through the bodies a cascade of swirling colors as the dancers kept time to the thunderous throb of a large drum which six men were beating in harmony while singing in high-pitched voices.

Goes In Lodge and Wolf Elk eased their way through the crowd, with younger people giving way in deference. Following behind these gentlemen, I was the object of attention from the youngest girl to the oldest matron, while the men glanced at me with understandable distrust, if not quite open hostility, considering that I was in "good company."

Finding space for the three of us to sit down on the earthen floor among the old men—for in those days the men and women sat and usually danced separately—Goes In Lodge directed my attention toward the dance floor.

A new dance was just starting and after four identical beats of the drum, men of all ages entered the circle and began to move and dance in the most complicated motions I had ever seen. Always circling clockwise, they would move a distance and stop, dancing in place, displaying quick and fancy footwork. Feet nearly collided with feet and yelping and howling filled the air as every part of their bodies, constantly in motion, strained in concert with the ever quickening beat of the reverberating drum. I was amazed at their stamina, for the dance was long, the pace furious and yet never a one seemed to stop or slacken.

I had seen many of the Indians while riding the range, and never imagined that the drab Arapahoes on horseback could transform themselves into the dancers I was now watching. It was as though the putting on of finery, yellow-, orange-, even purple-dyed feather bustles, war bonnets, jewelry and exquisitely beaded moccasins, changed their whole being. Here I was, surrounded by a happy, smiling, laughing people who were all-consumed in the beat of the drum and the jangling of sleigh bells fastened onto dancers' ankles. A people united in and by the feel—yes, the *feel*, not the sound—of the drum.

As I sat with the old men, listening to the drums and bells, the shouts and whoops of the younger men dancing in frenzy, I caught the hint of motion in the corner of my eye. Turning, I saw the most awesome piece of humanity I would ever encounter among the Indians. In the doorway stood a man who was at least six and half feet tall. A dark blue blanket shrouded his body and was pulled up over his nose. On top of his head was an eagle feather bonnet, not an heirloom but something this man had earned. The feathers of the bonnet were released from the constraints of the wind outside and slowly drifted into their intended, widespread circle. All in all, here stood about nine feet of Arapaho.

Wolf Elk nudged me and laughed. "That's Red Pipe. But he's just a baby. You should see his older brothers, Ice Man, Frying Pan and Painted Bear!"

Wolf Elk turned to Goes In Lodge and as the two of them talked they began chuckling. Suddenly, as if in response to a secret sign, Goes In Lodge grabbed my right elbow and Wolf Elk locked an iron-tight grip around my left wrist. For septuagenarians they had surprising strength. With a single motion, they lifted me from the floor and started walking toward the circle with me as their bewildered captive.

"He's my horse," Goes In Lodge cried, using an Arapaho idiom. "I can make him do what I want now. Maybeso, even teach him to dance!"

Although I was an unwilling participant, I knew the two old

men were having fun. So I did not offer much resistance, though my face was hot with the redness of acute embarrassment as I painfully tried to copy the fancy footwork displayed by my captors.

After what seemed to be an interminable time on the dance floor, during which every eye was focused upon me, I began to get the idea: one was supposed to feel the drum and release the body to its power. Eventually, I sat down to cheerful approval from the old men.

"Pretty good," Goes In Lodge said, beaming. "Yeah, pretty good."

This new world, I felt, was a wonderful place and I was having a grand time. But soon it dawned on me that I had to be up and working Irish Tom's cattle in a few hours. There was just enough time to make the long ride back to the cowboy camp.

I walked with Goes In Lodge to his tipi. "Few suns more, you come and visit?" the old man asked as we stood in the midst of the now sleeping village. The drum had stopped, the dance was over and the only sound, aside from the howls of the coyotes in the hills, was the jingling of sleigh bells as the last of the dancers made their way back to their homes.

I looked at him and it suddenly seemed the cultural allegiances which might have once kept us from understanding one another had vanished. It was somehow necessary to both of us that I be with him and among the Arapahoes.

"Yes," I answered, feeling a fullness within my heart.

"*Ethiti, ba!* Good, my brother! *Ethiti . . .*"

Little did I realize that in times to come Goes In Lodge and the other old men would dress me up in their cherished finery, paint my body red and enter me in dance competitions, betting heavily on their entrant and against their younger tribesmen. With Goes In Lodge's war bonnet snugly tied to my head, Wolf Elk's scalp shirt and matching leggings, Broken Horn's Washington peace medallion, Yellow Horse's hair pipe breastplate, Red Pipe's tomahawk, Ice Man's pipe bag and the moccasins presented to me as a gift by George Shakespear, and entered as a visiting southern Arapaho, I was not readily recognized as a white man cowboy.

Frequently I would win these competitions, whereupon the old men, having triumphed, would remove the war bonnet from my head, showing short, blond hair. Then, pointing to the younger Arapahoes, one of them invariably proclaimed, "What a fine herd of horses!"

A couple of weeks after I attended my first Arapaho dance, George Shakespear and I left Irish Tom and hired on at the Double Diamond, where preparations were being made for the fall roundup. This move was more than the cowboy's usual migration in search of a change of scene; the Double Diamond was closer to Wind River and I was able to spend more time among the Arapahoes. What I have previously described as a melt was, as the cowboys said, "startin' to begin to commence," and most of my free time was wisely spent at one or another of the several Arapaho tipi villages on the reservation.

In the beginning, I stuck to Goes In Lodge like glue. After a while he encouraged me to visit his friends by myself. Then, when I knew the old men and they knew me, Goes In Lodge was usually present, gently guiding the course of the conversation. The first few months of budding friendship were involved in what can only be described as an intensive indoctrination into what it meant to be an Indian.

Charlie Russell, the western painter and a man who knew the tribes of the northern Plains well, once observed of the Indians: "Their God was the sun, their church all outdoors. Their only book was nature and they knew all the pages." It didn't take me long to learn that they were not scholars in the white man's sense of keeping detailed records and preserving every scrap of minutiae; nor did they engage in endless debates of how many angels could dance on the head of a pin. What the Indian had that so many white men lack is that he remembered the basics, which to him were important: where the buffalo migrated, watering spots, how to tell a bird's call from an enemy's whistle and so on. It was the preservation of this knowledge which kept his tribe intact and made the continuation of his way of life possible.

It was clear from the many, many evenings I spent sitting beside tipi fires with them that, generally, the Arapahoes accepted reality without question and looked upon disaster and good fortune with much the same stoicism. It was, they reasoned, all part of the Great Mystery, the nature of which was amply explained by its name and pretty much beyond the ken of all but the most highly spiritual of the tribe.

They never doubted that it was the Great Mystery which made the universe; nor did they cease giving thanks for what they regarded as a perfect creation. The universe in which the old men had been raised was boundless and consisted of craggy mountains, vast unbroken plains, deserts and grasslands teeming with herds of antelope, deer, elk and buffalo. In the mountains were to be found grizzly bear and, still higher, the eagle, a bird of much power and great Medicine.

In every way, these men had tried to be as one with their world. Some believed that the war bonnet itself was a symbol of and the means toward attaining this goal, for the eagle feathers represented flight and the mountains, the cap the earth, and the plume in its center the sun.

Unable to match the skills of the animals in stealth, strength or soaring, they sought instead to emulate them by acquiring power. Thus, a scout dressed in skins and became the Wolf. A guard wore a tail and became the Coyote. And young warriors, desiring to strike fiercely and make a safe escape quickly, called themselves Kit Foxes and wore the skin of that animal.

The old men considered animals, rocks, plants, the very earth itself, living things, brothers possessed of as much life as themselves, and each a gift from the Great Mystery. It is therefore not in the least bit surprising that their initial reaction to the arrival and impact of the white man upon their field of experience was probably not so very different from what ours might be should an extraterrestrial choose to make an exploratory landing within our range of sight.

It took me some time to understand the old-timers were not talking specifically about me whenever they made it clear they had absolutely no use whatever for the white man. And, really, how could they have felt otherwise? What had the white man given them other than terror, confinement, venereal disease, smallpox—the scars of which the majority of the old men bore—a religion they didn't want, farm implements they couldn't have cared less about and death?

As they explained it, the big change in the tribe had come early in the eighteenth century, during what Goes In Lodge stated was "the time when my grandfather's father was a small boy." And what happened was the arrival of the horse. Instead of having to track, stampede and kill buffalo by foot, as was previously necessary, a devastatingly effective hunt could be made quickly by a few riders on horseback. Movement of camps could be made over a greater distance in a shorter time, since a horse could pull many times more weight than the previously used dog. Thus, the Arapahoes became more mobile in their nomadic existence.

Shortly afterward, guns, or "fire sticks" as Wolf Elk called them, were introduced, filtering to the Arapahoes from those tribes already contacted by early white fur traders. This affected two significant areas of Indian life: the hunt and warfare. Now full advantage could be taken of large wild animal herds prior to the arrival of the long, cold winter, a period during which the Arapahoes were largely immobile, spending the time in relatively sheltered encampments. Additionally, warfare, which had previously been almost a sporting proposition—with few casualties on either of the contesting sides—became a serious, intense and deadly affair resembling nothing so much as a vulgar brawl.

"We believed we could have the best of both worlds," Red Pipe explained one afternoon when I had used the excuse of scouting up a couple of stray horses to visit with him in his camp. "We thought we could use the white man's strong Medicine and still live the good life. But we were wrong."

Indeed they were. It was in the 1840s, and particularly during the California gold rush of 1849, that the Arapahoes started to feel the press of western expansion.

"I was just a boy," Goes In Lodge said, after agreeing with Red Pipe's analysis, "when the white man began bringing his wagons and *whoaha* across our hunting grounds. At first, we trusted them and were friendly to them. But then, more and more white men came and scared away the animals. Still, we wanted to be at peace, so we moved our camps. But wherever we went, the white man followed."

It didn'take the Arapahoes long to christen the white man with the name of *Niatha,* meaning both "clever" and "spider-like." It was not meant as a compliment.

It was inevitable that push would come to shove. In 1864, a camp of southern Cheyennes and southern Arapahoes at Sand Creek in eastern Colorado was the object of an unprovoked attack by a ragtag band of scum which styled itself as militia. Afterward, the militiamen paraded through Denver carrying the spoils of war: Indian testicles tied to poles and uteri fashioned into wallets.

"It was then clear to us," Wolf Elk said, "that the only way our way of life could be allowed to continue was to strike terror into the hearts of the white men. We joined with our brothers, the Sioux and Cheyennes, and showed the white men that our hearts were brave."

They did this by fighting the invader for well over a decade, contesting every hillock and coulee on the northern Plains. It was a period of lightning raids, during which no wagon train of immigrants or settler's cabin was safe from the threat of attack. Wolf Elk's words reminded me of something I had recently seen in Lander's Fremont County Pioneer Association museum. It was a man's skull, but a most peculiar one. It had once been the head of a young man named Harvey Morgan. In 1870, he and two other white men were jumped by an Arapaho war party and killed about six miles from the future site of the town of Lander. When Harvey Morgan's body was recovered, it was discovered that the skin of his back had been split the entire length of his torso and the neckyoke of the wagon he had been driving was nailed through his head. In my time, that neckyoke was still imbedded in the bone; one glance had given me an idea of what the Wyoming pioneers I often met meant when they described the Arapahoes as having been "somewhat hostile."

But within ten years of Sand Creek, the white man had retaliated with his own brand of savage and indiscriminate retribution by laying waste to the buffalo herds and decimating every Indian encampment within reach. It was because of this that something else became clear to the Indians: further resistance could never bring victory and would only guarantee the annihilation of the warriors' families.

Thus, it came about that the once mighty tribes were divided into widely dispersed, roving bands, split by the constant press of the white man, the scarcity of game and their own instincts for survival. In a sense, this instinct proved true, for a minority of the Indians did survive, though it was only a matter of time before they would be confined within the boundaries of reservations from which there was to be no permanent escape.

It was Goes In Lodge who gave the most succinct description of his people after their decade-long war with the white man: "We were poor and our moccasins were broken."

Summer turned to fall, fall became winter; then there was spring and another summer. When I wasn't working on the range, or mending fences, or constructing corrals at the Double Diamond, I listened to the old men and by listening to them gained their respect. If they did not choose to go into personal matters, it was not for me, a younger man, to begin a lengthy interrogation. Anyone who cannot fathom this point will never understand what George Shakespear described as "'Rapaho manners." Age commanded unbelievable respect among the Arapahoes, and I can remember more than one occasion when a younger Arapaho questioned the older men about some point. The old warriors would listen for a short time and then one, cutting the younger man off in the middle of a sentence, would say, with calm menace, "When we want to know what you think, then, maybeso, we will ask. But until then, *chiatayee*, little fat-bellied baby, shut your mouth!"

During the course of my association with these people, I met men whose names I see today in history books, men who were then just old fellows who sat inconspicuously around agency buildings or beside their tipis, puffing on their pipes. Had I been less green and a little riper with knowledge, I might have learned more.

What each of those eagle feathers on the war staff sunk into the ground outside of Goes In Lodge's tipi stood for I do not know, for I seldom asked about details not readily supplied.

It is true that the old men often enjoyed talking about the bygone days, for it was a time in which they were forever trapped beyond recall. Yet Goes In Lodge's and others' injunctions of "*Nahinan!* Stop!" brought many conversations to abrupt ends. The word was most often spoken by an old man whose eyes were beginning to float upon the sea of memory's tears. The gone days had been good times, as full as they were hard, while the present was not a thing these men had sought and one which they, having resisted its onslaught to the best of their abilities, profoundly resented.

Then too, it is the old thing of not knowing what questions to ask. I was not up on Wind River to write a book. I was there to make my living as a cowboy and, to my good fortune, found friendship with those remarkable men, to whom friendship implied the sometime relation of confidences but never any prying. Thus, I never asked Goes In Lodge how many men he had scalped, for that seemed a personal matter about which he would have spoken had he been so inclined. Had I asked, he would almost certainly have told me. But it was not for me to put the question. I did not ask Wolf Elk if he took part in the killing of Bluecoats. And I certainly never questioned Red Pipe as to his role, if any, in the working over of men like the unfortunate Harvey Morgan.

That I learned anything at all is due to the desire of the old men to pass along the memory of the way of life they had so enjoyed; that, and their openness.

Something more than their spirits alone went West when the old men died. It was as though the spirit of the entire tribe had also departed.

But the memory of it lingers . . .

CHAPTER SIX

Buffalo Dance

During the years between 1912 and 1916 I sometimes had occasion, while on cattle-buying trips or month-long respites from cowboying, to be in Cody, Wyoming, where Buffalo Bill could often be found in the bar of his Irma Hotel.

The hotel, named after Buffalo Bill's youngest daughter, and built by him at a cost of eighty thousand dollars, was opened on November 1, 1902. It was a pleasant oasis in one of America's wilder regions, just about fifty miles from Yellowstone National Park. As the Cody *Enterprise* described it three days after its opening, the Irma was

> New and Elegantly Furnished Throughout. The Celebrated Ostermoor Mattresses and Springs used exclusively. Heated by steam and lighted by gas. Telephone in every room. Elegant bar and billiard hall. Telegraph and public telephone. Barber shop and baths. Large Sample Rooms. All milk, cream and vegetables from its own dairy and farm. A Livery equipped with all kinds of rigs, saddle and driving horses, camp and pack outfits, with experienced guides for hunting and fishing parties and tourists in connection with the hotel . . . Everything is modern and first-class.

And indeed it was. The thirty-foot-long bar, aside from being functional, was a monument. It was hand-carved from cherry wood, cost a king's ransom and had been presented to Buffalo Bill as a gift by a queen, Victoria of Great Britain.

I can make no claim to having been a bosom buddy of the old showman, but whenever I was in Cody I made it a point to repair to the bar of the Irma and stand at or near his side as he delivered his accounts of history, stories to which all within earshot paid close attention. He was sixty-six years of age the first time I was with him at the Irma and a much older-looking man than when I first met him in Saginaw in 1898.

Still, he had not retired. In 1907 he merged with another first-rate wild West show entrepreneur, his former protégé, Pawnee Bill, and created "Buffalo Bill's Wild West and Pawnee Bill's Far East." Up until the time of his death in Denver, Colorado, on January 10, 1917, Cody continued with the tradition of showmanship he had established.

There was nobody even remotely like him. Cody had, after all, been on the scene during what his promoters enthusiastically billed as the "winning of the West." He *had* earned the nickname of "Buffalo Bill" in a contest on the Kansas plains in the late 1860s, bagging in a day-long hunt sixty-nine buffalo to Billy Comstock's forty-six. And he *had* killed the Cheyenne chief Yellow Hand. That particular event, which was immortalized in dime novels, posters and a re-enactment in his Wild West Show, had occurred on July 17, 1876. A party of soldiers, with Cody in tow, crashed into a band of Indians riding to join the victorious Sioux and Cheyennes who, twenty-one days before, had annihilated Custer and most of his command at the Battle of the Little Big Horn. Dressed in a Mexican *charro* outfit made of black velvet, trimmed with scarlet ribbons, silver buttons and lace, Cody met his adversary and, after killing him, took out his scalping knife and finished the job, "Injun fashion" as he once told me. Being nothing if not a studied showman, and a master at that craft, Cody then waved the bloody scalp lock above his head and hollered, "First scalp for Custer!"

He had his detractors, of course. They said he drank too much, saw too many beautiful women other than his wife, that sort of thing. But to the vast majority of Americans, including me, he was nothing less than a hero. It was both an honor and a pleasure for me to become reacquainted with him.

Cody was looked after by his ever present, faithful and ferocious-looking factotum, the Sioux chief Iron Tail, and surrounded at all times by old cronies such as the dapperly dressed Sherm Canfield, one of his most successful public relations men. I remember overhearing Sherm talking to a tourist from the East while standing beside him at the bar late one afternoon.

"Do you mean to tell me, Mr. Canfield, that you actually *know* Buffalo Bill?" the tourist asked incredulously.

"Know him?" Sherm snorted in response. "Hell, aside from shooting at targets from the back of a goddamned horse, I *am* Buffalo Bill!"

It was Sherm Canfield who, in a never-to-be-repeated slip of the tongue, stunned a British audience at Earl's Court in London by announcing Cody's entrance into the area by proclaiming: "Ladies and gentlemen, boys and girls, Colonel W. F. Cody—Buffalo Bill—will now shoot the glass balls off his horse."

Frequently, as Buffalo Bill stood beside the Irma's well-polished bar, he glanced at his reflection in the mirror. Being what Canfield described as a "great mirror fighter," he would slowly bring a hand up behind his collar and, with a grandiloquent gesture, fluff his long white hair into position. Then, his appearance in good order, he continued with the story he had been telling.

He had numbered the Sioux Medicine Man Sitting Bull among his friends. In fact, in 1885 the barrel-chested warrior had toured with Cody's Wild West Show and the two men knew, trusted and respected each other. It was as a result of this association that Buffalo Bill tried to save the life of the old chief during the Ghost Dance troubles.

In November of 1890, Buffalo Bill's Wild West Show was playing at Earl's Court in London. Cody began noticing articles in the papers about a new, mysterious "Indian trouble." A messiah, a Paiute Indian from Nevada, had proclaimed that the day of deliverance for the Indians was at hand. If the tribes would dance a certain dance, the Spirit or Ghost Dance, and sing prescribed songs, then a miracle would shortly take place: the white man would disappear and everything would be as it had been before he arrived. The buffalo would return and so would each person's dead relations. The Ghost Dance was drawing the Indians of the Plains much as a flame draws a moth, with, as it eventually turned out, similar results.

To Cody, who frankly admitted to me that he needed some publicity, the Ghost Dance was a godsend. He decided to take the first boat he could catch back to the United States and see if he could find a way to become embroiled in what promised to be a widely read story.

"I was having dinner with my good friend General Miles," Cody said, speaking to three or four of us who had formed a semi-circle around him at the Irma's bar early on an autumn evening in 1913. "We were in Chicago, enjoying the considerable hospitality of the Parker House. It was November 24 and four days before, the Army, at the insistence of those goddamned stupid *Indian agents*"—he spat the words—"made an unannounced and totally unnecessary show of force at the Sioux reservations of Pine Ridge and Rosebud. Those monkeys showed up with over two hundred infantry, two hundred black cavalry whom the Indians called buffalo soldiers because their hair reminded them of that on a buffalo, two Hotchkiss rapid-fire cannon and a Gatling gun. Christ Almighty, you'd have thought they were after a rampaging herd of Barnum's elephants!"

Slowly, Cody picked up his shot glass and drained the whiskey in a single gulp. The bartender, who knew the routine well, immediately refilled it.

"Do you young fellows know," Cody whispered, "that before that damn Ghost Dance business was finished among the Sioux, and by the time Wounded Knee had happened, over three hundred Injuns and about fifty whites had been killed, and over one million dollars had been thrown down a rathole? And all because of those stupid, panicky *Indian agents!*"

One of the cowboys beside me, growing impatient, waved his hand in front of Cody to gain the old man's attention and asked, "Yeah, but what happened after you got to Chicago?"

Cody smiled a thin, unfriendly smile, drummed his fingers gently against the gleaming top of the bar, looked up to the ceiling, stroked his moustache, fidgeted with his goatee and played with his hair. After a few minutes had passed he said to the rest of us, "You know, your acquaintance here reminds me of a fellow I once knew. We were sitting around in . . . well, I don't remember exactly now, but it was a hell of a long time ago, and we were listening to the scout Jim Bridger. He was telling us of a time when a little party he was with, which had been minding their own business and exploring the country, was jumped by a bunch of Sioux. Old Jim had gotten to the point in his narrative where hundreds of screaming savages had three or four of the white men, including himself, pinned behind some rocks. There were Injuns in front of them, Injuns to their left, more Injuns to their right and the solid wall of a box canyon at their backs. And when Bridger got that far, this young squirt popped off: 'What happened then? Tell us what happened then!' Bridger was thrown off the rhythm of his story and the only thing he could say was, 'Well, sonny, I guess they killed every damn one of us.' "

Buffalo Bill paused for another shot of whiskey. He had shifted gears but not forgotten where his original story had been headed. Cheerfully, he resumed. "Now, Miles and I," he said, "had always been good friends. I remember one time, we'd been up quite late. Yes, quite, quite late. We'd been refighting the Battle of the Little Big Horn and somewhere between Medicine Tail coulee and the last shot, we sort of drifted off to sleep. As a matter of fact, boys, I think we might even have been a bit drunk. So, the next morning, when I opened my eyes, there I was, lying on top of a table in Miles' suite, and there was the top-ranking general of our United States Army, stretched across the sofa. 'Miles,' I says to him, 'what the hell happened?' 'Cody,' he says to me, 'I think we died with Custer.' "

Cody allowed himself quite a chuckle over that one. Then, giving the man who had caused him to relate the Bridger story a sharp glance to make sure he wasn't going to be interrupted again, he cleared his throat. "But back to my story, boys, back to the story. Miles wanted to avoid a major screw-up among the Sioux. Like most of the Army officers, he didn't hate the Injuns. In fact, he respected them. And he knew a hell of a lot more about how their minds worked than all the honorary 'majors' who were supposed to be in charge. Miles says to me, 'Bill, we've got to have

Sitting Bull. Get him out of the hands of those agents and safe with the Army before something dreadful happens to him. Bring him in for a talk. Tell him he's going to have to leave his home for a while but ask him whether he would rather be in the clutches of the Indian Department or under our protection. You're the only man I can send to do this because you're just about the only white man he both knows and trusts. How about it?'

"'Course," Cody continued, "I thought that was a perfectly fine idea. I didn't want anything untoward to happen to old Bull. And after Miles and I shook hands and toasted the good luck of the coming adventure, the general wrote out an order on the back of the Palmer House's wine card. With that, I was off to Injun country."

As Cody told it to me, he left Chicago by train the morning of November 25 and journeyed to Bismarck, North Dakota. Then, driving a buckboard wagon filled with candies, he arrived at Standing Rock Agency late on the evening of November 27, where he presented his orders to the agent, "Major" McLaughlin, who, as might be expected, was not pleased.

"You know what McLaughlin tried to do?" Cody asked me, a tone of mock amazement running through his voice. "He ordered the officers at nearby Fort Yates to drink me under the table so I wouldn't be able to go out to see old Bull the next day. God, he was naïve! Not that they didn't try but I'll tell you this: early the next morning, when those young squirts were futilely attempting to find their way out from under their own table, I was driving my buckboard through snowdrifts, trying to make the twenty miles to Grand River, where old Bull was living in a little log cabin. But there was too much snow, so I had to make camp. And that's when McLaughlin outfoxed me."

According to Buffalo Bill, the main stratagem in this plot was the laying out by one of McLaughlin's minions of a false trail. It was made by a wagon drawn by unshod horses, and since Indian ponies were always without iron shoes, Cody was led to believe "old Bull" had already driven his wagon into the agency. In this manner was McLaughlin able to lure Cody back to the agency headquarters, where, upon arrival, he was presented with a telegram from Washington, D.C. The telegram, authorized by President Harrison at the insistence of the Secretary of the Interior—who had jurisdiction over the Indians and was fearful that this great pork barrel might be taken away from his control—in no uncertain terms commanded Cody to leave Sitting Bull to the tender mercies of McLaughlin, a man the Sioux detested.

"And that did it for old Bull," Cody explained sadly. "Early on the morning of December 15 the Injun police, at the direction of McLaughlin, arrived at his place on Grand River. They told him he was under arrest because of his espousal of the Ghost Dance. The old man was amenable to going in peaceful-like. But some of the couple of hundred Sioux who were camped nearby were a little suspicious about the whole business. There was a scuffle, some shots were thrown around and one of the Injun police blew old Bull's brains out. When that beautiful white horse I'd given him heard the shots, he started going through his routine of fancy tricks. By the time the smoke cleared and the 8th Cavalry came upon the scene, some of the Sioux and a few of the police were dead or dying. Among them, my friend Sitting Bull and his nice little boy, Crow Foot."

Cody looked sullen. "Goddamned Injun policeman," he muttered. "Put a uniform on him, give him a gun that'll blast through a wall, pin a badge on his chest and he just isn't an Injun any more."

By 1915 I was getting tired of working for other people. Fortunately, there was in those days an outlet for cowboys who wanted to have their own ranch someday, and, availing myself of this opportunity, I filed with the federal government for a 640-acre homestead on Owl Creek, about forty-five miles west of Thermopolis. The fee for such a claim was $27.50, or about four cents an acre. In order for the homesteader to maintain title to his land, all the government required was improvements totaling $1.25 per acre over a period of five years. These improvements almost always took the form of erecting a cabin, building a corral and constructing fences. Most of the cowboys who, like me, had filed for homesteads still worked for large outfits like the M-Bar. By doing this, and not trying to go it alone before they were really in a position to make it work, they saved their money and waited for the day when they would be able to buy a few head of cattle, hook up with a pool wagon and go into the cattle business.

At that time, my ranch had no name; it was barely even a place. But bit by bit the improvements were made and by 1916 it was clear to me, if to nobody else, that I would eventually make it work.

One day after visiting with Goes In Lodge, who could usually be found camped about fifty-five miles southwest of Owl Creek, I invited him to come and inspect my homestead. He asked me where it was and I gave him directions. Before I rode off he promised to arrive within two days.

He didn't make it in two days, three days or even four. Late on the afternoon of the fifth day he showed up, a tired man on an even more tired pony. When I asked him what the problem had been he shrugged his shoulders. "If you had told me to turn toward where the sun rises after passing the rocks where a war party I was with many, many years ago killed a big band of Shoshonis," he explained, "I would have known better how to get here." Or, he went on in a confidential tone, had I known and been able to inform him that a certain turn up a certain creekbed was "no more than the distance an arrow would fly from an elkhorn bow used by a strong man from the place where Yellow Calf received his Medicine from the Great Turtle," he would have had no difficulty in locating my homestead site.

There was no question that the old Arapahoes I knew thought along lines in no way related to those traversed by most white men. And one of the areas the white men would have had trouble in negotiating was a concept alluded to in Goes In Lodge's remark about "the place where Yellow Calf received his Medicine from the Great Turtle."

Medicine was viewed by Goes In Lodge and his brother warriors as a gift of power, bestowed by the Great Mystery upon the tribe or an individual. With power, truly wondrous things were possible; without it, Goes In Lodge often insisted, nothing was possible.

All that surrounded the Indians whispered that there was order to the universe. In winter, the snow came and covered the earth;

in spring, the snow melted, flowed downhill and joined with the rivers; in summer, after the buffalo cows had birthed their calves, game moved in unending herds of plenty across the Great Plains; then autumn arrived, cooling summer and soon to chill the land back to winter. These were not freak events. Autumn, winter, spring, summer, water, warmth and the animals, life and death came each year, every year. The sun rose in the east each morning, entered the tipis—for the lodges were erected to face in that direction so that the day might be greeted—and set in the West, dying at eveningtime only to be reborn when the moon, or Night Sun, gave way. The world, far from being filled with frenzy, was a highly ordered place. And they called it the Great Circle.

I have often thought one of the reasons the white man never really understood the Plains Indians was because while the white man thought linearly, in terms of squares and cubes and boxes, the Indian's conception of his surroundings was cyclical; the edges were softer. Time did not move from one point to the next in a great, logical line of progression. Time, for the Indian, was measured in seasons, events and natural phenomena. Life, when it changed at all for my friends among the old men, had changed slowly on the Great Plains.

"It is all the Circle," Goes In Lodge said to me during the course of an evening spent visiting in his tipi. "Everyone knows that. You stand on top of a mountain and what do you see when you look about? A circle, my brother, a circle."

Once the idea of a complete, self-contained circle, needing no further refinement, is accepted, it is a short, easy step to a belief in a power that made the well-ordered universe possible and maintains a hand in worldly affairs. It was, my friends knew, the Great Mystery that made all of this and if a man was given a small piece of power, that man might have some day-to-day control over the situations and circumstances in which he found himself immersed. Power was helpful, particularly when one was living the sort of life where it was necessary to contend with the vagaries of hunting or warfare.

At a time deemed propitious by an individual, usually when he was no older than fourteen or fifteen—the age at which Goes In Lodge insisted "any man who wanted to was ready to serve his

15. Several years later, when I was making a motion picture in northern Montana, General Scott and I rendezvoused among the Blackfeet. Left to right: Mud Head, Short Face, Wades In Water, General Scott, myself and Crow Chief, whose Medicine consisted of wearing the ear of a grizzly bear over his right ear.

16. While in Montana with Scott I was given a name by the Blackfeet: Black Eagle, the same one used by the long-dead brother of Lazy Boy, the man on my immediate left. While some of the articles worn by these Blackfeet are of late-nineteenth-century or early-twentieth-century manufacture, a number of the items are of heirloom quality. Seated left to right: Berry Child, Crow Chief, unidentified, Lazy Boy, unidentified and Jim White Calf.

17. Left Hand and I in 1922. He was one of five Arapahoes who fought against Custer at the Little Big Horn, though his coat was a reminder of his service as a soldier-scout in 1878.

18 & 19. Part of Left Hand's account of the Battle of the Little Big Horn, June 25, 1876. He is running his lance through a Sioux warrior he has mistaken for one of Custer's Indian scouts. The object in his hair is part of his Medicine, a morning star made out of buffalo hide with an eagle feather attached. Below him are some of the dead soldiers. This drawing was made about 1920 and forms part of an elkhide on which the old men of the tribe painted their exploits for me. The entire hide is shown below.

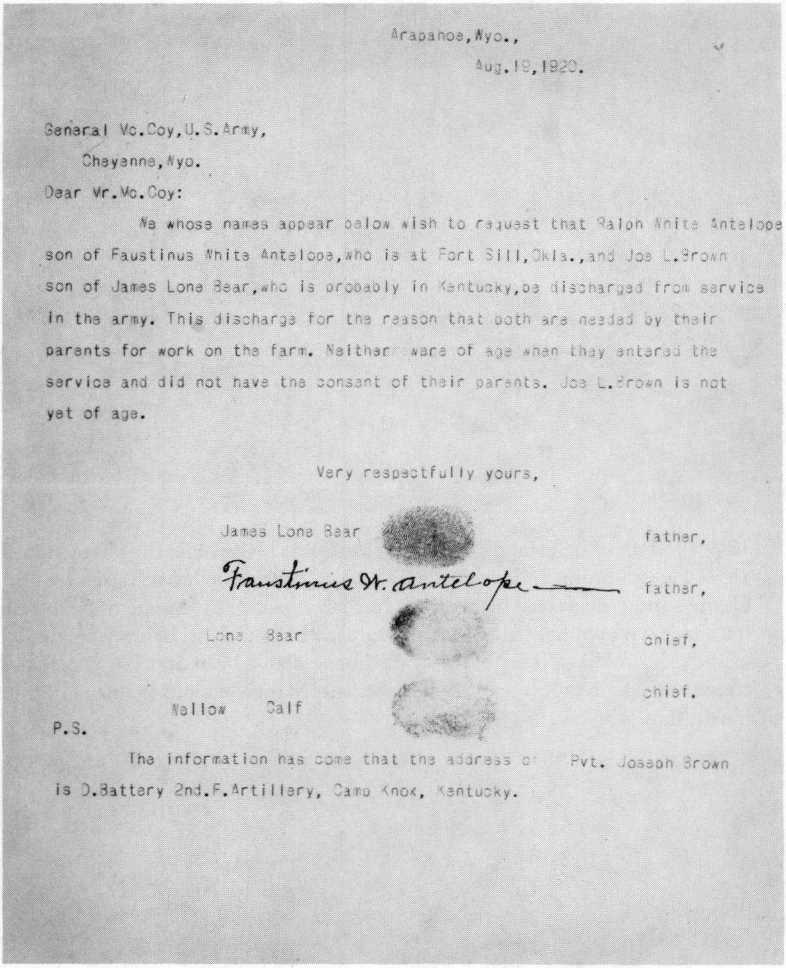

Arapahoe, Wyo.,

Aug.19,1920.

General Mc.Coy, U.S. Army,

   Cheyenne, Wyo.

Dear Mr. Mc.Coy:

     We whose names appear below wish to request that Ralph White Antelope
son of Faustinus White Antelope, who is at Fort Sill, Okla., and Joe L. Brown
son of James Lone Bear, who is probably in Kentucky, be discharged from service
in the army. This discharge for the reason that both are needed by their
parents for work on the farm. Neither were of age when they entered the
service and did not have the consent of their parents. Joe L. Brown is not
yet of age.

           Very respectfully yours,

James Lone Bear   father,

Faustinus W. Antelope   father,

Lone Bear   chief,

                                     chief.

     Yellow   Calf

P.S.

     The information has come that the address of Pvt. Joseph Brown
is D. Battery 2nd.F.Artillery, Camp Knox, Kentucky.

20. A request typical of many I received while adjutant general of Wyoming. It is
a good example of name changes among the Indians. Both boys, by the way, were
returned to their families.

21. Yellow Calf as he often appeared in council. In the background, a visiting white man's jalopy.

22. Recruiting among the Bannocks at Fort Hall, Idaho, in 1922 for Jesse L. Lasky's *The Covered Wagon*. The man to my immediate right wears the typical old-time Bannock hair style. To my left, his left hand wrapped in a blanket to hide his "bear claw," is Black Thunder.

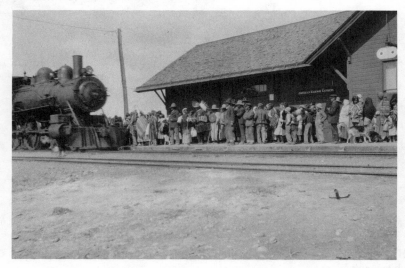

23. In April 1923 the train arrives at Arapaho, Wyoming, to take the Indians to Hollywood, where they will appear in the prologue to *The Covered Wagon*. Opposite, a collection of images from that day.

24. Charlie Whiteman, who became an Indian after being captured from a wagon train, and his
camera-shy son.

25. James Lone Bear, Mike Goggles, Painted Bear, the trader Pony
Hayes and Broken Horn.

26. Yellow Horse with his eagle wing fan and, in the background,
Goes In Lodge and myself.

27. Shortly after our arrival in Hollywood we met with the owner of Grauman's Egyptian Theatre, the frizzy-haired Sid Grauman; *The Covered Wagon*'s starch-collared producer, Jesse Lasky; and a somewhat rumpled James Cruze, the film's director.

28. Red Pipe in Hollywood. The six-and-a-half-foot-tall Arapaho had three brothers, all of at least equal height: Ice Man, Painted Bear and Frying Pan.

people as a warrior"—he would journey to a deserted place, some-times on foot but more often on a horse. This spot had to be soli-tary and the mood it inspired lonely, for the act of asking for at-tention from the Great Mystery was both desperate and intensely personal. Basically, I suppose the Indian was trying to get an an-swer to the age-old Who-am-I-what-is-it-all-about-and-where-am-I-going conundrum.

The process undergone by the vision-seeker varied with the indi-vidual, though some aspects, the old men informed me, were standard: no food, no water and no sleep coupled with plenty of sun, wind, cold and things that went bump in the night. It is hardly surprising that after a few days of this type of behavior a state of semi-consciousness or complete unconsciousness might come over the seeker. While in this state, the young man would experience his vision and come into direct, personal contact with the Great Mystery.

It is important to stress that the recipient of the vision did not, either then or later, ever view the experience as a dream. He had approached the Mystery with pure, noble intentions and his beg-ging for attention had been answered. It was not a "miracle," ei-ther, but simply one of the many possibilities in a world where anything was possible.

In a vision it was typical that an animal might speak to the young man, though sometimes a great warrior would appear, rid-ing through his enemies unharmed because of a particular Medi-cine object he was wearing in his hair or around his neck. This ob-ject, which might be a root, stone, feather, animal or part of an animal such as the head, skin, teeth or claws, would become the young man's Medicine, and, ever afterward, he would carry the token with him. In Goes In Lodge's case, it was inside the small leather pouch tied behind his left ear. For Left Hand, another of the old men, it was a piece of buffalo hide cut into the cross shape of the morning star and onto which was affixed a single eagle feather.

If the conquering warrior of the vision was meant to be iden-tified by the vision-seeker as a representation of himself, the young man would duplicate, to a high degree of exactitude, the trappings of the phantom rider. Not heeding the message in the vision was regarded by the old-time Indians as worse than simple stupidity. It was folly and viewed with emotions similar to those which prompted Euripides to claim, as Latinized by Plutarch: *Quem deus vult perdere, prius dementat*—Whom God would destroy, he first makes mad.

If words were heard during the vision they would be, to say the least, cryptic. As the young man made his way back to his village, he would ponder the experience, the full meanings of which he would soon learn when he discussed the matter with his father and other men wiser than himself.

Throughout their lives the old men placed complete faith in their Medicine. I remember asking Goes In Lodge whether if a warrior was wounded or killed the Great Mystery was at fault. He looked at me as though I had suddenly been transformed into an imbecile.

"Of course the Great Mystery would not be at fault," he finally answered, sighing heavily as though fearful he would have to begin to explain his view of the universe from the beginning. "If the Medicine failed, it could only be the fault of the warrior. Somehow, he must have made a mistake; perhaps he violated a provision of the power given him by the Mystery."

An example of this was a southern Cheyenne warrior named Sauts, or Bat, known to the white men as Roman Nose. Bat was killed at the Beecher Island fight in 1868, in spite of having the requisite mojos: a shield to which was affixed a dead bat, and a spectacular bonnet with a long trail trimmed with alternating rows of white and red-dyed eagle feathers grouped in sevens and attached to a cap of ermine tails which had a single buffalo horn protruding unicorn-style from the front. There was no question but that Bat's Medicine was strong. Unfortunately, prior to going into the battle he violated a provision of his power by eating meat which had touched metal. *Quem deus vult perdere, prius dementat.*

Early in 1916 I went through the first of many Arapaho Medicine ceremonies in which I would participate during the years the old men were alive. This particular one was called the *chibat*, or sweat lodge.

A *chibat* was constructed of branches about eight feet long.

The branches were anchored into the ground in the shape of a circle and then bent toward each other and tied. The structure looked much like an igloo, six feet in diameter. A small hole, a foot or so deep, was dug in the center of the enclosure. In this hole rocks, heated on an outside fire, were inserted by means of a long, forked stick. These rocks were placed atop other white-hot stones and sprinkled with water. The earth from this pit was removed from the sweat lodge, which faced east, and then used to construct a small mound on which was laid a buffalo skull. Though the rites conducted within the *chibat* were geared toward the making of Medicine, the structure itself was not unlike the white man's sauna, and through the ceremonies, participants received a sense of having undergone purification.

I had ridden to the Arapaho encampment along Little Wind River intending to visit with Goes In Lodge. When I found him, he was walking toward the sweat lodge, which had been erected that morning at the northern edge of the village, close by the river.

"Come on," he said, not breaking his stride. "You come to *chibat*, too!"

I dismounted, tied my horse to a tree and started to follow him but he turned and said, "No, you must take off those clothes. Put on a breechcloth. Then, you come to *chibat*."

After taking a towel out of my bedroll, which was tied behind my saddle, and changing in Goes In Lodge's tipi, I went searching for him and found him standing with Yellow Calf and three other old men beside the sweat lodge. The men had unbraided their long hair, letting it fall loosely over their shoulders and down to their waists. They were wrapped in blankets and underneath they wore only their breechcloths and moccasins.

Yellow Calf, I had learned from my friends, was the Arapaho equivalent of an early Archbishop of Canterbury. He wielded enormous political influence in council sessions because, first, he was an intelligent man and, second, he was a Medicine Man. Now I had discovered he was, among other things, a *Chi-natcha-chibat-ina*, or Old Man Priest. As such, he frequently conducted the Arapaho men in the sweat lodge ritual.

He was holding a ball of red clay paint, mixed with grease.

After scooping out a clump of it for himself, he passed the ball to Goes In Lodge. At about that time, I heard a woman's voice calling my name. As I turned, I saw Julia Lone Bear, daughter of old Wolf Moccasin, running toward our little group. She stopped about fifteen yards away and shyly beckoned me toward her.

"This *chibat*," she informed me, "is for my son. He is coming home from a visit to Pine Ridge, so Yellow Calf is making Medicine to be sure his journey is safe. It makes me very happy you are going to be in there with the others. Would you wear these?"

She held out a pair of moccasins which she had made. They were new and stiff and embellished with a background of white beadwork setting off bold, geometric designs in blue, red, yellow and green.

"You keep them," Julia continued, putting them into my hand. "Good Medicine for my son."

I thanked her, put on the moccasins and walked back to the old men, who by this time had dropped their blankets and, covered from their heads to their feet with red paint, were preparing to enter the sweat lodge. Yellow Calf looked at the moccasins on my feet.

"Nice," he said, "but you got to take them off. Put them here." He pointed toward the entrance, where the other men's moccasins were in a line. Then he handed me the lump of red paint, which I smeared on my face, chest and legs.

Inside, the *chibat* was a cozy but not uncomfortable fit. Upon Yellow Calf's spoken signal, somebody outside let a leather flap fall across the entrance and we plunged into thick darkness. There was not a single beam of light in that place and I think I might have begun to feel a little panicky and claustrophobic but for suddenly noticing the heat.

It was coming from those white-hot rocks in the central pit and was, truly, incredible. During his chants, which he accompanied by shaking a rattle made from a buffalo's scrotum filled with shot, Yellow Calf dipped a horn ladle into a bowl and threw water onto those stones. This action was met almost simultaneously by loud hissing and waves of steam which hit my body like stiff breakers against a rapidly eroding rock, nearly knocking me out.

After this had happened a couple of times, I felt a strong hand across the back of my neck. It was Goes In Lodge, who was sitting beside me. With a single motion, he pushed my head down toward my crossed legs. Then, taking my hand in his, he moved it so that I touched his head, which was bent low, almost touching the ground. It was as though he was saying, "My friend, if you do not do as I am doing, pretty soon you will be hard asleep."

It *was* cooler if you kept your head low, and as I discovered later, none of the Arapaho participants in the ritual had ever even considered holding their heads erect. "I thought everybody knew about that," Yellow Calf said in a puzzled tone when we were through.

The ceremony lasted about half an hour, and when the ritual was concluded, the leather flap was lifted and we walked outside, squinting. I followed the lead of the old men by running like a demon toward the Little Wind River and plunging into the chilly waters. It was both a shock and a relief.

Over the years, I was inside the *chibat* many, many times and it always struck me as an eerie place. At times I had the distinct impression there was an indefinably mysterious, non-human presence; there was, in the darkness, a strange sense of motion, as if something was moving through the circle. Little gusts of wind seemed to brush along my body and, all too often for comfort, I actually *felt* something like fingers touching and stroking my hair.

Because he was a Medicine Man it happened in the old days that when game was scarce the focus of the band's attention fell upon Yellow Calf.

"Sometimes we would go for many days without meat and have to eat roots," Yellow Calf explained as Goes In Lodge and I sat with him outside his tipi one cool afternoon. The husky man picked up a small stone, observed it carefully, weighed it in his hand and continued scornfully, "I remember times when there was not *this* much food."

"What happened then?" I inquired.

"I have always had power, from when I was just so small," he answered, indicating with his right hand. "Why, I do not know. It is a gift from the Great Mystery, who gives some of us strong eyes to see over hills, while others have big ears to hear sounds way off. Goes In Lodge has power for running so fast a bird could not catch him; while I, Yellow Calf, can talk to our four-legged brothers who are far away and ask them for their aid.

"When the *etheninon*, buffalo herd, would disappear, it was I who asked the people of the village to come with me to a hill. There, on the highest point, I placed a painted buffalo skull inside a circle of special stones. I would ask the people to think of the buffalo and thank them for giving us food for life, shelter for protection and clothing for warmth."

Yellow Calf went on to describe how he used his Medicine rattle, the same one with which he conducted *chibat* ceremonies, sang songs and stared at the skull.

"I called to the buffalo," he said solemnly, "and I would say: 'My brothers, it is Yellow Calf. My people are hungry. Maybeso, we will die unless you help us.'

"Then the people outside the circle of stones around the buffalo skull moved inside the circle and shouted: '*Nechawunania!* Have pity on us! *Nibithi!* We have nothing to eat! *Nechawunania! Nibithi!*'"

Goes In Lodge murmured the Arapaho words. There was a short period of silence before Yellow Calf continued.

"Then," he said, "I would sit down beside the skull, knowing the herd would come. If not that day, the next or the day after. But they always came, until there were no more buffalo to hear our cries."

Buffalo, however, was not the only source of meat for the Arapahoes. In the old days they used to eat dog, and occasionally I got the impression they were still doing so in my time. I recall once when I was sitting with Lone Bear, the last of the great Arapaho council chiefs.

"I am told," I said to him, "that the Arapaho used to eat dog. Is this still done?"

"*Ahh-h, natchakaw*, a long time ago. But these young women, they don't know how to cook dog any more," the old chief replied, shaking his head. Then he gestured toward an iron pot bubbling away over the fire in his tipi and a smile filled his lean face. "But young pup, he's pretty good!"

Still, they had preferred to eat buffalo meat and did so

regularly, up until the 1840s when the white man began his invasion of the Great Plains. At that time, there were probably upward of 75 million buffalo roaming the heart of the continent. They moved in herds numbering anywhere from several hundred to one hundred thousand or more animals. Aside from being an obvious provider of meat, the buffalo served a myriad of purposes: they supplied hides for winter robes, leggings, shirts, dresses, pipe bags, quivers, moccasin tops and even dolls; rawhide for moccasin soles, parfleches, shields, ropes, quirts and belts; hair for pillows; tails used as fly brushes and whips; horns to be transformed into spoons, cups and ladles; hooves for glue; muscles for bowstrings, sinew and thread; bones for awls, handles for quirts and war clubs; even excrement, called "chips," was utilized as good material for fires.

Thus, from the tipis they lived in to the clothes they wore, the weapons and tools they carried and the food they ate, the buffalo was the greatest of the Great Mystery's gifts to the Arapahoes.

For the white man, if the buffalo was a nuisance to incoming farmers, it was also a source of plunder. They were shot from passing trains, sniped at by sportsmen and stalked by professional hunters. Sometimes the shaggy animals were hunted for their robes, less often their tongues, regarded by both the Indian and the white man as a delicacy. In the end, their bleached bones were collected and ground into fertilizer. Whoever did the killing, and for whatever ends, the frequently stated purpose of the hunt was to deprive the Indians of the means to continue their way of life while making a buck on the side.

If the eradication of the buffalo was not formally promulgated as official government policy, it came close. In 1873, Colonel Richard Dodge, speaking with a group of buffalo hunters who wondered if they would be prosecuted for trespassing on hunting grounds guaranteed to the Indians by solemn treaty, said, "Boys, if I were a buffalo hunter, I would hunt buffalo where the buffalo are."

And they did, until by 1890 there were fewer than one thousand of these creatures in the United States, struggling survivors of the greatest slaughter of animals mankind has yet witnessed.

The reader may well wonder just what point I am trying to

make here. It is this: in 1916 I was able to arrange for my friends to have a buffalo hunt, the first they had experienced in over forty years.

About a week before Fourth of July festivities in Thermopolis I had taken the train from that town to Denver, intending to buy, from a rancher who was selling out, some good breeding heifer stock to beef up the small herd I was running on my Owl Creek homestead. Since the terms of the agreement were "cash and carry," the rancher had his stock corralled in a pen at the Denver railroad yard. Together, we surveyed his herd, which consisted of about fifty head of cattle and two one-ton, three-year-old buffalo bulls. The rancher had once held high hopes of breeding buffalo with his cattle. Since I never made a similar attempt, I do not know all the ramifications but throughout my days as a cowboy and rancher all I heard about breeding "beefalo" or "catelo," as they are sometimes called, was that the business was at best an unsure proposition. By the time I had agreed to purchase ten or twelve of his cattle, those buffalo were beginning to fascinate me.

"What will you take for them?" I asked, motioning toward the two shaggies in a corner of the corral.

"You want to *buy* them?" he said, a look of perplexed amazement coming across his face.

"Maybe. How much?"

"Cash?" The tone of his voice had changed and while he may have been surprised at my interest in those buffalo, he was no longer astonished. The horse-trader instincts within him had resumed control.

I nodded.

"Well, you know, those animals, they're mighty valuable creatures. Not many of 'em left in these parts. 'Sides, over the years I've grown kinda attached to 'em. Yes sir, fine, friendly fellas they are . . ." and on and on, to the point that you never would have guessed he had been negotiating with a couple of zoos to take them off his hands for nothing.

"Would you take a hundred and fifty dollars for the big one?" I asked. Those were the days when you could get a full-course steak dinner in Lander or Thermopolis for fifty cents, and I could about as well afford to buy a bull buffalo for that price as I could to make an offer for the M-Bar. It should, however, be quite clear by now that I tend to be impulsive.

"Well . . ." he started.

"Look," I interrupted him sharply, "I'll give you three hundred for the pair."

"What are you gonna do with 'em?" he asked suspiciously, as though I had figured out some way to corner the non-existent buffalo market.

"I don't know," I replied. "But I've got some friends who'll know *exactly* what to do."

"Don't worry about shipping," the rancher said, as he merrily stuffed his three-hundred-dollar windfall into his shirt pocket. "They're plumb gentle critters."

He was using the exact terminology I had heard applied to innumerable broncs, including Appaloosie. But he turned out to be correct, for the train arrived in Thermopolis in time for the Fourth of July, with both cattle car and buffalo intact.

The next morning I rode to the Arapaho encampment at the edge of town. The Indians could usually be found near Thermopolis during Independence Day celebrations. It wasn't only that they enjoyed the unending feasting and dancing; some of the older men, Goes In Lodge, Painted Bear and Left Hand among them, were United States Army veterans, having served as scouts for General Crook in 1878.

Goes In Lodge, Red Pipe, Yellow Calf, Wolf Elk, Painted Bear and I sat inside Red Pipe's tipi, smoking the pipe. They could all tell I was excited but it was not their way to inquire too directly.

"Where you been?" Yellow Calf asked.

"Denver," I replied.

Yellow Calf nodded.

"Have a good time?" Wolf Elk asked.

"Yes," I answered. "I bought some cattle for my homestead. And I brought the Arapahoes a present."

Each one of the old men looked up in anticipation and grinned.

When we came to the railyard, I took the five old men to the corral where the cattle and buffalo were being held. "There," I said, pointing toward the two bulls. "That's your present."

Yellow Calf leaped from his pony's back, landed hard on his feet, grabbed me by the shoulders, pulled me from my saddle, embraced me in a rib-shattering bear hug, lifted me high in the air and said, over and over again, "That's my baby! That's my baby!"

The six of us herded the buffalo across town to the Arapaho encampment without difficulty and stored them in a pen beside the nearby race track. While the tribe poured from their tipis to see the animals, Goes In Lodge set about making some buffalo arrows, like the ones used in the old days. They were just under thirty inches in length, with a wide, flat head. The range of these arrows was not significantly greater than that of the arrows normally used in warfare and deer or elk killing, and nowhere near the six hundred yards some modern authorities have claimed. But their striking force was considerably more powerful. On occasion, such arrows would actually pass entirely through the animals.

By the next morning, Goes In Lodge had prepared six such arrows, keeping one for himself and distributing the others to Painted Bear, Red Pipe, Wolf Elk and Yellow Calf. With a grin, Goes In Lodge handed me a bow and one of the arrows, saying, "You help kill buffalo, too!"

Everyone wanted to have a hand in the afternoon killing, but the old men exercised their prerogative and gave the young men the opportunity to run, rather than actually bring down, the buffalo. Charlie White Bull and some of the younger Arapahoes mounted their ponies and herded the two bulls out onto the race track, where there would be room to maneuver.

"Now," Goes In Lodge said, an enormous smile crossing his face, *"we are going to hunt buffalo!"*

I was not exactly confident of my ability to shoot buffalo bulls with a bow and arrow while riding bareback on an Indian pony. Yellow Calf sensed this and had some words of advice.

"Just hold the reins in your mouth," he said, "ride alongside a bull, lean over his back and drive that arrow all the way in . . ."

This was starting to sound like serious business.

"If you get thrown, or that bull goes into your pony . . ."

Goes into my pony?

". . . lie on the ground very, very still. That way, buffalo won't be able to tell you from a rock."

I was getting a familiar sinking sensation and could not help looking at him in amazement.

"You know," he said impatiently, "play dead."

This was beginning to look like a fairly dangerous proposition, so while the old men trotted their ponies out toward the unsuspecting buffalo, I made my entrance onto the track with a tightly reined, slow-walking horse.

Suddenly Red Pipe let out a bloodcurdling scream that sent tremors down my spine. As he kicked his pony toward the bewildered buffalo, Goes In Lodge and Yellow Calf circled behind, calling, "*Hu! Hu! Hu!*", while Wolf Elk and Painted Bear galloped in a wide, flanking movement toward the other side of the animals.

Not knowing what to do, and not really having a burning desire to find out, I sat on the pony, buffalo arrow in hand, watching while clenching the bow hard. I expected at any moment to see a gut-shattering collision of five old Arapahoes and two bull buffalo with a combined weight of four thousand pounds.

The buffalo slowly, almost with boredom, raised their massive heads, snorted disdainfully, trotted off about twenty yards and stopped. The Arapahoes pulled their ponies into wheeling halts almost simultaneously.

"We try again!" Goes In Lodge shouted.

Galloping, yelling and weaving behind, in front of and to the sides of the buffalo, the five old warriors tried to get the animals to move. Each time, the initial performance was repeated.

Losing patience, Yellow Calf rode up to one immobile bull, stopped his pony, leaned over and let fly with his arrow. The bull raised its head slightly as the arrow slid into his hump with a dull *thwack!* and made a quick thrust with his left horn, narrowly missing Yellow Calf's pony. Then, arrogantly, he walked a short distance away.

Red Pipe, howling the whole time, raced by the wounded animal and fired his arrow into its side. The bull bellowed, lowered its head and started pawing the ground.

Goes In Lodge galloped past the other buffalo, which was doing absolutely nothing but standing and staring ominously at me, smacked it across the nose with his bow as he went by and headed for the other, cornered animal.

After circling it a couple of times, and calling on it to charge, the old man finally drove his arrow deep into the bull's shoulder.

Wolf Elk and Painted Bear were set on bringing the other bull to the ground, and after circling it a few times, each placed an arrow in its hump.

Still, after about twenty minutes of this, both buffalo were on their feet, very much alive and growing increasingly cantankerous.

"No damn good," Yellow Calf muttered when he rode up beside me.

"What's the problem?" I asked, mystified at the inability of these former buffalo hunters to kill off the two buffalo.

"First thing," he answered, his voice quivering with rage, "those buffalo don't act right. Been in a cage too long. And the ponies. They don't steer by the knees, they're not real buffalo ponies so they don't know what to do."

That I could understand.

"And second thing," he continued, working himself into a rage, "those buffalo don't run right."

"What do you mean, 'don't run right'?" I asked.

"When you're on the edge of a herd," he explained, "and lots of buffalo are moving very fast, bumping into each other, snorting, bellowing, knocking into each other, hooking their horns—when there are thousands of buffalo and plenty of noise and action, it's different.

"But these buffalo," he said, giving the bulls an angry look, "they just don't know how to run right. Understand?"

I did.

Goes In Lodge jumped from his pony, stomped over to the fence, borrowed a rifle from Charlie White Bull and strode over to the first bull. He dropped the animal with a single shot, moved over to the second bull and crumpled him with another.

Then the women and children clambered over the fence and the women began butchering the two animals on the spot. I had an idea the owners of the race track would not be pleased when they heard their establishment had been turned into a slaughterhouse, rendering yard and butcher shop by the Indians. However, it was impossible to convince an Arapaho with warm buffalo liver in his mouth that this was neither the time nor the place for butchering his spoils. They were so excited that my pleas for them to move the buffalo carcasses to their encampment were greeted by smiles, pats on the back and promises of "Soon, soon."

As the butchering process was going on, some of the women took their babies' hands and gently rubbed them along the bull's fur. For years afterward, Arapahoes who had been there said that they, too, had once touched the sacred *ha-natcha*.

Milling on the outside of the crowd which had gathered in a circle around the buffalo, I saw the old men bend down, put their hands into the open throats of those bulls, cover their faces, breathe deeply and cry.

That night, after the butchering was completed, the Arapahoes struck their tipis a day earlier than expected, mounted their ponies and rode far out of Thermopolis. They went to a valley where the white men would not bother them and, for the first time in a very long time, danced the dance of the buffalo hunt and ate the meat of the great provider.

CHAPTER SEVEN

Forty Miles a Day on Beans and Hay

The First World War was, for over two years, perceived but dimly by those of us in Wyoming. Soon, however, heated arguments were taking place in the recesses of Happy Jack's saloon in Thermopolis, where the question signaling a point of departure in opinion was whether the United States should remain neutral or enter the growing and increasingly bloody conflict then known as "the European War."

"Of course I'm neutral," I overheard one fellow explaining to a friend at the bar. "I'm so damned neutral I don't care *who* kills the Kaiser."

Irish Tom, who was still operating his pool wagon business, was the source of several inspirations. One evening he hatched a deadly plot.

"We Irish," Tom snorted, "will take care of everything. We've just invented a new weapon. As a matter of fact, they're just beginning to come out with it now. It's a square cannon that shoots bricks."

On another occasion, the talk turned to the German navy, which, using U-boats and converted freighters capable of coursing the high seas at remarkable speeds, was sinking a prodigious amount of British shipping.

"Ah, but there'll be an end to those sea raiders soon," Tom said. "You just wait till the Irish navy comes out."

"Irish navy?" somebody cried in disbelief. "Who the hell ever heard of it? Aren't they the ones that go home for their lunch? Where is the Irish navy, anyway?"

"And do you think," Tom replied, arching an eyebrow and staring slyly toward the unbeliever, "that I'd be tellin' you, you damned German spy!"

Officially, the United States was neutral but public opinion was strongly anti-German. In retrospect, it is clear that the war drums were being beaten long and hard by journalists and editors in the press of the day. The great propaganda target, aside from the individual German soldier, who was pictured as more beast than man, was Kaiser Wilhelm, or, as he was sometimes called, Willy the Head Hun.

The debates in Happy Jack's frequently turned on the fate of the Kaiser.

"He should be shot by a firing squad!" shouted one man.

"No! He ought to be drawn and quartered!" ranted another.

"Hell," observed Irish Tom dryly, "you fellows are being too lenient. The punishment should fit the crime. And I say, he ought to have his ass kicked!"

It was only about half a mile from the M-Bar bunkhouse to the Em-Bar post office, where mail was delivered three times a week by the stagecoach from Thermopolis, and many of us cowboys would ride over at least a couple of times a week for the mail, which might bring news from family or friends and, almost surely, newspapers only a few days old. No news might be good news, but after looking at cows all day, every day, even bad news from the outside world was eagerly sought after.

Around late January 1917, when the snow was thick upon the ground, I picked up my mail and that evening, while lying on my bunk and reading the Denver *Post*, noticed an article which dealt with the latest exploits of the flamboyant former President of the United States Theodore Roosevelt. Ever anxious to be in the midst of whatever action was currently at center stage of the public's attention, "Teddy" had decided he could win the war.

According to the article I was reading, Roosevelt was proposing that a full division of soldiers be raised and sent to aid England and France against the Hun. In addition to the division of infantry, he wanted some cavalry whose speed and maneuverability would make it possible for them to punch a small hole in the heretofore impregnable German Western Front. These Rough Riders were to be drawn primarily from America's hard-riding cowboy population, much as the Rough Riders Roosevelt had helped organize during the Spanish-American War had been. The intention was that they would fan out behind the German lines and live off the country while wreaking havoc upon the enemy's lines of communication and supply. Then other Allied forces would concentrate on expanding this little hole into a wide gap. According to Roosevelt's theory, this was the only way the interminably static European war could be swiftly brought to a successful conclusion.

At the time I read that article, I was twenty-six years old, bursting with energy, enjoying good health and filled with that roving spirit which has always constituted a substantial part of my make-up. And, like many young people, I had the brashness, or spunk, that comes when you've passed most of your time on life's hills rather than down in the valleys.

Throwing caution to the wind, I got up from my bunk, walked over to the coffee table, took a piece of paper and a pen and began to write a letter to Mr. Roosevelt. In my letter I offered to recruit a full squadron of four hundred cavalrymen from among the cowboys of Montana and Wyoming. Having no idea where T.R. lived, but deciding that someone in the post office was bound to know, I addressed the envelope to "The Hon. Theo. Roosevelt, New York City, New York."

Two weeks later, I received a telegram from him which was brought up by a rider from Thermopolis because, as the cowboy explained, "It looked mighty important." It was. Roosevelt had replied to my letter with six words: *"Bully for you! Do proceed! Roosevelt."*

My job as a recruiter was a simple affair. Armed with the newspaper article outlining Roosevelt's plan and his directive to me to go ahead with recruitment for the operation, I spent the next two months riding to the towns and ranches of northern Wyoming and southern Montana. It was winter, there was little to do at the M-Bar but sit in the warm bunkhouse and peruse the catalogues of western wear and equipment, or, as the cowboys termed them, "wishin' books": "Gee, I sure wisht' I had a pair of them Angora chaps." Besides, my employers were not immune to appeals to their patriotism.

I rarely had trouble getting recruits and my effort in Thermopolis was typical. I rode into town on a Friday and made the rounds of the saloons. There, surrounded by tobacco smoke and whiskey fumes, I knew I was sure to find many eager recruits. With cheers and raucous shouts of approval, cowboys in town for the long weekend would sign their names to a plain sheet of paper. There were very few who hesitated to pledge leaving the monotonous life of a wintertime cowboy and saddle tramp to become one of Roosevelt's Rough Riders. In two months, I had signed up the full squadron of four hundred men.

While I was engaged in recruiting Rough Riders, the tide was beginning to turn against Roosevelt. In order for him to cut through the Western Front he first had to receive permission to embark his division from an American port and that required the approval of the still officially neutral United States government. The court of final appeal for Roosevelt's request was the President, Woodrow Wilson.

In an effort to grease the wheels of bureaucracy, Roosevelt arranged for an appointment with Wilson at the White House. During this interview, he did not receive a definite answer. Several years later one of Roosevelt's friends, General Leonard Wood, told me what had transpired during that interview.

"Well," Roosevelt had said to Wood in recounting the meeting, "if I were President and I told somebody what Wilson told me, I would have meant 'yes.' But since I'm not President and I'm not Woodrow Wilson, I really don't know what the hell he meant!"

Wilson meant "no" but I was ensconced in comparative isolation from the outside world, and thought everything was set until the ax fell in the form of another telegram from Roosevelt, which reached me in late March 1917. There were no marching orders, his plan had been rejected, the Rough Riders would remain cowboys and nobody was going anywhere.

Two things had happened. There was some doubt among Army strategists and tacticians as to whether cavalry could do any better other than be demolished by German machine guns. Also, Wilson felt that favorable publicity for Roosevelt—who was still a power in national politics and a natural, obvious rival to the Democratic President—was not to his own advantage. Thus did politics and technology doom my chance to ride in an old-time cavalry charge with Teddy Roosevelt. It would certainly have been, as he was so fond of putting it, "Bully!"

On April 2, 1917, Congress declared war on Germany, and, with the failure of Roosevelt's plan, I felt much like the man in the air who suddenly discovers he is without his trapeze. The middle of Wyoming was not the place to find out what sort of units were being recruited. Most of my Arapaho friends, however, could hardly have cared less. They were exempt from the draft, for, though natives of this country, they were not yet citizens of it. Over the years, their status had changed from "members of sovereign nations" to "hostiles" to "prisoners of war" to "wards of the government." It was not until six years after the First World War had ended that they were finally granted full citizenship.

The Army needed men badly. So, citizens or no, a special commission of civilian politicians and officers in blue uniforms with much gold braid was sent to Wind River Reservation to rouse the fervor of patriotism among the young, enlistable but as yet undraftable Arapahoes.

A council was held one afternoon at a circular dance arbor which had been erected for a powwow at Ethiti. Poles had been driven into the ground and leafy branches laid over the top to give spectators and participants some shade. The commission was seated at a table in the center of the dance area, facing about two hundred curious Arapahoes, who sat cross-legged on the ground. As I viewed this scene from the outer fringes of the crowd of Arapahoes, I was reminded of photographs I had seen of white man-Indian parleys during the 1860s and 1870s.

The speeches given by the white man commissioners were reminiscent of both the old peace commission pleas and latter-day Rotary Club orations.

"The Great White Father needs the help of his Indian children," said one.

"We must join together, red and white, to fight our common enemy!" cried another.

"The red man and the white man are brothers!" and on and on.

The only speech that made sense to me was the one given by Lone Bear. It was logical, short and struck at the very heart of the matter.

The tall, dignified chief rose, dropped his blanket and spoke, using signs and the rarest form of communication employed by the old men, the English language.

"A long time ago," he said, "we 'Rapahoes fought you white men. We were brave but there were more of you. Your Medicine was good and though we fought hard, many of our friends were killed. A lot of Bluecoats also died during those fights. Then we were beaten and you told us to follow the white man's road. You told us to putem down our tomahawks forever and pickem up plows. Yeah, 'Pickem up plow, live in peace.' That is what you said then.

"But," Lone Bear continued, his voice rising, "now you come here and tell us, 'Injun, putem down plow, pickem up tomahawk!' Lone Bear is an old man and, maybeso, Lone Bear is stupid, but Lone Bear no savvy!"

I am not certain that I "savvied" any better than old Lone Bear did, but my days with the G.A.R. and aboard the *Yantic*, as well as the recently aborted Rough Rider recruitment effort, took hold and I became determined that I would somehow join the Army's elite corps, the horse cavalry.

Within a week of the council at Ethiti, the stagecoach brought another edition of the Denver *Post*, which contained an article explaining that since the Army was expanding at an unheard-of rate, the War Department was going to open several officer training schools. Qualified candidates, which meant able-bodied men between the ages of eighteen and thirty-five, were urged to apply to one of these schools if they desired a commission. The alternative was to wait until the draft notice came and you were thrown into the ranks of the infantry, a branch of the service which in the First World War was even more a mass of cannon fodder than it is today. I had no idea where these schools were located but I knew they sure as hell were not up in the Big Horn Basin.

The following Saturday I was standing in front of the Emery

Hotel in Thermopolis, which was where I had a room for the weekend. It was three o'clock in the afternoon and the south-bound train for Cheyenne and Denver would be coming through in half an hour. Figuring I could get the information I needed about those training schools down in Cheyenne, I made my decision. Counting my money while running inside the hotel, I put on my one blue suit, packed my clothes into a small suitcase and made arrangements with the manager to take care of my saddle and bridle after telling him he could ride my horse if he'd see it was fed and cared for. I left a message with the desk clerk for George Shakespear, asking him to watch after my homestead for a few days until I returned. Then I walked briskly to the railway depot, where I boarded the train for Cheyenne. It would be almost two years before I returned to the Big Horn Basin.

The train pulled into Cheyenne early the next morning and, armed with the telegrams from Teddy Roosevelt, I made my way to the capitol building with the intention of seeing the governor. Since the day was just under way, and not much of anything was going on, the governor's secretary, Charlie Thompson—a former journalist who had witnessed and reported the hanging of the bushwhacker Tom Horn—took me in to see him.

Governor Frank Haux could not have been more friendly, though he had no idea what he could do to help me out. While the three of us were sitting in the high-ceilinged office, Charlie Thompson spoke up.

"Somewhere," he said, "I read one of the posts where they're examining prospective officers is at Fort Logan, which is not far from Denver . . . Frank, why don't you give this fella a letter of recommendation?"

The governor wrote the letter and, patting me on the back and wishing me the best of luck, showed me out of his office.

While sitting on the Denver-bound train that afternoon I suddenly had the props knocked out from under me. The Denver *Post*, which seemed to be determining the course of my life at that time, informed me that the examinations for would-be officers had been completed and terminated as of the previous night. Still, after coming that far I had no intention of turning back and admitting that I was a beaten man. Life, I knew even then, brims with possibilities and, even more, is constantly in a state of change. So after I reached Denver the following morning, I boarded another train for the short ride to Fort Logan. When I arrived at the post a soldier told me that the name of the commanding officer was Colonel Robert Getty. I walked to the headquarters building and asked the sergeant at the reception desk if I could see Colonel Getty. He smiled, shook his head and directed me to the office of the post adjutant, Captain Walter Scott Fulton. With his short-cropped black moustache, dark hair brushed straight back and horn-rimmed glasses, Fulton looked the perfect adjutant. When I told him I wanted to see Getty he said that the colonel was out on an inspection of the post and invited me to sit down on one of the several high-backed chairs lining one wall of his tidy office.

Fulton cast an eye over in my direction several times while working on a small mountain of papers in front of him and, after a few minutes, asked, "Do you mind if I inquire as to why you wish to see Colonel Getty?"

I told him I was trying to get into the school for officer candidates.

"You should be advised," he said stiffly, "that entrance examinations for the school were discontinued as of two nights ago." He paused, tapping his pen lightly against his pile of papers. Clearing his throat he said, "Having noted your Stetson hat and cowboy boots, might I presume that you would be for the cavalry?"

Upon my nod, he picked up his telephone, asked for an extension and, before being connected, stage-whispered, "Captain Ralph Hayden, the examining officer, is a cavalry classmate of mine. Perhaps he can come up with something."

They had a brief conversation and in a few minutes a personable, heavy-set yet handsome cavalryman stepped into Captain Fulton's office and glanced at me with the studied but not genuinely hostile look of disdain affected by the old-time horse soldiers. They viewed themselves, always, as the elite corps which traveled, as one of their songs so aptly put it, "Forty miles a day on beans and hay in the Regular Army-o." During joint maneuvers with infantry troops they delighted in galloping down roadways and across fields, splattering the foot soldiers with mud. It was a friendly rivalry, with the cavalry calling the infantry "mud-eaters" and the doughboys returning the compliment by nicknaming the cavalry "leather-assed-sonsofbitches"; but a rivalry nonetheless. Though the mounted troops would eventually be phased out, former members never forgot that they were, first, last and always, *cavalrymen.*

I had no sooner told my story to Captain Hayden than the desk sergeant brought word that Colonel Getty had returned. Fulton and Hayden escorted me into his office, where I presented my case to the white-haired colonel, known to intimates as "Gentle Bob."

I did not know then that Colonel Getty, as a young lieutenant in 1890, had been involved in the mess that the Department of Indians Affairs had created during the Ghost Dance among the Sioux. Getty had been second-in-command of Lieutenant Casey's Cheyenne Scouts. When Casey, who was on a peacemaking mission, was shot in the head and murdered outside a Sioux village by a hot-blooded young buck eager to make a name for himself, Getty had taken over command.

Colonel Getty heard me out and answered my pleas by repeating the disappointing information that there would be no further examinations.

I was getting pretty desperate by this time and asked him if under the unusual circumstances—Owl Creek's being too far from the mainstream for me to get timely information, my letter from Governor Haux and my telegrams from former President Roosevelt—it might be possible for him to request some sort of special permission to allow me to take the examination.

Getty was at heart a kindly man, but he smiled a thin smile and coolly informed me that things were not done that way in the United States Army. A directive, he explained, was an order, an order was to be obeyed, and he had a directive in black and white discontinuing further examinations.

Just when I thought I had run out of moves and the game was up, Captain Hayden stepped into the breach, ending the awkwardly heavy silence by saying, "Colonel, I know we can't take such steps, *but* there is nothing to prevent this cowpuncher from requesting special permission on his own."

Captain Hayden had an expectant look upon his face, the likes of which I was to see many times as the men of the Army took special delight in changing the intended result of an order by obeying that order to the letter.

"Right you are, Hayden!" Getty exclaimed, his eyes gleaming. "Take this young fellow to the telegraph office. Help him compose a properly worded wire to the Commanding General, Central Department, Chicago, requesting—on his own, mind you—that a special order be sent to you as examining officer, directing that he be given an examination here at Fort Logan."

Each of the three officers seemed to get caught up in this mini-conspiracy, their grins becoming increasingly sly.

"And good luck to you!" Getty gruffly said as Captain Hayden escorted me out of his office.

When Hayden and I reached the post telegraph office, the captain drafted a strongly worded telegram to the commanding general in Chicago, to which I affixed my name. Since it would be some time before a train came through to Denver, where I was to await a reply, he invited me to join him in his quarters for lunch.

"Now," he said, sipping on a straight whiskey and hungrily eying the lamb chops his orderly set before us, "you will just have to sweat it out at a hotel until the reply comes through."

At about nine that evening, when I was in my room at the Oxford Hotel in Denver, where I had been pacing back and forth like a wild animal in a cage, there was a knock on the door and a bellman slipped a piece of paper onto the floor. It was the reply from Chicago authorizing me to report to the "proper authority" at Fort Logan—Captain Hayden—"anytime before ten o'clock tonight."

It was nine o'clock when I received this and no train was going to Fort Logan until the next morning. I had traveled from the bunkhouse at the M-Bar, barged into the office of the governor of the state of Wyoming, cajoled my way into the presence of the commanding officer at Fort Logan, got involved in an order-changing scheme, and now it looked as if all my efforts had been in vain.

Clutching the telegram in my hands, I raced down the three flights of stairs to the lobby of the Oxford, where I placed a telephone call to Hayden. I learned later than an officer's dance was in progress at the headquarters building but Hayden had asked his wife to go without him. "Something might come up for this cowboy that would need my immediate attention and I'd hate to miss it," he explained.

Hayden asked me to reread the telegram to him over the phone. There was a long pause before he said, "Well, it doesn't say *how* you are to report, so I am now taking your report by telephone. Come out in the morning and I'll date your papers as of the time you reported, which is tonight. Now, go back to your hutch and get some sleep."

The next morning I reported to Hayden, who handed me an official order to "proceed immediately to Fort Snelling, Minnesota, where you will present yourself to the Commanding Officer for admission to the Officers Training Camp at that post."

Nothing was said about travel expenses, which was disconcerting because I was in Denver, Colorado, and Fort Snelling was near St. Paul, Minnesota. Besides, I was fresh out of money.

Whenever, during the course of my life, I have found myself in a jam, especially one of the financial variety, I have tried not to panic. It does no good to get upset because all perspective, save for the most debilitating and self-defeating sort, vanishes in the haze of confusion and the road ahead assumes the proportions of a quagmire. It is bad for the morale.

Faced with this latest dilemma, I decided to take a walk down the street from my hotel. The street was crowded but through the throng I spied two tall Stetson hats and headed straight for them. The hats were perched atop the heads of two cattlemen I knew from Thermopolis, Charlie Anderson and "Big Bill" Clayton. I don't think I have ever been so glad to see anyone as I was to run into those two that Sunday morning in Denver.

After the initial "What the hell are *you* doing here? We thought you were keeping the calves company up on Owl Creek!" I explained my predicament and put the touch on them for twenty-five dollars to pay my fare to Fort Snelling.

Big Bill answered for them both. "You know," he said, "I'm too big and fat to go to war and Charlie here won't go, so I guess we'll just have to send you to do our fighting for us!"

I asked them to deliver a message to George Shakespear: if he would pick up my horse, saddle and bridle from the owner of the Emery Hotel and still keep watch over my homestead, when I returned to the Big Horn Basin I'd give him a bull for every year and a cow for each three months I had been gone.

I was on my way.

Disembarking from the train two days later, I took the main streetcar line from Minneapolis to St. Paul, got off close to the fort and climbed into a little taxi car that stopped in front of the post headquarters, by which time I had exactly twenty-five cents in my pocket. However, while I was on the streetcar, I happened to pick up a newspaper and a startling item caught my eye: the number of candidates for the Officers Training School outnumbered the barracks capacity at the fort and some of the candidates were going to be turned away. I had been getting so much bad news from the papers lately that I began to wonder if the gods were conspiring against me. There was no doubt that my luck was beginning to wear extremely thin.

When I arrived at headquarters, I joined a two-hundred-yard-long queue of fellows of all shapes and sizes, all carrying suitcases similar to mine and all waiting patiently in line. I soon noticed the intense interest the obvious-looking city boys displayed toward my Stetson hat and high-heeled boots and, fearing they might cut the queue, I decided to play the Important Cowboy and bull my way into the Army.

Passing up the throng, I barged through the headquarters door. An armed sentry tried to stop me but I could tell he was a recruit and not too sure of himself, so I impatiently pushed him aside and walked to the table from which the endless queue emanated and where a young lieutenant was checking papers and making room assignments. I slammed my telegraphic order down hard on the table and bellowed, "*Here I am!*"

The lieutenant was obviously accustomed to normal procedure and my performance startled him. He caught his breath and stammered something about, "But where is your form A-728-B? Also, you seem to have no C-27-9372-X. Please step aside!"

Having come this far, I had no choice but to give him an argument that held up the entire line. This commotion went on for a few minutes and I could sense that my time was drawing to a close, as the element of surprise was about to pass through a bureaucratic maze from which it would never emerge intact.

"What's the trouble, Lieutenant?" boomed a strong, commanding voice. The lieutenant jumped sharply to his feet and there was an immediate silence. As I looked around slowly I saw a cavalry captain standing in an open doorway.

The lieutenant tried to explain what was happening but the captain cut him off, called an orderly, reached out his hand, snapped his fingers, received my papers from the lieutenant and, turning to the waiting orderly, snapped, "Take this to the colonel for his OK!"

Within five minutes the orderly returned on the run. My papers were endorsed and I was finally in the Army.

The course which had been devised for prospective officers during World War I was probably the most intensive training program ever undertaken by the Army. For the first few weeks we were trained as infantry. It was the same indoctrination program given to all recruits: up at five-thirty in the morning, physical exercise followed by a breakfast of ham and eggs, toast and coffee, after which we engaged in close-order drill and the usual monotonous military routine. Our afternoons were spent in classrooms listening to interminable lectures on tactics, strategy, map reading, care of troops and sanitation. At night, until "lights out" at ten-thirty or eleven, we studied for the next day's classes.

Each company of candidates numbered slightly over one hundred men, 25 per cent of whom were "benzined"—washed out —before the course was over. Each company was commanded by a captain, some of whom had been captains since the time of the Spanish-American War. At that time, promotion in the Army was to a limited number of positions and always made on the basis of seniority. As in peacetime armies, advancement crept along at a snail's pace and many promising men finished their decades-long service as captains; majors were considered high-ranking and colonels and generals just slightly less rare than a passenger pigeon.

The man in command of my company was Captain Phil Remington. Remington was a gruff, strict disciplinarian who never seemed to have a whole hell of a lot to say and constantly carried with him a thick, pocket-sized notebook. After calling a recruit out to take command of a platoon, or the entire company, he would usually make a sour grimace and write in that little black book, which, in a short time, we christened "the Doomsday Book."

Remington, although he ostentatiously refused to wear even a single decoration, had an enviable record. He was regarded as a top-rank pistol shot and during the Philippine campaign in the 1890s had personally killed the notorious Dato Ali. Later, when we were more or less on an equal footing, at least rankwise, I asked him about it.

"It is one thing," he said, "to make a great score on the pistol range, but when some madman, his eyes bulging with fanatic blood lust, jumps out of the jungle, swinging a razor-sharp bolo sword, it's an entirely different situation. When Dato Ali came at me, I aimed at his belly to slow him down, but, you know, the damnedest thing happened: I hit him right between the eyes!"

It was Remington who, when I later asked for leave, inquired, "What for?"

"Marriage, sir," I replied. For some time I had been corresponding with a girl I had met while she was staying at a dude ranch near Jackson Hole, Wyoming. Her name was Agnes Miller and she came from a prominent New York-London theatrical family. "Marriage," I repeated.

"What for?"

"Well, sir, I don't know . . . why does anyone get married?"

Remington snorted, glanced at his gold pocket watch and said, "I really can't imagine."

A few days later, Agnes and I were married at Fort Snelling. We set ourselves up in an off-base rooming house run by the widow of an old-time Army Indian fighter. Army pay and benefits then were not what they are today and at the end of each month Agnes had to take our twenty or so remaining cents and make liverwurst and cheese last until my next payday. We were young, full of hope and happy. But liverwurst has never tasted the same to me since.

After about twelve weeks, those of us who had not been benzined were sent to the branches of the Army in which we had requested permanent assignment. Those of us who were bound for the cavalry reported to an ancient barracks at Fort Snelling.

One of the aspects of military life which our superior officers tried to instill in us was a respect for the code of honor. Theoretically, as "officers and gentlemen"—the standard joke being that, according to certificates of commission, one had been created an "officer and a gentleman by Act of Congress"—we were to respect not only ourselves and our superiors but also the enemy. The fact that the last war in which any real degree of chivalry had been evident was our own Civil War, and that warfare had become increasingly slovenly since the British first used gunpowder on the French at the Battle of Crécy in 1346, seemed to make no difference. But it did, as the story of a visiting French cavalryman illustrates.

This diminutive officer with a pencil moustache had been brought to Fort Snelling to tell us what war was really like.

"Ah, yes, the code of honor," he replied to my question during a classroom session. "A wonderful thing. Chivalry! Comradeship! The brotherhood of arms! But very difficult to keep in mind during the heat of battle."

He paused a moment and gave our instructor a nervous glance. "I remember," he continued, "early in the war. It was late summer 1914, and my regiment was ordered to intercept a marauding group of Huns. We eventually crashed into each other. This big Ulan with an enormous sword came at me on the gallop. All I had to combat him equally, as the code of honor directs men at arms to do, was a fragile *épée*. I was scared, I tell you, but honor was at stake . . ."

"What did you do?" I asked the Frenchman impatiently.

"I pulled out my revolver and shot him, of course. What else could I do?" he replied, grinning and holding his arms out in a gesture of helplessness.

Shortly afterward, I was awarded one of the ten commissions which were issued granting captaincies of cavalry. Aside from me, the others who had been promoted to captain were mostly old-timers whose advancement had been held up by the seniority rule.

After serving as an instructor in bayonet drill at a new officers training camp, and a brief interlude on the recently promoted General Getty's staff at Camp Dodge, Iowa, I was assigned to a newly formed regiment of cavalry at Fort Riley, Kansas.

Fort Riley was the home of the Officers Mounted Service School, the core of the cavalry. It was the post to which officers of cavalry and the horse-drawn field artillery were sent for their higher military education in equitation, hippology, horseshoeing and the other subjects an officer in constant contact with horses had to know. American Olympic teams trained there because great stress was laid on jumping and learning how to sit a horse in the accepted fashion.

The cavalry regiment we new officers were to train at Fort Riley was composed of enlisted volunteers, mostly town boys from the East who had, in many cases, never even ridden a horse. The situation I was faced with in having to train these extremely raw recruits reminded me of a story I heard about an old cavalry character, Major Michael Cooney.

When, in the early 1900s, the cavalry was expanded from an original ten to fifteen regiments, Major Cooney was ordered to Fort Mead, South Dakota, to command the 1st Squadron of the newly formed 12th Cavalry. He, much like ourselves, received a batch of raw recruits from Jefferson Barracks, horses from the remount station at Fort Robinson, Nebraska, and a cadre of lieutenants just out of West Point. This prompted him to send the War Department a telegram which, unfortunately, is not capable of being reproduced in his thick Irish brogue:

I HAVE BEEN ORDERED TO THIS POST FOR THE PURPOSE OF ORGANIZING THE FIRST SQUADRON OF THE TWELFTH U. S. CAVALRY. FOR THAT PURPOSE, THERE HAS BEEN GIVEN ME THREE HUNDRED MEN WHO NEVER SAW A HORSE, THREE HUNDRED HORSES WHO NEVER SAW A MAN, AND TWENTY-ONE SHAVETAIL LIEUTENANTS WHO NEVER SAW EITHER A HORSE OR A MAN. FOR GOD'S SAKE, SEND HELP.

One day while at the remount depot to collect my troop's mounts, I noticed that most of the men stationed at the depot were cowboys from the West, the right kind of men for the job, which was, as always, a rarity in the Army. I introduced myself to the commander of the depot, told him of my problems, which by then were quite literally of the Major Cooney proportion, and let him know that if he would approve the transfer of two of his men to my outfit I would promote them to sergeant. He liked the idea and gave me Harry Shuler, a native of Cheyenne, and a lanky Arizonian, Dave Blair. Both were top hands.

Shuler became stable sergeant and Blair was promoted to duty sergeant. It was only with their help that I was able to get the "bulls"—as officers referred to troops in those days—accustomed to horseflesh. It wasn't long before the bull ring, or enlisted men's riding course, was filled with courageous recruits galloping along, standing upright on their saddles, Cossack-fashion.

In addition to the bull ring, Fort Riley boasted an officer's riding hall. It was an enormous building with a high, domed ceiling. The interior walls were covered with long mirrors in which we observed our form while taking the jumps. While I was at Riley, a Lieutenant Sloan Doak steered his horse toward the last hurdle at the far end of the hall. The hurdle had been placed too far down and, as a result, Doak underwent a rare experience.

His mount cleared the final hurdle and Doak was about to make a sharp left turn, preparatory to circling back along the outer reaches of the hall, as was normal routine. However, his high-spirited horse, evidently seeing the jump he had just gone over reflected in the mirror, galloped forward, taking Lieutenant Doak with him, crashing into the mirrored wall. There was a great shattering of glass and the accompanying teeth-shattering sound of flesh, bone and saddle leather crunching together. Somehow, both the unfortunate Doak and his somewhat dazed horse survived.

The saddle we used in the cavalry was called a *semur* and was of the French cavalry school. It was flat, like an English saddle, but longer and made of pigskin. One of the informal requirements of the cavalry was *élan* and it was this never-ending expression of the devil-may-care attitude that caused us to remove the stirrups from our *semurs,* tie a knot in the horse's reins and make the final turn at the end of the hall with the intention of taking the next four jumps at a full gallop. It was while making the approach that we began removing our shirts which we used as our blindfolds. Then, kicking our mounts with our short cavalry spurs, praying constantly that we would stay aboard, we shouted at the top of our lungs an old toast that went back to Civil War days: "Here's to victory . . . or death!" In this way, as the veterans put it, we learned "to sit a saddle properly, *sir!*"

During evening meals in the officers' mess some of the older cavalrymen kept us younger men enthralled with tales of what life in the cavalry had "really been like" before it was expanded to meet the needs of the First World War. Cliquishness and rivalry seemed to have dominated the force before the war. And while the cavalrymen refused to entertain the possibility of competition with such lowly branches of the service as the infantry and artillery, the rivalry between the different regiments of horse soldiers was, to say the least, intense. I remember one story told to me by a captain who had served under Colonel Tommy Tompkins, commanding officer of the 7th Cavalry at Fort Bliss, Texas, shortly before the war.

Colonel Holbrook, commander of the 8th Cavalry, also stationed at Fort Bliss, sent an orderly bearing an invitation to Tompkins. "The Commanding Officer and Officers of the 8th Cavalry request the presence of the Commanding Officer and Officers of the 7th Cavalry at a Controlled Ride on Saturday next. R.S.V.P."

Tompkins was a veteran of Wounded Knee and gave his officers as free a rein as possible. Unlike Holbrook, he disdained formality. His reply, which was given to Holbrook's orderly and forwarded to the colonel, read: "The Commanding Officer and Officers of the 7th Cavalry wish to thank the Commanding Officer and Officers of the 8th Cavalry for their most generous invitation to join them on Saturday next for a Controlled Ride and have the honor of accepting their invitation. In return, the Commanding Officer and Officers of the 7th Cavalry request the presence of the Commanding Officer and Officers of the 8th Cavalry at an Uncontrolled Drunk immediately following the Controlled Ride. R.S.V.P."

Holbrook's immediate response was not recorded. But during World War One, he was promoted to general and made chief of cavalry. His first action upon assuming command was to have Tompkins removed from command of the 7th Cavalry; his next was to have Tompkins transferred to Camp Stanley, Texas, an obscure field artillery post.

General Pershing, commander of the American Expeditionary Force in Europe, was a cavalryman. He adhered, as Teddy Roosevelt had, to the by then antiquated notion that when a breakthrough occurred on the Western Front, masses of cavalry would be needed to pour into the rear of the German lines, where they would raise hell. The British also subscribed to this tactical theory and maintained large bodies of cavalry in reserve for the day when the German wall would be cracked. The problem was that in four years of war nobody had figured out a way to do much other than dent it slightly.

In Washington, D.C., the Chief of Staff, General Payton Marsh, found this idea ludicrous. Being an artilleryman, he believed, and rightly so—though few cavalrymen dared to admit it at the time—that it was useless to prepare for an action which would take place after the German defenses were broken if there was no plan for breaching those defenses. The only way to slice into German-held territory, he reasoned, was to blast a huge hole in the lines, a job requiring guns and more guns. So he converted a large number of cavalry regiments into field artillery regiments. This news was not well received among the cavalrymen, who had often joked that a position in the field artillery required a scale of equal parts, horn-rimmed glasses and a degree from Harvard.

When word reached us that the bulk of the cavalry forces were to be converted into field artillery, we were stunned. Gone were the days of the glorious, thundering, saber-wielding cavalry charges. It was an emotional low point for all of us, but particularly for the older officers and non-coms.

In the summer of 1918, and shortly after being transferred to West Point, Kentucky, I led a funeral march in which hundreds of troops participated. Wearing black arm bands, with our heads bowed, we moved slowly through the post to the tune of a dirge. In the center of this procession was a caisson with a casket draped in black, and on a black-bordered white streamer which lay across the coffin were the words: "United States Cavalry. Died 1918. RIP."

I was shortly afterward ordered to the Artillery Officers School of Fire at Fort Sill, Oklahoma, and before I had finished the course, was promoted to major of field artillery in command of a battery of horse-drawn French .75's. By the end of the war in 1918, I had attained the rank of lieutenant colonel.

I was still at Fort Sill when word reached us that the armistice had been arranged and the war was finally over. The Kiowas, who lived on a reservation near Fort Sill, staged an old-time scalp dance. Drums were beating and women danced around a tall center pole, screaming and yelping. Each of the women was carrying a stick, and when the drums stopped at irregular intervals, they rushed toward the center pole and beat hard on a weathered scalp dangling from the top. To them, the end of a war meant that a scalp dance was required, and the function of a scalp dance was to demonstrate that the enemy had been conquered. That scalp, an old Kiowa warrior explained to me, represented the hair of the Kaiser.

Later, I learned of Goes In Lodge's reaction. The old Arapahoes were sitting and smoking one evening in council, solemnly debating what they would recommend to the Great White Father should be the punishment for Kaiser Willy, now that he had finally been brought to bay. There were as many suggestions as had been floated around Happy Jack's saloon before war had been declared.

Finally, Goes In Lodge, growing weary of the endless discussion, said, "This is what we should do if we really want to punish that man: send him to an Indian reservation and make him live like us."

The question I had to answer at this point was whether I would stay in the Army, which, as always, was a bastion of security, and face the boredom of peacetime soldiering, or go back to ranching; the lure of Wyoming remained strong within me. In an effort to make up my mind, I took leave and along with my wife returned to my homestead in the Big Horn Basin.

George Shakespear was as happy to see me as I was to see him. He had taken good care of my homestead and was a satisfied man when he left our company after a few days with one bull and six cows in his possession. After arranging with the M-Bar to purchase from them an additional four hundred acres with our savings, Agnes and I settled back in our little log house on Owl Creek to think about our future.

Shortly after our return I was offered an appointment to the position of adjutant general of the state of Wyoming by the new governor, Bob Carey, an old friend of mine from roundup days. The job carried with it the rank of brigadier general and it took me no time at all to accept this offer, for it made me a one-star general at the age of twenty-eight.

The position was a truly choice assignment, because while my headquarters was inside the state capitol building at Cheyenne, I was given wide latitude in movement. I could perform my duties of recruiting squadrons of reserve troops and still get around the state to explore historical sites or *chibat* rituals, and run down some of the last of the old-timers who had played roles in the events which were rapidly becoming a part of the history of the West. Besides, I could maintain and improve my ranch while keeping my friendship with Goes In Lodge and the other Arapaho warriors.

I was now interested in the "how" and "why" of the heritage that surrounded me and not just in the fact of its existence. Now I was confident enough of myself to ask questions. For me, this was a change in attitude, emphasis, outlook and awareness which had come about because of my association during the war with one of the most remarkable men I had ever met.

CHAPTER EIGHT

Good Medicine

Today, his name is close to unknown, though at the time I met him General Hugh Lenox Scott was regarded throughout America as a truly unusual character and an intriguing combination of soldier, statesman and scholar.

It was impossible for me to mistake him for anybody else when I spotted him walking with three staff officers across the post parade ground at Fort Sill, Oklahoma, in 1918. At sixty-five, he was a tall, broad-shouldered, barrel-chested man who carried about him the unmistakable aura of unquestioned and unquestionable authority. His inner nature, as I would eventually discover, was considerably less formidable and intimidating than his stern, impressive and seemingly impassive exterior. In fact, upon close observation, he wore his personality and the elements of his make-up rather well: his wire-rimmed spectacles hinted at the scholar, his uniform proclaimed his life of military service; his white moustache was cut to a fine, disciplined trim and it was clear that, physically, this rugged man more than lived up to his Blackfoot name of Strong Bear.

After I had introduced myself to him and he learned that I was from "Indian territory," as he called it, our friendship, which was to last until his death in 1934, began.

Sometimes, over the years, he would prod me by saying, "It's a pity. You're just like the Indians. You know how to make the signs but you don't know why. I really wish, for your own sake, you'd find out because when I go you'll be the last sign talker who really knows what he's doing."

He was in a position to judge the matter well, for at that time he was the world's foremost authority on Indian sign language, though he had but three fingers on his left hand, the other two having been shot off during the Philippine war. The absence of those two fingers did not hinder him from making rude comments in sign language to me across the room while listening to a particularly boring series of speakers during dinner at the officers' mess. Our common interest in sign language livened up many evenings for both of us and helped to develop, in spite of the differences between us in age, rank and experience, a particularly close relationship.

It had been Scott's custom during his days on the Army's frontier posts in the West to offer a cash prize of five dollars to any Indian who could make a sign with which he was unfamiliar. During the time I knew him I only saw him pay out this bounty once. This occurred when a Kiowa came into Fort Sill and, in rapid succession, made the signs for "elk" and "dog." Scott was stumped and the triumphant Kiowa, five dollars richer, explained that the first sign language term his tribe had had for the horse was derived from the fact that the animal looked like an elk and did the work of a dog by pulling the travois.

Besides our common interest in sign language, Scott and I also shared an unquenchable desire to learn as much as we could about all matters Indian. One day, Scott, in the pursuit of helping to further my education, introduced me to a tall, thin Kiowa warrior who must have been about his own age, proclaiming him to be, "Sergeant I-See-O, United States Army, Retired; my right-hand man on the southern Plains."

I-See-O told a remarkable and sad story, concerning a Kiowa he had known called Dau-te-kaun, or Keeps His Name Always. As the result of a vision in 1881 he changed his name to Pau-tape, Buffalo Bull Returns. He claimed he had been shown the hole in the ground to which the buffalo had gone to escape the white man hunters and he also claimed that he had the power to open the hole, free the buffalo and thus guarantee the Kiowas a continuation of the way of life to which they were accustomed.

He gathered together his followers, among them I-See-O, and began to make his Medicine on the banks of the Washita River.

The Great Mystery demanded sacrifice and Buffalo Bull Returns complied. He removed quarter-inch strips of skin from his arms, shoulders, legs and ankles and then he directed a follower to cut a large piece of skin in the shape of a buffalo from his back. These he wrapped around a pole in front of a tipi he had erected beside the sealed-up buffalo hole.

"Buffalo Bull Returns lay on the ground with his ear to the earth, listening as his followers chanted," I-See-O recalled as the three of us sat together in the shade of a large elm near the parade ground at Fort Sill.

"But you see," he said, "they were not chanting loud enough and the Medicine was not working. So Buffalo Bull Returns told them to sing louder and to believe harder.

"Suddenly Buffalo Bull Returns lifted his head and looked at us with bright eyes. 'The Medicine is working!' he said. '*The Medicine is working!*'

"Soon he was making buffalo noises. *Hurrumph! Hurrumph!* I put my ear to the ground where his had been and I, too, could hear the buffalo. They were calling to Buffalo Bull Returns to make his Medicine stronger. 'It will take much Medicine for us to get out of this hole. Make it stronger, Pau-tape, bring us back to you!'" I-See-O recalled the buffalo as saying.

"But," I-See-O said sadly, "there were not enough of us there. The Medicine was good and I know this, because I, too, could hear the buffalo. But there were not enough Kiowas with faith. And so, Colonel," he said, looking directly at me, "the buffalo were sealed in that hole forever."

I-See-O was one of the many Indians whom General Scott felt it would be instructive for me to meet. Scott belonged to the "You Are There" school of history and it was because of this that in 1919 he and I, accompanied by men who had been there, traversed the route taken by Custer and his doomed troops to the Little Big Horn.

On June 25, 1877, exactly one year after the battle, Lieutenant Scott had arrived at the site of the carnage to try and identify and recover, if possible, the bodies of the officers and rebury those of the enlisted men. He found identification to be an almost totally futile effort. The graves, owing to a lack of tools the year before and the near-granite quality of the ground, were nothing more than scatterings of dust and the placing of rocks over bodies. Thus, wind, rain, coyotes and wolves had been able to hasten the natural processes. It was not a pleasant assignment, so Scott occupied himself with discovering whatever diversions the place had to offer. These were few and consisted of scouting the terrain, absorbing the lay of the land, and making a personal survey to gain insight into the probable answer to that often asked question: what actually happened at the Little Big Horn?

The best summing up of the battle I ever heard came from the great Cheyenne war chief Two Moon. When I met him at the semi-centennial of the battle he said in quick, strong sign language, "Long time ago, the white man soldiers came here. There was a big fight and we wiped them out."

But this was not the sort of explanation which would suit a man as concerned about detail as General Scott. So in the summer of 1919, when I was adjutant general of Wyoming and he was a member of the Board of Indian Commissioners, he invited me to accompany him to Crow Agency, Montana, where we met with White Man Runs Him, one of Custer's surviving Crow scouts, and retraced the path of the boy general's last ride.

White Man Runs Him was an impressive man. He stood over six feet tall, his body was well muscled and lean and his face and hands had been burned dark by the sun under which he had ridden across the Great Plains for well over seventy years. In 1876, as a scout for the Bluecoats, he was paid thirteen dollars a month plus food for himself and his horse. It was his job to fan out ahead of the regiment and, acting as Custer's eyes and ears, check for signs of the numerous bands of hostile Sioux and Cheyenne who had refused to go to reservations or, having gone and not liked what they found, left to have a crack at the free life once again. As a scout, White Man Runs Him was not paid actually to fight for the Bluecoats and, like most of his cohorts, was more than willing to abide by that provision of his contract. What he received, aside from money, was the gratification of aiding in the striking of a mortal blow against his ancestral adversaries and, if all went well, a chance to run off his enemy's pony herd.

Thus, in August of 1919, General Scott, White Man Runs Him,

another scout named Curley—who had been a young buck at the time and later made some preposterous and quickly discredited claims of being the sole survivor of the battle—a stenographer, Russell White Bear who acted as interpreter to ensure absolute accuracy, and I rode horseback along the trail that the 7th Cavalry had followed.

It was a hot day, perhaps not so different from the day of the fight. We began at the Crow's Nest, a hill from which the scouts had attempted to point out the cooking fires from the distant village to the disbelieving Custer. He simply could not fathom that what lay before him was the largest number of Indians ever to come together at one time on the North American continent. The year after the battle, Scott explained, he had counted fourteen hundred wikiups at the campsite, little protection hovels made of twigs by single warriors without families. He had also measured the camp as being approximately four to five miles long. As White Man Runs Him explained, the scouts tried without success to make Custer cognizant of the size of the Sioux-Cheyenne pony herd. "They looked," White Man Runs Him said to us, "like worms, thousands and thousands of worms on the hill behind the camp." Together, he, Scott and I calculated that there were at least fifty thousand animals in the herd.

Throughout the day we maintained our march, trying to stick as closely as possible to the actual timetable of the battle. Eventually, we came to Medicine Tail Coulee, where there was a path from the high bluffs leading down to the waters of the Little Big Horn. It was there, forty-three years before, that White Man Runs Him and the other Crows, some of whom were already singing their death songs, decided to see if their presence was still required; for Custer had split his command some miles back and was now preparing to ride against between four and seven thousand warriors with fewer than three hundred men.

After reining their ponies tightly, the scouts halted and took a position on the bluffs. From the high ground they watched as Custer and his men descended into Medicine Tail Coulee. Then, Mitch Boyer, Custer's half-breed Sioux scout, rode up to the Crows. White Man Runs Him recounted their conversation. "Mitch Boyer said to us, 'You scouts need go no farther. You have guided Custer here, and your work is finished, so you had better go back to the pack train and let the soldiers do the fighting.' He said that he was going to join Custer and, turning his horse, galloped away. That is the last time we saw Mitch Boyer."

White Man Runs Him stared toward the hill where the gleaming white monument marking the spot where Custer's body was found stands. Leading up to it from the river are stone markers placed on the exact spots where over two hundred men fell. Each marker bears an identical inscription: "U.S. Soldier, 7th Cavalry. Fell Here, June 25, 1876." Those stones illustrate better than any account the speed and confusion of that fight, which, as one Sioux veteran later told me, "didn't last long enough to light a pipe." The Bluecoats were rolled up and fell fast. Many of the markers are huddled in little groups where the men were wiped out as soon as they had formed the regulation defensive position, one man to hold the horses, three in a skirmish line. Some stones are pitifully alone.

Looking from the top of the ridge from which he had watched the beginning of the fight, White Man Runs Him said, "Every man who rode down Medicine Tail Coulee with Custer died with Custer." Then, with a sudden sadness in his voice, he gave thanks to a friend who could no longer hear his voice. "If it had not been for Mitch Boyer," he said, turning to look at us, "I, too, would be buried over on that ridge."

There was nothing more to be said. The next day, our interview with the scouts completed, Scott returned to his home at Princeton, New Jersey, and I returned to my position as adjutant general.

Not long after the visit to the battlefield, I was sitting in an Arapaho village near Ethiti by an evening fire, visiting with some of my friends and discussing those matters usually gone over by friends who have not seen each other for a while. Eventually I was asked where I'd been and told them Scott, whom they knew as Strong Bear, and I had gone up to the country of the Crow and traveled across the place where Long Hair, who was also known as the Son of the Morning Star, had been rubbed out in that big fight with the Sioux and Cheyenne.

"Heard about that fight," a couple of them said, staring intently into the embers.

There was a brief silence before Goes in Lodge threw a twig into the fire, saying, "You ought to ask Water Man about that fight."

"Why Water Man?" I asked.

"Because he was there."

"But, my brother," I insisted, "there were no Arapahoes in that fight, just Sioux and Cheyenne, as many as the grasses."

"It is true about the Sioux and Cheyenne," he replied, turning to stare into my eyes. "Many, many of our friends. And if they were as the grasses, then the Arapahoes were like little stalks, scattered here and there. But the Arapahoes were there. You ask Water Man. Then you talk to Left Hand, because he was there, too."

Water Man, who was seated at the far end of the circle around the fire, watched with interest as the two of us talked. I turned to him and asked in signs if Goes In Lodge's information was correct. Water Man made a quick sign of affirmation.

I was well acquainted with the tendency of many warriors to build up their coup counts and war stories. They were not lying as they saw it, just making a good story. So I was suspicious of this business of Water Man and Left Hand having been present at the Little Big Horn, for, officially, it had been a Sioux-Cheyenne affair to which others had been invited but chose not to attend.

In the dirt by the side of the fire I began to sketch a map of the battlefield with a sagebrush stick. Water Man watched closely, concentrating on details in the emerging picture.

"Here," I said, pointing to an area of my map showing the location of the Miniconjou Sioux circle, "was the Hunkpapa camp."

"No," Water Man said emphatically, "Hunkpapa Sioux up here."

"Okay. Now, Water Man, where did the Bluecoats who were all killed cross the river?"

"Didn't cross the river. They tried to cross . . . *here!*" he replied, pointing to the ford by Medicine Tail Coulee.

By his answers to these and other questions, Water Man demonstrated a knowledge of the battle which he could have obtained only by having been there. Also, his story was independently supported, in all its particulars, by Left Hand.

As the embers of the fire began to die, Left Hand told me his story.

"I was born in what is now called Powder River country. My father's name was Cherry. I am part Blackfoot and part Cheyenne, but I have always lived among the Arapahoes. When I was a small boy, I always used my left hand instead of my right, and as that was strange for an Indian, I was called Left Hand. That has always been my name."

He looked at Goes In Lodge, who nodded, as if to say that it was all right for him to continue to tell his story.

"The Arapahoes," he said, "were camped at Fort Robinson, where they drew their rations from the government, and I, with four other young bucks, slipped out of the agency to go on a scouting party for Shoshonis. With me were Yellow Eagle, Yellow Fly, Water Man and a southern Arapaho named Well-Knowing One who was sometimes known as Green Grass.

"We rode north into the buffalo country, and one day, near the Little Big Horn River, we met a small party of Sioux. They told us they were going to have a Sun Dance, and said we should come with them to their village and have a good time.

"So we rode along with them and as we came near the village, a great many Sioux came out of the camp to meet us. They took all our guns away, and made us prisoners. They said that we were scouts for the white man and that they were going to kill us. That night we were guarded so we would not escape, and in the morning, Two Moon, chief of the Cheyenne, learning that we were Arapahoes, went to the Sioux chiefs and made them give us back our guns and set us free, for the Cheyenne and Arapahoes have always been brothers."

"We were lucky," Water Man said.

Left Hand nodded his agreement and continued, "The Sioux gave us our guns, but they kept a close watch on us so we could not get away. We remained in the Sioux camp and saw the sun rise twice. Then the whole village moved farther down the river and made another camp. It was the biggest camp I ever saw. There were thousands and thousands of warriors. I do not know how many. When the sun came up again that was the day of the big fight.

"The first attack," he said, picking up a twig and pointing to the map I had drawn on the ground, "was made at the south end of the village. The soldiers fired a few shots but when we rushed them they became frightened and started back across the river. Many of them lost their horses and had to swim across. They climbed up on a high ridge and built a barricade. There were many soldiers killed there, the Sioux were all around them."

I remembered General Scott telling me of his friends who had been in that particular place. The Sioux had been so close that they were actually pelting the soldiers with stones while the besieged troopers tried to dig protection pits with knives and forks from their field kits, the only tools they had.

"When the sun was straight up," Left Hand continued, "we heard shooting at the lower end of the village and knew it must be more soldiers. I went down through the village, crossed the river with a large party of Sioux and Cheyenne. We Arapahoes had all gotten separated during the first fight."

Left Hand's words were giving new life to the story I had heard from White Man Runs Him. The time of which Left Hand was now speaking was obviously immediately after Mitch Boyer had told the Crow scouts they could return to the pack train, which was some distance from the area of danger.

"By the time we got there," Left Hand said, "the soldiers were up on the ridge and the Indians were all around them. There was lots of shooting all around, and the Indians were yelling. Everyone was excited.

"I saw an Indian on foot who was wounded in the leg and, thinking he was one of the Crow or Arikara scouts with the soldiers, I rode at him, striking him with a long lance I carried. It struck him in the chest and went clear through him. He fell over a pile of dead soldiers. Afterward, I found out he was a Sioux, and the Sioux were going to kill me because I had killed their friend. One Sioux tried to take my horse away from me, but I would not give him up.

"Everyone was excited. The hills were swarming with Indians, all yelling and shooting. Many of the Indians had bows and arrows. As I came up on the ridge, one soldier, who was on the ground, handed me his gun. I took the gun and did not kill him, but some Sioux who were behind me killed him. I went back and took his belt, which had many cartridges in it."

I knew from talks with Scott that the soldiers were armed with single-shot, .45-.70 Springfield rifles. After firing, the used copper shells were ejected by a narrow ejector. In many cases, the shells, having expanded after the initial explosion, were not expelled from the breech but, instead, tore the ejector mechanism, jamming the gun. The result was that many of these weapons were found on the field, abandoned by the Indians as useless. Scott felt that the soldiers behaving in the manner described by Left Hand were probably either trying to surrender or dazedly handing a non-functioning weapon to the first body that happened to be passing by. There had been talk earlier, Scott had explained to me with disgust, of arming the troopers with Spencer repeating rifles but such plans were abandoned because, it was reasoned, the soldiers "would only waste the ammunition."

Water Man had obviously decided it was time for him to add something to the story. "During the earlier part of the fight," he said, "I was with some Indians in a small gulch below the hill where the soldiers were, but later we moved up the hill and closed in on the soldiers. There was a great deal of noise and confusion. The air was heavy with powder and smoke and the Indians were yelling. Crazy Horse, the Sioux chief, was the bravest man I have ever seen. He rode closest to the soldiers, yelling to his warriors. All the soldiers were shooting at him but he was never hit.

"The Indians on horseback," he went on, "had shields and rode on the sides of their horses so the soldiers could not hit them. The soldiers were entirely surrounded, and the whole country was alive with Indians. There were thousands of them.

"A few soldiers tried to get away and reach the river, but they were all killed. A few did get down to the river, but were killed by some Indians there. The Indians were all running around. We were all very excited.

"I know of one soldier that I killed," Water Man said, bringing his tightly clenched right fist down hard on the palm of his left hand. "It was just at the last of the fight, when we rushed to the top of the hill and finished all that were still alive. I killed him with my gun but did not scalp him because the Arapahoes do not scalp a man with short hair, but only long hair."

Water Man, finished, motioned to Left Hand, who resumed his story. "Once I saw Custer. He was dressed in buckskin. It was almost at the end of the fight and he was standing up with his pistols in his hands, shooting into the Indians. I did not see him again until it was all over. I walked around and saw him lying there. He was dead. Most of the soldiers were all dead, but some still moved a little.

"The Sioux scalped a great many," he continued, "and then the squaws crossed the river and took all the soldiers' clothes. What they did to those dead soldiers I do not know, because I went back across the river to the camp and joined the other Arapahoes. Some of the Indians went back and fought the soldiers who were barricaded on the ridge at the south end of the camp, but I did not go with them.

"The next morning, the Sioux broke camp and started for the mountains. We heard that some soldiers were coming up the river and the Indians were very scared. That night, after they had made camp and it was dark, we five Arapahoes crawled out to the pony herd and, each mounting a pony, slipped away. We traveled as fast as we could back to Fort Robinson.

"During the fight," he announced proudly, "I counted thirteen coups. I was dressed in a shirt and breechcloth. My Medicine was a piece of buffalo hide made into a cross with two feathers in it which I wore in my hair.

"I was a young man," he sighed, "and there were lots of Indians. The white man used to trade us guns for buffalo robes but now that is all changed. The Indian is like a prisoner on his reservation. The buffalo and the antelope are all gone and now we old men can only sit by the fire, singing our war songs and dreaming of the past."

The fire died and, one by one, the old men drifted away into the night. As I escorted Goes In Lodge back to his tipi, I was already planning how I would arrange to have a stenographer take down the accounts of Water Man and Left Hand. The thought of sending transcripts to General Scott gave me much excitement.

"Why didn't you tell me about these men before?" I asked Goes In Lodge.

"Because, Banee-i-natcha, Soldier Chief," the old warrior replied, using the name that had recently been given me by the old men, a twinkle in his eyes and the traces of an imminent smile upon his lips, "you never asked me about it."

Before the First World War I had been known to the old men of the tribe simply as Ba, or Friend. But after the Arapahoes saw me in an Army uniform and observed the single star on my shoulders, they decided to give me what they called a "real" name. This pleased me greatly.

In the old days, an Indian usually received his name by performing a particular action or by being involved in a dramatic occurrence, and the utterance of that name forever proclaimed the event. Lone Bear, for instance, received his name of Woq Niasi, One or Lone Bear, by using only a knife to kill a grizzly single-handed. Goes In Lodge, on the other hand, was a good example of a man acquiring his name through warfare. Once, when he and a small Arapaho raiding party were attacking a Shoshoni village, he stepped into a chief's tipi to untie the string by which a pony outside was attached to its owner's wrist, and finding five sleeping Snake warriors instead of the expected one, silently dispatched them, one by one, to the Great Mystery with his stone-headed war club. After that, he was known as the Man Who Goes Into The Lodge Alone, or Goes In Lodge.

After the First World War, several of the older warriors were entrusted with the task of thinking up a name for me. Within a month they returned to the council and agreed that because I was a soldier, and had attained the rank of brigadier general at the age of twenty-eight, which they considered unusual, the name Banee-i-natcha, Soldier Chief, would be appropriate. Thus, one evening in April 1919, Goes In Lodge led me to the center of the village, where my friends were seated cross-legged upon the ground around an outdoor fire.

Yellow Calf, the Medicine Man and Buffalo Caller, explained

to the assembled Arapahoes that I was a brave soldier and now, truly, a warrior. He talked for some time and finally motioned for a younger man who was seated at the outer fringe of the circle to hand him an heirloom eagle feather war bonnet borrowed from Painted Bear for the occasion. Quietly, gently, Yellow Calf placed the bonnet on my head and, at that instant, proclaimed me Banee-i-natcha.

It was customary for an Arapaho to change his name once or even many times during his life, for while Kills Enemy might once have brought to the fore memories of a particularly exciting event, Strikes Twice might, following a recent occurrence, more accurately describe the warrior. I had been known as Banee-i-natcha for not more than a year before the old men felt another name was required. By that time I had traveled considerably—the visit to the Little Big Horn was a part of the educating process General Scott had inspired—and spent time among the Sioux, Cheyenne and Blackfeet. I had also become completely fluent in sign language and was, therefore, able to communicate with all the older men of the Plains tribes and, fortunately, enjoyed the reputation of being a "good white man."

"A man's name, like his arrow, should strike directly at the mark," Goes In Lodge said, preparing me for the new name, "and Soldier Chief does not make a good target any more."

The ceremony in which I received my second name was similar to that when I was named Soldier Chief. It was nighttime, there was a central fire and around the fire old men sat in a circle. Once again, Yellow Calf stood beside me in the center of the circle and explained why a name change was necessary.

"Once," the Medicine Man said, "we called our friend Soldier Chief. In those days, that was enough and whenever anyone said Banee-i-natcha, all of us knew who that was. But now, time has passed, and Banee-i-natcha has gone to the tribes of the Four Directions. He has traveled much and learned many things. It is as if he were a bird, an eagle, able to soar high into the sky and look at all the people of all the tribes. He needs a new name now and so we have met in council and smoked on it. Now I will give him the name we have agreed on and he will be known from now on as Nee-hee-cha-ooth, High Eagle."

Yellow Calf took the same bonnet that had been used at my first naming ceremony, placed it on my head and brought his hands down both sides of my body in a broad, sweeping motion. Suddenly a young man darted out of the crowd. It was old White Bull's son, known to the government as Charles W. Bell and among his own people as Charlie White Bull. He ran to me, bent down and seemed to pick up something from the ground, which he clutched tightly to his chest. Charlie turned to Yellow Calf and they spoke for a few moments. Then Yellow Calf said something to the onlookers in Arapaho. The old men in the circle nodded and Charlie, grinning, ran off into the night, an obviously happy man.

I was puzzled by Charlie's behavior at the ceremony and later learned what had happened. When Yellow Calf gave me the name of High Eagle, my other name fell to the ground. Before the spirit of Soldier Chief died, Charlie scooped it up and hugged it to his breast, keeping it warm and alive. He then asked Yellow Calf if, because I would not be using the name any longer, he might have it to keep as his own. Yellow Calf asked the old men if they agreed to the request, they offered no objection and Charlie finally had what in the days to come he would proudly call "a real 'Rapaho name."

In the summer of 1920, General Scott, in his capacity as a member of the Board of Indian Commissioners, was making a tour of inspection of various western reservations. He visited me one afternoon in my office in the capitol building. Later, during dinner at the Plains Hotel, he inquired about the progress of my "education" and I was able to tell him, with pride, that I now possessed an Arapaho name. Since this was in the days before every visiting politician and dignitary received "Indian names," Scott was impressed.

"Well," Scott smiled, "you're the only blue-eyed Arapaho I've ever seen. But, tell me, General, have you seen *Seicha?*"

"*Seicha?*" I asked, bewildered.

"*Ahh-h,*" he exclaimed, imitating the tone of the old warriors, "you're not an Arapaho yet!"

"Well, what is this *Seicha?*" I questioned.

29. While Mike Goggles dances to the beat of Charlie Whiteman's drum, Painted Bear, Yellow Horse, Left Hand and Rising Buffalo look on. This scene was typical of the life the Arapahoes led at the encampment near Cahuenga Pass.

30. After their arrival in London in early November 1923, the Arapahoes were greeted by a number of unfamiliar sights, among them this World War I tank in Hyde Park.

31. Soon after setting up camp on the grounds of London's Crystal Palace, Charlie White Bull and Jack Shavehead took a break from one of their marathon poker games to pose for this picture. Shavehead is holding a peyote rattle, fan and staff.

REGISTRATION CERTIFICATE No. 196480

ISSUED AT _Bow Street Station_

ON _6 November 1923_

NAME (Surname first in Roman Capitals) _LODGE Goes in the (Mrs)_

ALIAS ....

Left Thumb Print (if unable to sign name in English Characters).

8-11-23

Signature of Holder ....

Nationality _American Indian_

Born on .... in _Indian Country USA._

Previous Nationality (if any) .... _Actress_

Profession or Occupation ....

Address of Residence _52 Guilford St., Russell Sq. WC1_

Arrived in United Kingdom on _27. 8. 23_

Address of last Residence outside U.K. _Wind River Reservation, Wyoming USA._

Government Service ....

Passport or other papers as to Nationality and Identity. _Husbands Passport USA No 333369 Washington 16-8-23_

REGISTRATION CERTIFICATE No. 196479

ISSUED AT _Bow Street Station_

ON _6 November 1923_

NAME (Surname first in Roman Capitals) _LODGE Goes in the_

ALIAS ....

Left Thumb Print (if unable to sign name in English Characters).

8-11-23

Signature of Holder ....

Nationality _American Indian_

Born on _1845 Wyoming USA._

Previous Nationality (if any) .... _Actor_

Profession or Occupation ....

Address of Residence _52 Guilford St., Russell Square, WC.1._

Arrived in United Kingdom on _27. 8. 23._

Address of last Residence outside U.K. _Wind River Reservation, Wyoming USA._

Government Service ....

Passport or other papers as to Nationality and Identity. _U.S. Passport No 333369 Washington 16-8-23._

32 & 33. By terms of the British Aliens Order of 1920, the Arapahoes were issued certificates of registration from London's Bow Street Police Station. The birth date given for Goes In Lodge is approximate and about two years later than the actual event.

34. In March 1925 I escorted a mixed party of Arapahoes and Shoshonis to Los Angeles for the prologue to John Ford's *The Iron Horse*. When Goes In Lodge, who is partly hidden on the platform of the railroad car, was asked how the Arapahoes and Shoshonis could travel together, given their ancient animosity, he pointed to me and replied, "We're not with the Shoshonis. We're with him."

35. A scene from my first film, M-G-M's *Warpaint*. It was shot on location at Wind River in August 1926. In the background are old-time warrior Shoshonis and Arapahoes and, to the extreme right, Goes In Lodge.

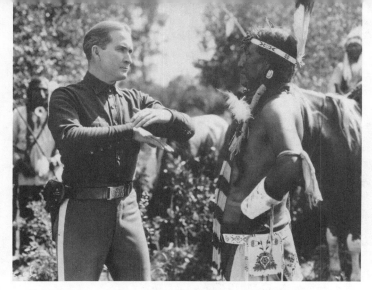

36. Another scene from *Warpaint*, in which I am speaking in signs
to one of my Arapaho friends, White Horse, a son of the Cheyenne
war chief at the Little Big Horn, Two Moon.

37. Joan Crawford and I take a bow in M-G-M's 1927 production
Winners of the Wilderness.

38. One of my favorite leading ladies was the aristocratic and beautiful Claire Windsor. She is shown here in a scene from *The Frontiersman* (M-G-M, 1927).

39. Between films, I often returned to Wyoming and my ranch, the Eagle's Nest. While there I could visit with my Arapaho friends, among whom the years were beginning to take a toll.

40. A poster for *Two Fisted Law* (Columbia, 1932).

41. Getting the best of a tough hombre (Billie Seward) in *Riding Wild* (Columbia, 1935).

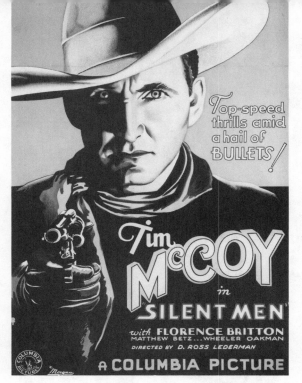

42. The inspiration for this poster from *Silent Men* (Columbia, 1933) must have been an old Uncle Sam recruiting card.

43. My best friend among the Hollywood crowd was Ronald Colman, shown here with his wife Benita and their daughter, my god-child, Juliet.

"*Seicha*," he answered, "is only the central core that binds the entire Arapaho tribe together. Each tribe of the Great Plains has tribal Medicines, usually wrapped in hides and guarded most carefully lest bad times descend upon the people. For the Sioux, the Sacred Bundle consists of a pipe given them by the White Buffalo Woman. For the Cheyenne, it is the Sacred Buffalo Hat and Four Sacred Arrows. While for the Arapaho, it is *Seicha*.

"The *Nan-ah-eh* or Keeper of *Seicha*," Scott said, warming enthusiastically to his subject, "has to be an honorable and virtually holy man. In the old days, when the Arapahoes moved camp, the Keeper was forbidden to ride horseback while carrying the Bundle and so he walked to the next campsite, cradling *Seicha* in his arms."

"What does the Bundle contain?" I asked.

Scott leaned back in his chair. "I don't rightly know," he replied. "I was told many years ago that if I had hung around Wind River long enough I would probably have had the opportunity to see it. But you know how it is, watches, schedules, time. We white men are always in too much of a hurry to be somewhere else. So I missed out on that one and I've regretted it like hell ever since."

He paused, deep in thought, and then put his hand on my arm. "But I think if the old men will let anyone see it, it's going to be you."

One evening, several weeks later, I was sitting in Goes In Lodge's tipi near Ethiti when Yellow Calf joined us. He had agreed to answer my questions about where the Arapahoes had come from. After we had exchanged pleasantries and smoked the pipe, Yellow Calf started to tell the story.

"A long time ago, there was no land, only water," Yellow Calf said, perhaps speaking the liturgy with the exact words his father had used in telling him the tale when he was a boy. "And floating on top of the water, with a flat, stone pipe cradled in one of his arms, was the first man, Arapaho.

"One day, when he was tired of floating on top of the water, he called to Duck: 'Will you dive to the bottom of this sea and bring me some mud so I can make Earth?'

"Duck answered: 'Yes, I will try,' and dived under the water.

"Arapaho waited but Duck never came back so Arapaho knew that Duck had died trying to get the mud. 'Poor Duck,' Arapaho said, shifting that heavy stone pipe to rest on his other arm.

"Arapaho floated on the water until he saw Turtle. He called to Turtle and said: 'My friend, I am tired of floating on this water. I must have mud from the bottom of this sea so I can make Earth. I asked Duck to get me some and he tried, but he dived under this water and did not return. Do you think you could get me some mud?'

"Turtle said, 'I will try,' and dived under the water.

"Arapaho waited until he knew that Turtle, too, had died trying to bring him some mud. 'Poor Turtle, he was my friend and now, like Duck, he is dead.'

"Suddenly he saw something floating in the water. When he looked carefully at it, he saw that it was Turtle, dead. But in his mouth was mud from the bottom of the water. There was not much but just enough for Arapaho to make Earth.

"So, while it was Arapaho who made Earth, it was Turtle who gave his life that this thing could be done."

The three of us sat by the fire in silence. Finally, Yellow Calf shifted his weight and said, as if in passing, "We have the Flat Pipe Arapaho carried when he floated on the waters."

Quiet words spoken in their language passed between Goes In Lodge and the Medicine Man. Then Yellow Calf said, "We also have some other things that come from that time. You are an Arapaho, High Eagle, and I think you should see them."

"Maybeso," Goes In Lodge said, turning to Yellow Calf. "We ask Oscar White."

And so it was to Oscar White, the Keeper of *Seicha*, that Goes In Lodge and Yellow Calf went the next day, seeking permission for me to view the Sacred Bundle.

By now I knew that only one other white man had been allowed to view the unwrapping of *Seicha* and the unveiling of its Medicine. That man was John Roberts, D.D., LL.D.

Dr. Roberts was a bearded, balding and white-haired old man when I knew him. The red-faced Welshman had been born in 1853, attended and graduated from Oxford University and, in 1883, founded a school for Shoshoni girls near Fort Washakie on the Wind River Reservation. By 1890, he had built St. Michael's Episcopal Mission, where he conducted the services of his faith, and from which he spread much good will to both the Shoshoni and Arapaho, journeying from the two-story red brick Georgian building he called home and traveling to the scattered Indian encampments, where he visited Episcopalian Shoshoni and Catholic Arapaho alike. No Indian was ever turned away from John Roberts' green and white door; always, within the mission house, there was nourishment for both stomach and spirit. As a result, Roberts was highly regarded by both tribes.

There is no question that John Roberts was a special, almost saintly, individual. It was undoubtedly this impression that he radiated at all times, combined with the innumerable kindnesses he had shown the Arapahoes, which in the 1880s caused old Weasel Bear, then Keeper of *Seicha*, to suggest to the council that the minister be allowed to view the Medicine. It was an extraordinary request, for no white man had ever been so honored.

After receiving Goes In Lodge's invitation I rode my horse to Fort Washakie and then northwest over to St. Michael's Mission to seek advice from Dr. Roberts.

"What should I do?" I asked Roberts over afternoon tea, a week or so after Yellow Calf and Goes In Lodge had opened negotiations with Oscar White.

The old man's eyes sparkled as he carefully placed his bone-china teacup upon its saucer. "First of all," he replied, "this is a most unusual honor. It means you are viewed by the Arapahoes as one of them. You will be, as well, one of a select group, for not every Arapaho has seen Flat Pipe."

He picked up his teacup and swallowed some of the amber mixture before continuing. "I would strongly advise you to give the old men a feast," he said. "These are, after all, what the white man insists on calling a 'primitive people' and every celebration or special observance for them is tied to food. It's not really primitive, but just a matter of norms. Have some fried bread and thick chunks of juicy, roasted beef prepared and give them coffee with as much sugar as they want. They mix it about half and half, you know."

I nodded.

"Then," he said, sitting back in his armchair and hooking a thumb in the gold watch chain which stretched across his black vestments, "savor every moment of the experience."

He smiled, and as he paused I thought I detected a slight glistening in his eyes. "You see, Tim, what they are going to show you is their ark of the covenant. Intact."

Within a month after approaching Oscar White, Yellow Calf and Goes In Lodge informed me that the Keeper thought late spring 1921 would be an auspicious time for me to see *Seicha*.

So on a pleasantly warm, sunny afternoon nearly six months after the initial approach, the feast was held.

Afterward, Yellow Calf, Goes In Lodge, Red Pipe, Painted Bear, Little Ant, Wolf Elk and I followed the Keeper into the tipi where *Seicha* resided. We watched in silence as the Bundle was carefully unwrapped and, in an atmosphere thick with holiness, solemnity and the scent of burning sweet grass, its contents revealed.

There have been numerous accounts in ethnological journals which claim to describe what is contained within *Seicha*. If one reads these accounts carefully, it soon becomes apparent that disagreement among the "experts" is rampant. This is just as well, for to describe in meticulous detail, viewing with a jeweler's eye, these holy objects would be a disservice to the memories of the now dead old buffalo hunters who honored me by inviting me into the Keeper's tipi that spring afternoon so many, many years ago. More, it would violate a sacred trust, upset the children and grandchildren of the old men and give to the white man information which he has no right to ask after.

So all that need, or should, be said is that Reverend Roberts was right: *Seicha* was the ark of the covenant. Over the years, my respect and awe for this Medicine has not diminished and has, in fact, progressively deepened.

And while my heart had been opened to Medicine, I was still adjutant general of Wyoming, and soon I would be far from Wind River though not from the Arapahoes.

CHAPTER NINE

A Ticket to Hollywood

"How would I go about acquiring five hundred Indians?"

I stared at my questioner, a slightly built, dark-haired and bespectacled man sitting in front of me. We were in my office in Cheyenne's capitol building. It was early fall 1922, and I am sure we presented contrasting images. He was nattily, if conservatively, attired in a red and white polka-dot tie and a pin-striped Brooks Brothers suit and carried an alligator-skin briefcase. I was wearing the khaki, high-collared uniform of the United States Army, a shiny silver star fastened to each shoulder strap, and my feet were encased in knee-high cavalry boots.

I had been adjutant general of Wyoming for just under three years. I was thirty-one years old. I owned a ranch on Owl Creek that had been expanded gradually to a twenty-five-hundred acre spread with an additional twenty-five hundred acres of leased government land, and ran a herd of three hundred and fifty cattle. I was married and by now had three children, two boys and a girl. But I was bored.

"Have you ever heard of Famous Players-Lasky?" the little man, who looked like nothing so much as a diligent, high-priced accountant, asked.

"Nope," I answered, staring out the window at the well-manicured grounds of the capitol.

"It's a production company operating out of Hollywood. We make motion pictures and are currently engaged in filming a Western, The Covered Wagon. It's based on a novel by—"

"Emerson Hough."

"Yes, correct, sir. And we need five hundred Indians if the picture is ever going to be finished. The problem is, we don't seem to be able to get them. We've sent talent agents up to Wind River, over to Fort Hall, to any number of reservations, and they all come back with the same story: they ask the Indians if they're interested in appearing in the film, the Indians agree, but nothing ever seems to come of it."

I chuckled, imagining some fellow from Hollywood talking to an old longhair, proposing a role in a picture, and the former buffalo hunter smiling politely, nodding and saying, "Yeah, good idea!" And then the Indian agent, putting the kibosh on the whole project by insisting that the Indians were going to be farmers and not run all over the country playing at being wild men.

But, the man from Famous Players-Lasky explained, it was not a laughing matter to the people in Hollywood. *The Covered Wagon* had originally been budgeted at just over $100,000, hit the $500,000 mark in no time and, owing to delays in production because of the problem they were having in latching onto the required number of Indians, Famous Players-Lasky was about to get caught holding a three-quarter-of-a-million-dollar baby.

"We became aware of you," the little accountant continued, "as a result of a newspaper article describing the survey of the Custer battlefield you made with General Scott and the Crow scouts. It must have been an interesting experience."

"It was," I replied, almost absently, remembering White Man Runs Him pointing a long finger toward Medicine Tail Coulee, the jaws of death for Custer and his men, the last place the Crow saw the soldiers alive.

"Anyway, the point is, you seem to know all about the Indians. Is that correct?"

For some reason I was now regarded as an "Indian expert." "What are the Indians like?" I had been and would be asked that inane question thousands of times. Usually I replied by asking my interrogator, "What are *people* like?"

"I don't know 'all about the Indians,' as you put it," I replied. "I have some friends who happen to be Indians, I speak sign language and their history interests me. But if you're searching for an

'Indian expert,' I suggest you forget it. The fellows who tell you they're great Indian authorities probably won't know what the hell they're talking about. It's the old thing of a little bit of knowledge being a dangerous thing."

"All the same," he said insistently, "you are uniquely qualified for the job we have in mind."

"Which is . . . ?"

"Going to reservations, talking to the Indians and hiring them as extras for *The Covered Wagon*. You see, Mr. Lasky wants this picture to be as authentic as possible. He doesn't want to hire Filipinos, slap wigs on top of their heads and call them 'Indians.' No sir, Mr. Lasky wants the real thing. Veterans of the battles with the white man, that sort of authenticity."

"You realize, don't you, that those longhair types are getting pretty old?" I replied. "There probably wouldn't be one of them much under seventy-five or eighty now."

"But don't some of the younger ones also wear their hair long?"

"Some."

"And you speak that sign language of theirs?"

"Yes," I said flatly.

The little accountant smiled. "Then you're the man we're looking for. But will you do it?"

"How much will the Indians be paid?" I asked suspiciously, knowing that too many times the white man had taken them to the cleaners. I had spent a considerable portion of my time as adjutant general trying to rectify some injustices that had been done to them in the past. For instance, when Goes In Lodge and a number of other Arapahoes who had served as scouts for the Army were mustered out of the service, nobody bothered to inform them they might be eligible for pensions. My position had given me access to War Department files, and after scanning these records, it was clear to me that some back money was due these Indians. Eventually they had been presented with their decades-in-arrears checks, some of which amounted to as much as eight hundred dollars. Following this episode, the tribal council sent a delegation of old warriors to me requesting that I become their agent. It was with some regret that I refused. My reasoning, I did not doubt, was accurate: as an Indian agent I would be called upon to enforce the government's policies toward them and I would be damned if I was going to participate in anything that would leave a bad taste in the mouths of my friends.

If there was one sign the man from Famous Players-Lasky knew, it was that of the dollar. "On the basis of a seven-day week," he replied, "we are prepared to pay five dollars a day to each adult Indian, fifty cents to each child, one dollar per day for each horse they bring with them, and one dollar a day for their tipis. Thus, General, an adult man and woman with one child, one horse and a tipi will receive eighty-seven dollars and fifty cents per week."

That was more than most of them saw in a year.

"And their food?" I inquired.

"We'll feed them."

"Yes, but *what* will you feed them?"

"Beef, bread, canned fruit, coffee. They'll be eating just what everyone else on the picture will be eating."

"Where will they have to go to do this filming?" I asked.

"Milford, Utah," he replied.

"How do they get there?"

"Special trains, which you will be authorized to hire."

"How do they get back to their homes?" I asked.

"The same way they got to Utah," he answered, as though talking to what my father, working up his Irish, would have termed an "eejit."

"You'll put all of this in writing, and make it legal?"

"Of course."

The little accountant snapped open his briefcase, sifted through his well-organized file of papers and handed me a sample contract which would be signed by Famous Players-Lasky and each individual Indian. I read the document carefully, as I have always been leery of the death pits created by small print. Everything he had said was covered by the contract. In short, the whole thing seemed "legit."

"Oh, yes," he said, as I folded the paper and put it into my pocket, "you will also be empowered to hire up to three other men to assist you in supervising the Indians. Additionally, we will expect you to act in the capacity of technical adviser."

"And how much do I get paid?"

"Fifty dollars a week, plus expenses."

"Even if I bring my own tipi?"

The little accountant smiled. "Fifty dollars a week, plus expenses," he said.

What the hell, I thought. Wyoming's getting settled, the range is closing, life might be a bit more interesting on this film. "We've got ourselves a deal," I said, rising from my chair. The little accountant and I shook hands. "Would you mind telling me one thing?" I asked him. "*Who* is Famous Players-Lasky?"

When formed in 1913, Famous Players-Lasky comprised a glove salesman, Sam Goldfish, his vaudeville producer brother-in-law Jesse Lasky, and a starved-to-death Broadway playwright and director, Cecil B. DeMille. Each man provided $5,000 for the kitty, though DeMille had to go into hock to be able to do so.

Shortly afterward, Lasky approached Dustin Farnum and asked him to star in the company's first, as yet undetermined, film. Farnum, like most stage actors of the day, looked askance at the infant film industry; there existed some question as to whether a thespian would be stooping to unheard-of depths by appearing in a "movie." But Farnum, who was not working at the time, succumbed to the temptation of filthy lucre and replied that if Lasky could secure screen rights to Edwin Milton Royale's *The Squaw Man*, he would play the lead.

The Squaw Man, which had recently been a smash on Broadway, starring Farnum's rival, William Favershant, did not come cheap, and cost the fledgling entrepreneurs almost their entire starting capital.

Farnum, who had understood filming would take place about twenty-five minutes from Broadway, was nearly apoplectic when he was told to pack his bags for Flagstaff, Arizona.

While Goldfish and Lasky remained in New York City, De-Mille took the train West. Flagstaff, he had been told, was the perfect place for outdoor shooting. Lots of sun and no rain. But when he arrived, in early winter 1913, rain was giving way to snow and the entire production was in peril.

DeMille had no choice but to continue moving west, and the

farther he traveled from New York, the deeper became Lasky's despair. But DeMille soon found just the place. A little town, populated by a few retirees, surrounded by orange groves and out in the middle of nowhere: Hollywood, California.

On the corner of Selma and Vine streets, which, like all roads in Hollywood, were unpaved, DeMille rented a green barn for $75 a month, and it was there, on December 29, 1913, that filming began on *The Squaw Man*, with DeMille directing and, to save money, stepping in front of the camera to play a faro dealer.

The Squaw Man was released in 1914 and immediately achieved both financial and critical success, becoming the first of many nuggets in the gold mine that was Famous Players-Lasky. Within two years, the studio had produced twenty-two films. And when Sam Goldfish was forced out of the corporation in 1916, he sold his original $5,000 interest for a tidy $900,000.

These, then, were the roots of Famous Players-Lasky. And of Hollywood itself. For as Sam Goldfish became Samuel Goldwyn and Famous Players-Lasky was eventually transformed into Paramount; as Louis B. Mayer would leave his nickelodeon in Haverhill, Massachusetts, far behind, form his own film company and combine with Goldwyn to create Metro-Goldwyn-Mayer; so, too, the orange groves, the green barn and the pepper trees lining the dusty street called Vine would be replaced by sprawling new studios, thousands of actors, directors and film hands, tons of concrete and a rapidly developing metropolis.

But in late fall 1922, I was not concerned with such matters. I had a more immediate task: five hundred Indians were needed for the filming of *The Covered Wagon*, and they had to be on location in Milford, Utah, yesterday.

The day after my talk with Lasky's accountant, I resigned the post of adjutant general, packed my uniform away, somewhat sadly placed the two silver stars in a jewelry box and arranged for a foreman and a couple of cowboys to take care of my ranch on Owl Creek. Then, after saying farewell to my wife and children, I made my way to Wind River.

"*Five hundred!*" my friend Paul Haws, the agent at Fort Washakie, exclaimed. "I don't think there are that many long-haired Arapahoes in the entire world. Why not five thousand?"

"I didn't say they had to be Arapahoes, Paul. Just Indians," I explained. "Arapahoes, Shoshonis, Sioux, Cheyenne, I don't care. Just so long as they've got long hair and can ride a horse bareback."

"I see, Tim, you're going to put the Arapahoes and Shoshonis together," he said derisively.

I could understand his doubting attitude. Goes In Lodge had once told me about an event the Arapahoes had named the Battle of Tabasco Sauce. Shortly after the Arapahoes had arrived at Wind River Agency in 1878, Captain Brown, commander of the U.S. garrison at Fort Washakie, thought it would be a good thing to see if differences between the co-inhabiters of the reservation could be patched up. He deemed the first step in achieving harmony to be a summit conference between Washakie and Otai of the Shoshoni and Sharp Nose and Black Coal of the Arapaho.

A feast was prepared in the officers' mess at Fort Washakie. During the consumption of much food, many words of praise, admiration and budding friendship passed between Sharp Nose and Washakie, who sat across the table from one another.

A young Bluecoat lieutenant, hoping to have some fun, reached for a bottle of tabasco sauce which stood with other condiments in the center of the table, held his thumb over the spout and pretended to take a swallow. Then he offered the bottle to Washakie.

Believing a present of firewater had been made, the old chief grasped the bottle and took several quick gulps. Putting the bottle down, he sat back to savor the sensation. Soon, however, tears came to his eyes and began streaming down his reddened face.

"Why," Sharp Nose asked with feigned politeness, "does Washakie weep?"

Ever the stoic, Washakie replied, "I was thinking of my brother. He was killed a long time ago by the Blackfeet. And whenever Washakie thinks of his brother, Washakie weeps."

Grabbing the bottle, Washakie pushed it across the table to Sharp Nose, who, not to be outdone, swigged with abandon. Soon Sharp Nose was also crying.

Washakie, with just the trace of a sadistic grin coming across his lips, stared triumphantly at the devastated Arapaho chief.

"And why does Sharp Nose weep?" he asked.

Sharp Nose gulped, waiting for the fire within to die. Finally, he replied, "I was thinking it is too bad Washakie did not die with his brother at the hands of those Blackfeet."

Thus ended the Battle of Tabasco Sauce and with it any further co-operation between the two tribes.

I mentioned the story to Paul Haws, who countered with a more recent one from his own experience. He explained that the chief draw for the Indians to participate in the white man's Fourth of July celebrations had always been the issuing of special rations. Still, each tribe refused to have much to do with the other and the Arapahoes traveled to Riverton while the Shoshonis made their way to Lander, at opposite ends of the reservation, where they would pitch their tipis, charge money to be photographed with tourists, dance and have a fine time. They thoroughly enjoyed this most welcome respite from the crushing monotony of reservation life.

"A couple of years ago," Paul said, "I became obsessed with what I viewed as this elitist attitude between the two tribes. Finally I came up with what I thought was a solution." He paused, lit his pipe and nodded knowingly when I told him he should have known better.

What Paul did was gather the headmen of the two tribes together for a council on the lawn outside his office.

"The time has come," Paul said, "for the Arapaho and Shoshoni to join in celebration. After all, this is one country. So I'll tell you what we're going to do. This Fourth of July, both tribes will come to Fort Washakie, camp and join in the festivities. It'll be an All-Indian celebration!"

This vision of harmony was greeted by stony silence until Yellow Calf stood up and, after edgily eying the Shoshoni delegation, said, "That sounds like a good idea to me. Now, let me see if I got it right. On Fourth of July, the Arapaho and Shoshoni will celebrate together, here at Fort Washakie?"

Paul Haws, unable to hide his glee, answered, "You've hit the nail right on the head."

"Okay with me," Yellow Calf replied, resuming his seat on the ground.

Then Dick Washakie, son of the now dead Washakie, got to his feet. "Mr. Haws, this is a good idea," he said. "For too long we and the white men fought these Arapaho. They were a very bad people. My father, whom you all remember, killed many of them and I, too, have sent many of them into the Great Mystery. The Dog Eaters, before coming to us as beggars and pleading for land that was not theirs and food they had not hunted for, killed many of my people. But that was a long time ago and times have changed. Now all Indians must live in peace with the Great Father and if the Great Father wants us to live in peace even with these Arapaho, well, we can do it. I think we should do just as you ask and so the Arapaho will camp at the east end of Fort Washakie and we will camp at the western side. The first day, Arapaho celebrate. Next day, Shoshoni celebrate. Yeah, an All-Injun celebration!"

After telling the story, Paul held out his hand and said, "Let me see that contract again, Tim."

I handed him the agreement. "It's not a bad deal," I said.

Paul read it slowly, three times, looked up and answered, "Actually, it's a hell of a good deal for them. What would they be doing if they weren't in the film? Sitting around up here with no place to go, nothing to do, eating their hearts out. This way, at least they can do some traveling, see new country, eat well and not have to play at being farmers."

As I left his office to see if any of my friends were interested in becoming actors, Paul called out, "You'll have no trouble from me. I just hope you can avoid an 'All-Injun celebration'!"

I left the government compound at Fort Washakie and climbed into the convertible car the film company had provided. And even though the frontier had changed and there were now fences, paved roads, automobiles and other "civilized" trimmings, I felt like a free man. It was good to be back in cowboy boots, wearing a Stetson, and surrounded by change; for to me, change has often been the handmaiden of adventure. And now I was going to the movies.

There was no problem in getting Arapahoes to sign on for roles in *The Covered Wagon*. A few, however, were deeply suspicious of what the white man intended to do with them once they'd left Wind River, but they trusted me and I knew that once they had agreed to participate they would never change their minds.

Within two weeks, I had rounded up every available Arapaho

and Shoshoni—among them Goes In Lodge, Yellow Calf, Red Pipe, Wolf Elk, George Shakespear, Broken Horn, Painted Wolf and old Washakie's sons, Dick and Charlie—and was still about three hundred Indians shy of Lasky's required five hundred. Paul Haws had been right about one thing: there were simply not enough Indians of the right type at Fort Washakie.

I sent a telegram to General Scott and another to Wyoming's Senator Warren, General Pershing's father-in-law, requesting their assistance in securing the co-operation of the Indian agent among the Bannocks at Fort Hall, Idaho, a man and a place enjoying a particularly poor reputation with the Lasky people. They had already sent a man to the reservation who had signed a number of Indians and then the agent intervened and refused to give the Bannocks passes to leave the agency.

I left a friend of mine, Ed Farlow, to oversee preparations for the journey the Indians of Wind River would soon be making. Ed was a beefy, jovial fellow with a salt-and-pepper moustache. He had left his native Iowa in 1876, when he was fifteen, and emigrated to Wyoming, where he became a miner, rancher and, later, mayor of Lander for six terms. His wife was Lizzie Lamoreau, a half-breed Sioux and the daugher of Woman Dress, a sister of the war chief, Gall, who led a substantial number of warriors against Custer at the Little Big Horn.

Upon my arrival by train at Fort Hall, for the Union Pacific ran through the reservation, I found the agent had received telegrams from Scott and Warren, asking him to "co-operate to the fullest extent." The extent of his co-operation consisted of not getting in my way. This was some help but I still had to deal with the Bannocks, a tribe among whom I then had no contacts.

It was Saturday and I leaned against a hitchrack at the agency headquarters, watching the Bannocks riding their horses in to collect rations. There were quite a few longhairs among them. They were big men, somewhat larger than their Shoshoni relatives, wrapped in Hudson Bay blankets, wearing reservation hats and riding bareback. These Bannocks, I thought, would match the Arapahoes and Shoshonis waiting at Wind River.

About twenty yards from the headquarters building, fifteen Bannocks were standing in a circle around a gray-haired old man who seemed to be some sort of chief.

I walked over to the circle, listened to the incomprehensible
language, and waited for an opportunity to address the old man.
Finally, when he gave me a glance, I asked him in signs—left
hand held flat, palm down, in front of my body, and the index
finger of my right hand extended and tapping against the palm of
my other hand—"Are you a Touch-the-Clouds, a Bannock?"
He looked at me, surprised. "*Ahh-h*," he said, and then, in
signs, asked me how I could speak sign language.
"I'm an Arapaho," I replied.
Puzzled, he asked, "Are you a half-breed?"
"No," I answered, "I'm all Arapaho."
The old man and I were soon the center of attention, as Bannocks flocked from every direction to watch an Irish Arapaho talk
to them in a language many of them could understand. Some of
the younger Indians, however, did not know signs, and I heard a
voice behind me interpreting for them. I turned to look at the
translator. He was a round-faced, husky fellow, wearing a high-
crowned Stetson and white man's clothes. I asked him his name.
"Black Thunder," he replied in signs. Then, speaking perfect
English, he extended his right hand and as we shook, he said,
"My name is Randall."
"My name is McCoy."
"You speak pretty good signs," he smiled.
"And you speak pretty good English," I replied.
We laughed together and, as one thing led to another, I knew I
had found my contact among the Bannocks. I explained the pro-
posal being made by Famous Players-Lasky and asked Black
Thunder if he would be one of the men the company had author-
ized me to sign on to help manage the Indian camp which would
be made down at Milford. He agreed and we went to work.
The next day being Sunday, we toured the various spots where
the Bannocks were gambling, playing cards and stick games. I
spoke in signs and he, in his own language, gave the Indians a
more detailed idea of what they were being asked to do.
As we traveled from one place to another, I noticed Black
Thunder always kept his left hand concealed under a blanket.
And after we'd been together a couple of days, I didn't feel too
out of line in asking him why.
"Shot it all to hell with a shotgun one time," he explained,

discreetly removing the blanket for just a moment so I could see the mangled flesh.

But to the other Bannocks, it was a more mysterious thing than that. And during the next two months, when I was in close, day-to-day association with them, they would take me aside and, in signs or whispers, explain that Black Thunder had not blown his hand to pieces with a gun; no, what he concealed under that blanket was the fact that his left hand was not a hand at all, but a grizzly bear claw. Big Medicine.

Along toward mid-October 1922, Black Thunder and I watched as about three hundred Bannocks boarded the Union Pacific at Fort Hall. At the same time, Ed Farlow and two hundred Arapahoes and Shoshonis from Fort Washakie climbed into trucks and drove to Rawlins, where the railroad spur was located. Upon arrival, they linked up with a group of younger Indians who had taken their herd of three hundred ponies overland.

During my days as adjutant general, I frequently had to order special trains, tracks cleared and other courtesies from the Union Pacific. It was thus not a difficult job to get the superintendent of the line at Cheyenne to order and have ready the necessary cars—about thirty coaches and fifteen stock cars—waiting for the Wind River contingent when they arrived at Rawlins.

The two special trains traveled clear rails and, a day later, met in Salt Lake City, Utah. When the five hundred Bannocks, Shoshonis and Arapahoes, and their four hundred horses, were off the trains, the ponies were herded overland and the Indians once again climbed into trucks. Eighty-five miles later, Indians, ponies and tipis arrived safely in Milford, where *The Covered Wagon* was being filmed.

When Jesse Lasky read *The Covered Wagon* on a westbound train in 1922, it was at the suggestion of his secretary, who had also lobbied for him to purchase screen rights to *The Sheik*. Riding across the expanse of the West, Lasky was struck by Emerson Hough's tale of the Oregon Trail, wagon trains and Indian attacks; it would, he was sure, make a fantastic movie. But only if it was authentic. Cast, director and location had to possess like standards of excellence. But excellence cost money, and even before the film was off the planning boards, Lasky realized that the initial budget of $100,000 was inadequate.

During a trip to New York, he discussed the matter with Adolph Zukor, who, having replaced Sam Goldfish, was running the distributing company, Paramount. When Jesse handed Adolph a sheet indicating a budget of $500,000, Zukor gasped, "Don't you think you've got the decimal in the wrong place?"

"What you don't realize, Adolph, is that *The Covered Wagon* is going to be an epic," Lasky coolly replied.

"Well," Zukor shrugged, "I guess that's different."

And it was. For *The Covered Wagon* was a colossal picture which ran ten reels—or one hundred and eight minutes—and a decade after it had been released, remained one of the top five all-time grossing films, having drawn over $3.5 million into the coffers of Famous Players-Lasky.

But in late October 1922, in Milford, Utah, there was no sign that anything of that magnitude was about to occur. The director, James Cruze, a veteran of playing in Shakespearean plays with repertory companies and medicine shows, was on the verge of tearing out the last vestiges of his once full head of hair. Nothing seemed to be going right, and after spending over half a million dollars, Cruze and Lasky had a lion by the tail which they could not afford to let loose.

In Milford there were over three thousand extras, not counting the Indians, five hundred tents, not counting tipis, hundreds upon hundreds of horses, and the food bill alone was nearly driving Cruze mad. But he hadn't counted on the Indians, who soon after their arrival began carting off sides of beef from the cook tents, cutting the meat into slivers and jerking it by drying it on outdoor racks beside their tipis. In fact, when we left location after eight weeks in residence, I had to arrange with the Union Pacific for two extra railroad cars to transport the canned goods they had stashed in their blankets back to Wind River. I certainly raised no objection to this; the Hollywood people could afford it and the food would undoubtedly do much good back on the reservation. Sugar, too, proved enticing, for it was a key ingredient in the moonshine the Arapahoes began manufacturing in the surrounding hills. The ringleader in this operation seemed to be a young man from Wind River named Anthony Iron, whom Ed Farlow and I immediately christened "Chief White Mule," after a brand of booze then popular.

I met James Cruze the evening of the day the two "Injun trains," as he called them, arrived. After riding in the trucks to Milford, the Indians set about making camp, and that night I was asked to attend a screening of the day's rushes. Fifteen or twenty of the cameramen, actors and actresses joined Cruze in a large tent and, almost in a state of depression, watched the reel silently spin its tale.

The scene we viewed was the crossing of the Platte River, in truth a nearby reservoir. One of the local extras had painted his initials on the side of his covered wagon, and Cruze jumped out of his chair when he saw the wagon, with the initials "L.M." painted in big, bold letters across the canvas, come bounding out of the river and up the bank.

"Jee-zus Christ!" he moaned. "*Everybody* knows!"

"What do you mean, Jim?" the handsome leading man, J. Warren Kerrigan, asked.

"Don't you see? L.M. Lasky's Mistake!"

But for all his apparent cynicism, Cruze was determined to bring in a winning film. DeMille had been asked if he would direct, but felt he had bigger fish to fry. A number of other directors also turned down the project. An epic, after all, is not exactly an easy assignment. Cruze, who as a $200-a-week director had been low man on Lasky's totem pole, had, when offered the job, no choice but to climb into what all his colleagues assured him was going to become a death seat.

His salary was doubled for *The Covered Wagon* and he knew full well this film was his chance to make it into the big time. One year after the release of *The Covered Wagon*, he was able to command $7,000 for a week's work. But the glory and improved financial situation did not come easy for Cruze. When a snowstorm hit the camp at Milford, and before it became so outrageous that all shooting was canceled, Cruze did what most directors would not have done: he kept shooting and the scenes he finally captured of Conestoga wagons pushing relentlessly through the blinding sleet provided some of the film's most dramatic moments.

Jimmy Cruze may have understood the picture business but he did not understand the Indians.

"Look, Tim," he said to me one afternoon, speaking in a rapid-fire voice, his eyes, as usual, bulging from their sockets, "I want to shoot a scene tomorrow morning, and I want those tipis to be in a circle, with the entrances facing each other, just like in the old days."

"But that's not the way it was in the old days," I corrected him. "They always had the entrances facing toward the east."

"Why?" he asked sarcastically.

"To greet the rising sun."

"*The rising sun?* Oh, for chrissakes!" he said derisively.

"Yes, the rising sun," I replied.

"Well, that may be true, but it's also bullshit because this scene can't be filmed that way. Now, you just go and tell 'em what I want, how they gotta put those goddamned tents of theirs, and we'll have ourselves a few minutes in the can and ready to send back to Lasky."

"No."

"What the hell do you mean, 'No'? I want the tents the way I want them and that's the way they're going to be!"

"Fine, *you* tell the Indians," I said stubbornly. "It's taken me a long time to build some friendships with these people and I'm not going to ruin everything overnight by asking them to do something they're not going to do anyway."

"Great, just great!" Cruze roared, stomping back and forth like a bull elk in the rutting season. "We hire a technical director, we get ourselves an 'Indian expert,' and he's not gonna tell the goddamned Indians what to do. That's just *terrific.*" He paced back and forth a few more minutes, turned on his heel and bellowed, "Okay, you goddamned red-faced Irish sonofabitch, *I'll* tell 'em!"

By waving his arms and making numerous unintelligible noises, Cruze was able to attract a few hundred Arapahoes, Bannocks and Shoshonis to form an enormous circle around him. He singled out poor Black Thunder to interpret in signs and explained that the next morning he wanted the tipis in their usual circles, and everything just as always, except the entrances were to be facing toward one another and not east.

Most of the old longhairs smiled, nodded their heads and mumbled in low, gravelly voices, "Yeah, yeah."

"You see?" Cruze hissed at me. "All you gotta do is ask 'em right!"

I kept my distance from the entire transaction, and the next morning I happened to be coming out of the tent where I'd been watching rushes until the small hours. As I walked down a street of what by that time amounted to a Famous Players-Lasky tent city, I heard the soothing dawn shattered by a raucous, "*Keerist!*"

I ran toward the Indian encampment, and there, standing in the midst of generators, cameras, lights, prop men, actors, actresses, gofers and bewildered Indians, was Jimmy Cruze; a defeated man, for the tipis remained facing to the east.

"They're not going to change tens of thousands of years of habit for this picture, Jimmy," I said.

"But," he replied sadly, nearly on the verge of tears, and echoing Lasky's words to Zukor, "don't they realize this is an epic?"

We had been at Camp Cruze for about a month when a fierce blizzard came howling in from across the mountains, freezing everything in its path and making continued movement and filming impossible. Cruze had, as I've said, managed to get some impressive scenes in the can when the head of the storm had hit, but as the main body of ice clamped down on the camp, the entire production halted.

The only comfortable people in the entire outfit were the Indians, who were ensconced inside their tipis, where, quite content, they sat beside warm fires, eating, visiting and playing their shield drums. The Hollywood people and extras, however, were in Army-style tents, where they were cold, damp, thoroughly miserable and never much less than ankle-deep in drifting snow.

I moved in with Goes In Lodge for the duration and this particular day I was listening to him beating on his drum and singing. When he finished the song he said, "Maybeso, you ask Yellow Calf about this weather?"

"Why Yellow Calf?"

"He might be able to do something about it."

"What can Yellow Calf do about it?" I asked, almost insistently.

"You ask Yellow Calf about his Turtle Medicine," Goes In Lodge said, picking up his drum and resuming his singing.

You never knew with those old men when they were just playing out some elaborate joke or putting your nose to the ground where a valuable scent might be found. So I got up, put on my heavy overcoat, which had not dried even after a couple of hours in the tipi, jerked my hat over my head and walked out into the blizzard.

It was hard to see with the snow whirling around, but after some aimless prowling about, I found Yellow Calf's tipi, scratched at the entrance and, hearing the welcome call of "*Whoahai!*" from within, went inside, where it was both warm and comfortable.

After we had smoked and exchanged greetings, I told Yellow Calf what was on my mind. "I have been with Goes In Lodge and he says you might be able to do something about this weather."

Yellow Calf laughed. "This weather," he replied, "he's strong! What could I do about it?"

"Goes In Lodge said something about Turtle Medicine."

The Medicine Man smiled. "Oh, yeah . . . it's been a long time since I used that power. I don't know if it will work, but, maybeso, we give it a try."

One of the first things I learned about Indians was not to rush them. If they want to do something, they'll eventually get around to it. It was standard at powwows and dances to add the proviso that all times were "Indian time." Indeed, that phrase so often used by the old men, "maybeso," stands as a fairly good indicator of the uncertainty of any plans. Knowing this, I was not surprised when Yellow Calf pulled out his drum and began singing a slow, mournful song. After about an hour I figured it was time for me to leave and, bidding the old man goodbye, I started out again for Goes In Lodge's tipi. That was where I was later in the day when Yellow Calf poked his head through the entranceway and asked, "You ready?"

I had almost forgotten about this Turtle Medicine business, but since the weather was giving no sign of clearing and as I had, after all, sought him out, it seemed I had no choice but to answer, "Yes."

Outside, the wind was howling, having diminished not a whit over the course of the day. Yellow Calf, wrapped in a blanket, held a big ax in one hand, his drum in the other, and was surrounded by about twenty Arapahoes, a crowd Goes in Lodge and I soon joined.

"We gonna try the Turtle Medicine," Yellow Calf announced. The resultant nods and murmurs of approval from the Arapahoes left me with no doubt that I was the only one present who had not the slightest idea what he was talking about.

As I walked beside Yellow Calf, who was leading the procession through the encampment, I asked him, "Just what is this Turtle Medicine?"

"You ever kill a turtle?" he replied.

"No, can't say as I have."

"Well," he said, "Yellow Calf killed a turtle one time."

"And . . . ?"

"And that turtle says to Yellow Calf: 'I am sorry you kill me. But, Yellow Calf, you're not really a bad man, so I will give you my Medicine.' "

I was about to ask him what sort of things he could do with that Medicine—to which he probably would have answered, "Things"—but we had reached the center of the tipi circle and Yellow Calf motioned for everyone to halt.

Using the handle of his ax, the Medicine Man drew a large circle, about fifteen feet in diameter, on the ice-encrusted snow. In the center of the circle he drew out a four-foot-long turtle. After singing some songs, he took the ax in both hands and, winking at me, said, "Now we try Turtle Medicine!"

He walked with authoritative majesty to the center of the circle, raised the ax high over his head and quickly brought it down with a thud and a crunch into the back of the ice turtle.

"Pretty soon now," he said, turning to me, "we'll know if it works. Not too long. Just wait."

Within five or ten minutes the wind and snow stopped, the sun came out from behind the clouds for the first time in several days.

And within a short time, the ice turtle had melted and vanished. We were all believers.

After eight weeks in Milford, Utah, *The Covered Wagon*, as originally envisioned, and aside from a few interior shots, was finished. But a conference in Hollywood between Lasky and Cruze determined that this film was, indeed, an epic, and more scenes should be created and put into the can.

After accompanying the Arapahoes and Shoshonis back to Wind River, and traveling over to Fort Hall to make sure the Bannocks had arrived home safely, I took a train, at Cruze's command, and, in the first days of 1923, saw Hollywood for the first time. It was a place in which I was to spend a good many years. DeMille's green barn was no longer a sound stage, serving instead as a prop room. But, on the surface, little else about the picture business or the town itself had changed. Famous Players-Lasky consisted of a few two-story buildings flush against a wooden sidewalk leading to a dusty street dominated by pepper trees.

Cruze wanted me to be in Hollywood to continue as a technical director, figuring that, somehow, I would know the answer to such questions as how the teams of oxen which would draw covered wagons in the new scenes were to be broken. I didn't, but all it took was a little common sense: foot-rope two oxen, throw them, drag them toward one another, yoke them together, tie their tails so they couldn't spread out, and hope for the best. In Hollywood, such information was considered "expert."

One evening at Cruze's house on Mountain Street, as several of us were sitting in the director's living room, having a few drinks and listening to somebody playing the piano, a man came into the house, very excited.

"Are you Tim McCoy?" he asked, breathlessly.

I nodded.

"Mr. Clark wants to see you down at the studio, right now."

In those days, it did not take seventeen thousand producers and assistant producers to run a film company. At Famous Players-Lasky, there were three men: Jesse Lasky, who ran everything; Charlie Iten, who was responsible for the studio as a physical property; and Victor Clark, who might today be called an assistant producer but was, in essence, Jesse Lasky's right-hand man, his fixer.

A few minutes later, I arrived in Clark's office and he said, "Mr. Lasky wants to see you."

The snowball was gathering momentum as it tumbled downhill.

When we got to Lasky's office, the boss man said, "Mr. McCoy, we are in on *The Covered Wagon* very, very deep. We're going to keep it going, and I want you to go along with Cruze up to Bishop, as an assistant director, to help shoot the gold rush scenes."

I looked at Victor Clark, for the gold rush had not been in the script before now. But Clark's eyes had found some hidden wonder on the ceiling.

"This picture," Lasky continued, popping out of his swivel chair, "is going to be big and we're going to put it over bigger than anything that's ever been done before!"

Again, I looked toward Clark. His attention was now riveted upon a minute piece of fabric on the carpet.

"We're going to open at Grauman's Egyptian Theatre!" Lasky said enthusiastically.

I had, of course, heard of the place. It was the most grandiose piece of architecture in Southern California and, up to that time, had shown only one picture, *Robin Hood*, starring Douglas Fairbanks, Sr.

"What I want to know," Lasky said, stepping in front of me and waving his hands in my face, "is what all of this business I keep seeing in the rushes is all about."

"Indian sign language," I replied.

"Well, how's it work? I mean, how do you say . . ."

And for the next three hours, Jesse L. Lasky, Victor Clark and Tim McCoy went over some basic signs.

"Fascinating," Lasky, who was by then back in his chair, sighed. "When you get back from Bishop, you come to me with an idea for a prologue to *The Covered Wagon*. We want this film to be special, we want a prologue with you and as many old-time Indians as you can get, up on that stage. Let's teach the American people something."

As Clark escorted me out of Lasky's office, I heard the *Wunderkind* of Hollywood murmur, "Fantastic!"

I had plenty of time to think about Lasky's idea while in Bishop. The prologue seemed simple enough: have a few old Arapahoes on stage in their best dress, explain that these men were veterans of the wars with the white man and now they had acted in a picture recounting similar episodes. And, of course, plenty of sign language.

I decided against mentioning a specific sum of money to Lasky when I heard Ernest Torrence, one of the great stage actors of the day and now a player in *The Covered Wagon*, recount his experience with Hollywood high finance.

It was cold in northern California that winter, and we were sitting around an outdoor fire one afternoon, drinking coffee out of tin mugs. Torrence had heard about Lasky's interest in a prologue and he chuckled, "Don't even mention the subject of money. You've been on this film long enough to know that money means nothing to these fellows."

He took a mighty whiff of his brandied coffee and snorted, "When we got back from Milford, Cruze said, 'Ernest, they're pleased with your work. As a matter of fact, I wouldn't be surprised if they're gonna wanna talk money to you. Ask 'em for a grand a week.' 'A thousand a *week?*' I said to him. 'Cruze, they'll throw me out!'

"But when I got back to Hollywood," Torrence continued, uncorking his flask and pouring more brandy into his coffee, stirring it elegantly with his little finger, "Lasky called me in and said: 'Mr. Torrence, we'd like to talk long-term contract with you. We realize it has been a great sacrifice for you to leave New York and come out here to perform in this movie. But, unfortunately, our money situation is short at the present time and we will not be able to properly show our appreciation. Perhaps, at some future date, we can renegotiate and come up with a proposal a bit more tempting to a man of your stature. I'm afraid that at present all we are in a position to offer you is two thousand five hundred dollars a week."

"What did you do?" I asked the grand old man of the theater.

"What did I do?" he replied. "I swallowed my gum and asked for a pen!"

A week later, Jesse Lasky and I got down to the nitty-gritty.

"I like your idea," he said, and then, leaning back in his chair, inquired, in much the same tone of voice the captain of a ship might use when asking for a damage report, "How much is it going to cost?"

"Eight dollars a day for each and every Indian," I replied, clearing my throat and anticipating an early return to the Wyoming ranch life, "plus twenty dollars a week for their tipis, all transportation and food included on your side."

"And for you?" Lasky asked with a slight smile.

"To tell you the truth, I don't know what I'm worth."

"*Don't you ever say that to anybody else in this business again!*" he hissed. Then, rising from his chair, he composed himself, smiled warmly and said, "How about one thousand dollars a week?"

Like Ernest Torrence, I swallowed my gum and signed the contract.

Two months later, thirty-five Arapaho warriors, women and children, nine tipis and I arrived at the railroad station in Los Angeles, ready to begin our engagement as a prologue to *The Covered Wagon*.

I was still in the West and somewhat wet behind the ears. I was also in Hollywood.

CHAPTER TEN

Plainsmen in Piccadilly

The Covered Wagon opened on my thirty-second birthday, April 10, 1923, at Grauman's Egyptian in Hollywood, a theater which was, even by later Hollywood standards, opulent. It was not unknown for filmgoers to describe the edifice as "garish." And while it was not the sort of place in which I would choose to live, I could understand Lasky's reasoning. If one wanted to open a picture and ballyhoo it to the limit in a theater where it was bound to receive maximum attention, there was none better than Grauman's. I remember the first time I saw the building. It was bathed in the glow of massive, high-powered, aerial searchlights. Above, a turbaned Egyptian, a long-barreled flintlock cradled in his arms and a scowl across his face, walked back and forth, patrolling the parapets. Inside, it looked like nothing so much as a tomb a Fourteenth Dynasty Egyptian Pharaoh might have had constructed for himself during an unprecedented series of b.c. boom years. Pillars, colonnades, dripping velveteen, glittering gold, massive statuary and forbidding sarcophagi littered the enormous building.

Sid Grauman, whose place it was, knew exactly what he was doing. Like everybody else in Hollywood, he was there to make some money while bathing in the heady waters of glamour. And while men like Jesse Lasky received a thrill and, sometimes, a jolt out of taking the rags-to-riches-to-rags risks which making a picture entailed, Grauman would acquire his wad by showing their pictures in a theater at least as intriguing as the films themselves.

Sid Grauman was a slight, intense, highly alert and intelligent gentleman. His most outstanding characteristic, aside from always having his left hand shoved inside a pin-striped coat pocket—a mannerism which caused Goes In Lodge, remembering the Bannock Black Thunder, to ask with a wry grin, "He have bear claw, too?"—was his hair, which was, simply, incredible. The best way I can make the point is to recall an incident which took place at the Beverly Wilshire Hotel some years later, in the 1930s. Lionel Barrymore and I were ushers at the wedding of Lowell Sherman to Helene Costello. As we made our way to the aisle, preparatory to the wedding, we ran smack into the best man, Jack Barrymore. He was to begin shooting Warner Brothers' *Moby Dick* the next day and had gone into the studio earlier that morning to receive the frizzy coiffure required for his role as Captain Ahab. He looked like a drunk who had just stuck a finger into an electrical outlet.

Upon seeing us, Jack, his seventh or eighth martini glass in hand, planted both feet firmly upon the thick carpet, weaved ever so slightly, wiggled his eyebrows, pointed dramatically to his hair and resonantly intoned, "Made up for Sid Grauman, old boy."

While in Hollywood, the Arapahoes were camped in their tipis at Cahuenga Pass, a mile or so from the theater, and then a deserted spot which was bypassed by a dirt road leading to Universal City. I was living with my wife and three young children a block from Grauman's at the Hollywood Hotel, and at two-thirty in the afternoon and eight at night, the Indians and I had to be ready to make our entrance.

The prologue to *The Covered Wagon* was a simple affair. As the lights dimmed, the audience, which had paid the then princely sum of a dollar and a half to view the spectacle, hushed. An announcer's voice came from the depths of the orchestra pit, "Ladies and gentlemen, Famous Players-Lasky presents *The Covered Wagon*. This film, which is dedicated to the memory of Theodore Roosevelt, stars Miss Lois Wilson, Mr. J. Warren Kerrigan, and a cast of thousands, directed by Mr. James Cruze. As a prologue to this epic film, which may very well be the finest ever made, General Tim McCoy will now present for your elucidation, edification and entertainment a company of America's native sons, over thirty Arapaho Indians from the Wind River Reservation in Wyoming!"

The lights went up. They were so powerful that I often wondered whether I was facing a crowd of theatergoers or the core of the aurora borealis. And then the audience was greeted to the sight of a single white man clad in a white Stetson hat, white shirt, dark bow tie and dark pants tucked into black leather boots, behind whom stood thirty Arapahoes, arrayed in various stages of colorful dress and undress. The Indians were under no standing orders as to how to dress. I had simply asked them to show the white man audience how they looked when they felt beautiful. Eagle feathers, war bonnets, dentalium shell chokers, golden earrings, hair-pipe breastplates, Washington peace medallions, fringed buckskin shirts, beaded leggings and quilled moccasins erupted into a volcano of pure, joyous color.

"Ladies and gentlemen," I announced, without benefit of microphone, "the film you are about to see chronicles the path the white man made through the American West. The ladies and gentlemen standing before you are representatives of the Indians, who were overcome in the sometimes valiant, always tragic, struggle which that migration spawned."

Then I pointed to individual Arapahoes, who stepped forth to give their stories in sign language which I interpreted.

Goes In Lodge, who fought against the white man and later became a scout for the Army.

Charlie Whiteman, captured by the Utes from a wagon train in the 1860s, and later captured from the Utes by the Arapahoes. He was, to use Sharp Nose's description of him, "one-third Ute, one-third Arapaho and one-third white man." He was the only fully gray-haired Arapaho I ever knew, and certainly the only member of the tribe who had to shave every day. He spoke some English, but not much, and considered himself an Indian.

Lizzie Broken Horn, wife of old Broken Horn. A white girl, she was with her family when their wagon was attacked in 1865 by a group of Cheyenne and Arapaho dog soldiers in Wyoming. She was carted off, along with her older sister, who was eventually repatriated to her own people. But in 1902, when her sister finally tracked Lizzie down, she found the girl had gone Indian in a big way, to the extent of neither speaking nor understanding English. She was no longer Lizzie Fletcher, but Kills In Time, a redheaded Arapaho.

And others: the six-and-a-half-foot-tall Red Pipe, who had only to stand on stage to create a sensation; Left Hand, who had fought Custer, and stood before the audience in a blue Army coat with sergeant's stripes on his sleeve, symbolizing his service as a scout with the whites.

These, then, were some of the men and women with whom I performed the prologue to *The Covered Wagon,* each of whom enjoyed their stay in Hollywood. They were the center of attention, attended banquets, went to movies—which always fascinated them—saved money to send back to Wind River, ate well and never had to pretend being anything other than what they were: the last of a long line of buffalo-hunting Indians.

One of the high points of their stay was the day they were taken to see the ocean. Loading them onto the bus proved difficult because the stage manager at Grauman's, fancying himself an "Indian expert," had attempted to make mothers-in-law sit beside sons-in-law. In the process, he violated Arapaho etiquette so badly that the Indians refused to enter the bus until I came out of the theater and seated them properly. Eventually, they were driven along the dirt roads surrounding Hollywood, until they arrived at the beach. There they left the bus and walked along the sand to the edge of the Pacific Ocean.

I was standing beside Goes In Lodge, who stared at the sea, breathing deeply of the salty air. Slowly, he walked to the water's edge, gingerly put the tips of his fingers into the sea, paced along the shoreline and, finally, returned to where I was standing.

"Big lake," he said, nodding solemnly. "Can't see across."

The contract for the prologue ran four months, and in early August 1923, as our engagement in Hollywood drew to a close, the Arapahoes and I made ready to pack our gear and take the train back to Wyoming. But Jesse Lasky was busy broadening his horizons, as well as his financial base, and *The Covered Wagon* was due to open in September at London's Pavilion Theatre, in Piccadilly Circus.

"We've goosed it to death here. How would you like to take the Indians to London?" Victor Clark, Lasky's emissary on all delicate matters, asked me one afternoon early in August as we strolled through the Arapaho camp at Cahuenga Pass. The problem, I explained to Victor, was I had just told the Indians they would be returning to Wind River within two weeks, where they could spend the rest of their days with their grandchildren.

I was more than willing to make my first trip to Great Britain, and I knew my wife would enjoy seeing members of her family who lived in London. But as I explained at the beginning of my narrative, there were a good many Arapahoes who were not in the least bit anxious to travel across the Big Water. Thus, it was necessary for all of us to return immediately to Wind River to council on the matter. And if it had not been for Goes In Lodge and his the-night-is-upon-my-eyes speech, I doubt the European journey would have been made by a single long-haired member of the tribe.

But Goes In Lodge did make his speech, and as old men warded off evil spirits by burning tightly compressed balls of sweet grass from the observation platform of the last car of the train, and as they sang and danced up and down the aisles of the passenger cars throughout the journey, we made our way from the railroad station at Arapaho to the docks of Manhattan.

After pitching their tipis on the grounds of New York's Museum of Natural History, directly across from Central Park, the Arapahoes and I acquired our passports. The morning we did so, as we were standing in a line in the local Department of State office, Ed Farlow came rushing up to me, out of breath.

"I don't know what we're gonna do, Tim," he panted. "Some of the 'Raps are missing!"

"*Missing?* Ed, they're supposed to be here getting their photographs taken for their passports. No photo, no passport; no passport, no trip. Where are they?"

"I don't know," he wailed. "Off in Central Park or in some bar, I reckon. But they sure as hell aren't here."

"We're supposed to have thirty-five of them," I said, growing edgy.

"Right," he answered, "but we've only got thirty-two."

The ship was due to leave the next day and I had no illusions about the White Star Line: whether we were on board or not, it would depart on schedule for England. Just then, Goes In Lodge, wearing an eagle feather bonnet, passed by us after having his picture taken.

"Look," I said to Farlow, "borrow Goes In Lodge's bonnet, put it on Yellow Horse, tell them it's Shavehead or one of the other absentees, and see what happens."

"But . . . uh . . . ain't that kinda illegal, Tim?" Ed whispered.

"Ed, will this be the worst thing you've ever done?"

He laughed, parleyed with Goes In Lodge and commenced to play a game of musical war bonnets. I am not aware whether the statute of limitations has expired on that particular federal offense, but I do know that the government was never the wiser and none of the Arapahoes had to miss the boat for not having a passport.

The next morning we boarded the S.S. *Cedric,* a magnificent tribute to the effort by the White Star Line to permit its patrons to travel in luxurious comfort. I was amazed at the ease with which the Arapahoes adjusted to their new environment; no fear, no worry. They just stepped off the dock, walked up the gangplank and stood along the railings of the ship—though some managed to crawl up into the guy wires and shinny up the poles to get a precarious, but better, view of New York—waving to the crews of the tugboats which would guide the stately liner past the Statue of Liberty and into open sea.

It was only as the horns of the ship blared a farewell blast to the Big Apple and the liner slowly pulled away from the pier that the stunned expressions on their faces told me the plainsmen had thought they were still more or less on land and only waiting to board the tugboats, which they believed would take us to England.

On August 27, 1923, after an uneventful trip, we arrived in Liverpool and, that afternoon, having come by train to London, pitched a tipi camp on the grounds of the Crystal Palace. That day, while the Arapahoes were busily engaged in setting up their tipis and making themselves at home by stalking wayward, unsuspecting and unfortunate sparrows, I had an experience which, at the time, left me baffled and over the years has often caused me some small wonder.

A friend of mine, Oscar Solbert, a matinee-idol handsome fellow who was the American military attaché to the Court of St. James and when in full-dress uniform wore enough medals—or "gongs," as he called them—to topple a mere mortal, took me to luncheon at the Savoy. We passed a pleasant couple of hours and afterward he had us driven in a taxi to the house of a woman who called herself Madame Karma.

"Don't say a word," Solbert cautioned, as we waited for an answer to his knock at her door. "Your clothes look Bond Street"—I was no longer in a Stetson and boots, but a fedora and three-piece suit—"and while she may guess you're an American because you're with me, I don't want Madame Karma to be too sure of anything."

I looked at Oscar and laughed. "Would you mind telling me just what the hell it is we're doing here?"

"She's going to tell you your future," Solbert replied, muffling his words and sounding slightly embarrassed.

The door opened and a petite, long-nosed and dark-haired lady of indeterminate, but by no means youthful, age stood before us. She had a red and green bandana wound round her head.

"Yes?" she asked in a pleasantly clipped accent.

"We'd like to come in, if you don't mind, Madame Karma," Solbert said in his most diplomatic voice.

She escorted us inside to an ill-lit, slightly stuffy drawing room, bade us take seats and left to fetch some tea.

"Irish gypsy," Solbert mumbled.

"Oscar, I don't care if she's the Queen of Sheba . . ."

"*Shh-h!*" he whispered, putting a finger to his lips and opening his eyes wide.

"And what service may I perform for you gentlemen?" Madame Karma asked upon her return with an elegant tea tray, filled with those delectable goodies the British call biscuits. She stared at the two of us, though with none of the slyness or evil intent one sees displayed by the fortunetellers in films.

"To tell you the truth," Solbert said, nervously, as though his diplomatic habit of avoiding the truth as if it was the plague was at stake—for he was, after all, a uniformed spy with a fancy title —"I have heard you are able to read people's fortunes by looking at their hands."

"Sometimes," she said, brushing a lock of dark hair from her forehead with a thin hand, on which each finger bore a strikingly different ring. "Sometimes," she smiled.

"I would like you to read the fortune of my friend," Solbert said, pointing to me.

I coughed nervously and recrossed my legs.

Madame Karma stood up, moved her chair in front of mine, sat down and took both my hands in hers.

She looked at my open palms for some time and then said, "You are from America, not Britain. You are Irish and have lived for some time in the western part of your country. You are here for a visit which will last almost, but not quite, a year. Then you will return to your own country . . ."

Madame Karma closed her eyes and traced a line across my palm with her fingernail. "You are married, but before your life has finished its course, you will be married twice." This, eventually, was true.

"You have three children," she continued, "but someday you will have five." As it turned out, this was also right on the mark, though at the time I thought the two sons and a daughter Agnes and I had left with their grandmother on Long Island were sufficient.

"I can't quite explain," she went on, "but when you return to America, you will be surrounded by red people. I can see you in a big hat, riding a horse. You are bathed in lights and many red and white people are watching." I do not think I am going too far out on a limb to suggest that she could have been referring to Hollywood and the moving pictures.

"Beyond that," she sighed, gently placing my hands on my knees, "I can say nothing."

Solbert put a pound note into her hand and we left Madame Karma's. I was chuckling but Solbert was visibly shaken.

"But don't you see, Oscar?" I laughed. "She probably saw a picture of me and the Arapahoes arriving at Liverpool!"

"Not likely," he replied solemnly. "You see, Tim, there's been nothing about it in the papers. They're saving that stuff for tomorrow morning, after they have photographs of the tipis at the Crystal Palace."

We stopped at the curbside to wait for traffic to let up before crossing the street.

"Amazing!" Solbert muttered. "Just think of the military implications . . ."

The Arapahoes had been camped on the grounds of the Crystal Palace for a day and a half. It was raining hard and the dampness in the air, combined with the cold, was bone-shattering. Confident that the sparrows were safe once again, I went from one tipi to another, checking to make sure everybody was all right, had no serious problems, and that the plainsmen were adjusting reasonably well to Piccadilly.

After leaving Goes In Lodge's tipi, I happened to pass Jack Shavehead's tent. Jack had been to school, spoke English as well as I did and spent most of his time with Charlie White Bull, who was equally well educated. Perhaps one of the reasons for their close association lay in their mutual adherence to peyote religion. Together, Jack and Charlie led young Bill Shakespear, a bright and impressionable twenty-year-old nephew of George Shakespear's, down the road to civilization.

But London was not Lander or Riverton, much less Fort Washakie or Ethiti, and I was counting on Charlie and Jack to provide some guidance to assist the older Arapahoes while they were five thousand miles from home. As I passed the tent, I heard the unmistakable jingle of coins and some talking.

"Give me three," Shavehead said.

"Three it is," Charlie replied. "And you, sonny, what'll it be?"

There was a long pause before Bill Shakespear answered, "I think I'll stand pat."

"He still thinks a pair of deuces beats three queens!" Charlie laughed. A few moments passed in silence, and then he said, "Well, what are you gonna do about *that*?"

"What am I gonna do?" Shavehead replied. "I'm just gonna see that thin dime and raise you a sixpence!"

There was no question about it. They were adapting to being in London.

After three weeks at the Crystal Palace, it became clear that if the Arapahoes didn't move indoors, the English weather was going to do them in. Fog was everywhere and I had nightmarish visions of the Indians climbing into their cherabang—a long, open touring bus used to transport them from their camp to the Pavilion for matinee and evening performances—and ending up wrapped around a street lamp somewhere in the vicinity of King's Road. In due course, Ed Farlow and I found a suitable place, and during the third week of October 1923, the Arapahoes moved into a rooming house on Russell Square.

This establishment was operated, but not owned, by a rather nasty little Cockney lady, Mrs. Higgins, or, as she firmly put it, "'Iggins." For myself, I found digs at the Piccadilly Hotel, conveniently located across the street from the Pavilion Theatre. As for my removal from the Arapahoes, all that need be said is that Agnes made it clear she would prefer not to live in the same house with "those red men."

On weekends, the Arapahoes were invited to all sorts of festivities and banquets. They were the most unusual group of visitors to hit London since the Zulus. The British, aside from having a somewhat well-earned reputation for being reserved by American standards, were, as always, civilized and most curious about anything or anybody exotic.

One weekend, we drove down to the country estate of Lord Baden-Powell, hero of the seige of Mafeking during the Boer War in South Africa, when with one thousand men he had kept twelve thousand angry Boers from storming the town. Later, he founded the Boy Scouts. He was a small, cheerful and charming man and took great delight in wearing an eagle feather bonnet given him by Goes In Lodge.

At his invitation, the Arapahoes attended the International Boy Scout Jamboree in Gilwell, near London. They thoroughly enjoyed demonstrating for Scouts from every corner of the globe the proper way to make a bow and the arrows to go with it.

Once, after an evening's performance, the stage manager came into my dressing room and informed me that "the Honorable Cecil Baring is waiting to see you, sir."

"And who," I asked, "might he be?"

"Oh, sir, you've simply got to see him. He's up there," the stage manager answered, pointing a finger to the ceiling.

And, upon my nod, there was ushered in a character straight out of a Dickens novel. With a high silk hat, white tie, tails and midnight-blue evening cloak, the Honorable Cecil Baring, scion of one of Britain's most powerful banking families, stood before me. He was a sight that would have awed all but the most rabid Jacobin.

"Sir," he said, removing a white calf glove from his right hand and transferring it to his left, in which was held a gold-topped walking stick, "it is a great pleasure, indeed, to meet you. This is the third time I have come to see *The Covered Wagon*. This picture, and the prologue with those fine red gentlemen, if I may say so, sir, remind me of when I hunted buffalo on the plains of Wyoming."

"When was that?" I inquired.

"Let me see," he answered, his mind racing over a collage of memories comprising various and varied people, places and things. "I've got it! That was back in 1882."

Later, after honoring the Arapahoes with several dinners, Cecil Baring presented them with a special gift. Inside a polished mahogany box, to which was affixed a gold plaque reading, "From the Hon. Cecil Baring to the Arapaho Tribe of Wyoming," was a three-foot-long briar pipe in three separate pieces. The first segment, like the others, was nestled in its own red velvet-lined compartment, and consisted of a meerschaum bowl; the second was the stem of a briar from which a branch had, after growing outward, turned and re-entered its parent; and the third was a carved ivory mouthpiece.

The Savoy has always been one of London's more elegant hotels, and its rooms and restaurant are well appointed, as befitting one of the world's finest hostelries. It was customary in those days

for diners to come attired in evening clothes, and failure to do so
required the maître d'hôtel to refuse entry to anybody, be he a
prince or a commoner.

Shortly after New Year's 1924, Oscar Solbert arranged for three
or four of his friends to join Left Hand, Goes In Lodge, Yellow
Horse and myself for dinner. As we entered the hotel and
approached the maître d', I could see trouble was brewing.

"Sir," the maître d' said, almost in a whisper, "I'm afraid
these gentlemen . . ."—he paused and looked askance at the
three Arapahoes in their buckskins, headdresses and moccasins—
"are not properly attired."

"What do you mean, 'not properly attired'?" I asked him.

"Sir," he sputtered, "they are not wearing evening clothes."

"Let me tell you something," I answered in a loud voice as Solbert, who had risen from his table, arrived on the scene, ready to
join in the negotiations. "These gentlemen are from Wind River,
Wyoming. It is in the United States, but they are not really part
of it. Where they come from, they are well respected and, indeed,
they are wearing the only evening clothes they know anything
about. They would not dream of wearing anything else to an important occasion."

The maître d' bowed and escorted us to our table.

Left Hand, Goes In Lodge and Yellow Horse paid no attention
to the silverware, other than the knives, which they used to cut
their meat, but only after part of it was in their mouths. And
aside from picking up their food, gnawing on it and licking their
fingers, they behaved like the crème of society, taking particular
relish in the finger bowls, which, for them, were short-ration por-
tions of hot lemonade.

The roominghouse the Arapahoes occupied on Russell Square
was a comfortable place. It was a spacious, three-story building
with high ceilings, and in which the rooms were lavishly appointed with antique Tudor furniture and luxurious Persian carpets. Everything seemed in good order. But, unfortunately, the
Arapahoes and Mrs. 'Iggins did not hit it off.

"*Chaw-chaw,*" Goes In Lodge said with disgust when com-
plaining about the food she fed them. Steak and kidney pies and

watery beef stew were not quite what the Arapahoes had in mind when they thought of meat. For them, meat was thick, juicy and cooked over an open fire until it was just the dead side of alive. "No more *chaw-chaw*," Goes In Lodge grumbled, protesting he was an old man and didn't want the little Cockney lady to kill him off before he was ready to go to the Great Mystery. "*Ahsayna!*" he exclaimed, using the Arapaho word for beef, real beef. "We need *ahsayna!*"

The older Arapahoes often commissioned one of the younger ones who had been to school and could speak English—Bill Shakespear or, when they were not enmeshed in a poker game, Charlie White Bull or Jack Shavehead—to lead them down to a butcher's shop not far from Russell Square where they purchased enormous steaks.

Then, steak in hand, the old men returned to the rooming-house. Their pleas to Mrs. 'Iggins for more firewood had been greeted much as Oliver Twist's had when he asked for "more," so they loaded the little grates in their fireplaces with charcoal and the wood from the chairs they had shattered against the walls. After moving the grates into the center of their rooms and onto the Persian carpets, they would throw the raw steak onto the fire and sit in a circle, smoking their pipes, until their meal was ready.

When the Arapahoes finally left Russell Square, Famous Players-Lasky had to contend with a bill for over eight hundred 1924 dollars to repair the effects of their six-month residency.

The roof, almost literally, damn near fell in after the Arapahoes had been living on Russell Square for three months.

I was having a leisurely lunch with Solbert at the Savoy when the maître d' came to our table and informed me there was a telephone call for me and would I take it in the lobby. When I picked up the phone, I heard a great deal of noise and all the overtones of chaos coming through the receiver.

"Yes?" I said. "Tim McCoy here."

"Well, you better stop being there and be here right away!" It was Ed Farlow.

"What's the problem, Ed? Nobody's sick, I hope."

"Sick? Hell's bells, Tim, the Arapahoes have gone on the war-path!" he shouted desperately.

I hung up the telephone, went back into the dining room and explained to Solbert that I would have to excuse myself.

"What's the matter?" he asked.

"Well, Oscar," I replied, "I don't have all the details, but it seems the Arapahoes have hit the war trail down on Russell Square."

Solbert exhibited none of my worry and was, in fact, gleeful. "Let me go with you," he said, as excited as a child at the prospect of Christmas. "*Please?*"

I nodded and, together, we hailed a taxi and made our way to Russell Square. When the taxi stopped in front of the rooming-house, we could see many shadows dancing spasmodically across the windows. From within came the sound of singing, drums, laughter, shattering furniture, screams and shouts.

Opening the door, Solbert and I were greeted by the sight of the seventy-five-year-old Yellow Horse riding the banister rails down from the third floor. He was stripped to a war bonnet, breechcloth and moccasins. His body and face were painted green, with yellow dots. In one hand was a nearly empty bottle of gin and in the other a tomahawk.

When he arrived at the foot of the stairs, after negotiating some sharp turns, he leaped off the banister he had been riding with commendable dexterity, straightened up and with a degree of courage and dignity imposed upon him by the contents of the bottle he was clutching, walked to the door leading to the room occupied by Mrs. 'Iggins. Carefully, he put his bottle down, bent low and began uttering a frightful war whoop which, as he straightened up, turned into a horrible howl, tapering off into a mere shriek. This performance was followed by the crash of his tomahawk as it was slammed into the door.

Slowly the focus of my attention expanded, and I saw the entire house was littered with broken furniture, bottles of every size and description and gleeful, painted Arapahoes. The sole bastion of normalcy seemed to be at the top of the first landing of stairs leading to the upper floors. There Goes In Lodge was sitting on his haunches, smoking his pipe and grinning demonically.

I walked over to Yellow Horse, who put his arm over my shoulder, nearly toppling us both.

"*Ahh-h*," he smiled. "You help us. We teach old lady a lesson.

No more *chaw-chaw*. No more cold in our rooms. No more little old lady," he laughed, turning to bury his tomahawk in her door once again.

Russell Square became a reasonably respectable place again, but only after I had convinced the Arapahoes to take their party upstairs and have a dance. I sent Farlow down to the butcher's to pick up fifty pounds of beef, partly to give them some decent food and partly to soak up their drink. When all was quiet downstairs —though the noise from the floor above was considerable—I spoke through the door to Mrs. 'Iggins.

"You can come out now, ma'am."

"Bloody 'ell!" she roared.

Solbert gave himself the role of a British bobby and informed her in his best East London accent that all was well and she should come out to make a report of the afternoon's festivities to the proper authorities.

"I'll 'proper authorities' 'em, I will," I heard the poor lady muttering just over the crash of a bolt being thrown back and the rubble of furniture being pushed away from the door. Then the door opened.

Mrs. 'Iggins' appearance alone would have satisfied even the most disgruntled of the Arapahoes. Her wispy red hair, which had previously been carefully piled onto a well-collected bun on top of her head, was hanging in ringlets over her ears, with a few sweaty strands pasted across her forehead. She was shaking, scared and angry.

She didn't even notice there was no policeman present, and was content to turn her considerable wrath upon me.

"What the 'ell do you think I'm running 'ere?" she screeched. "A bloody carnival? Those savages were going to kill me, they were. And I've 'ad it, positively 'ad it. I want all of your sarky ruffians out of 'ere now. Do you 'ear me? *Now!*"

Solbert walked into her room, a mess testifying to the general state of confusion and hysteria that had prevailed for the previous half hour. In her rush to push a bureau, table and several chairs against the door to stem the onslaught of the barbarian hordes, Mrs. 'Iggins had scattered papers, bedspreads, sheets and clothing across the floor.

Gingerly stepping over the pile, Solbert made his way to the telephone, asked her for the number of the man who owned the roominghouse, dialed and, in his most soothing tone, began to make his pitch. "Sir," he said, "I am Oscar Solbert, military attaché of the United States of America, accredited to His Britannic Majesty's Government. In that capacity I have taken the responsibility of guaranteeing the safety, security and well-being of some of my countrymen who are in Great Britain on a special mission of friendship."

Oscar turned to me, winked and gave Mrs. 'Iggins, whose mouth was agape, a sly look.

"Unfortunately," he continued, "the lady who operates your establishment on Russell Square, Mrs. Higgins, seems ill-prepared to cope with the situation of living with people from another culture. Through her general ignorance, total incompetence, lack of tact and arrogance of manner, she has caused to be incited this afternoon a general riot.

"The damage to your property has been . . . uh . . . rather extensive," Solbert said, listening to the receiver and glancing around the room.

"Yes? . . . Yes? . . . Oh, definitely, sir, they were provoked, of that there can be no question . . . Tomorrow morning? Very good! Thank you, sir, and have a pleasant evening."

Solbert, an expression of undisguised triumph on his face, placed the receiver back upon its hook, walked over to Mrs. 'Iggins and put a hand on her quivering shoulder. "Mrs. Higgins," he said, smiling sweetly, "I'm afraid you, and not the Indians, will be leaving Russell Square tomorrow morning."

After we had been in London for about six and a half months and when our day of departure was still some three weeks away, Jack Shavehead came to my dressing room at the Pavilion.

"High Eagle, we have a problem," he said, helping himself to a seat on the floor, crossing his legs and playing with the toes of his moccasins.

"And what's that?" I asked.

"Well, you know that gee-gaw store a couple of blocks from our hotel?"

I knew it well. The place was run by a man and his wife and

they had, during the Arapahoes' stay in London, amassed quite a tidy sum by selling sequins, bolts of outlandishly colored and patterned cloth, cheap perfume, ostrich feathers, tinkling bells, finger paint, velvet gloves, scarlet garters, spangled earrings and all the other items which the Arapahoes viewed as the finer joys of civilization.

"Ever seen their daughter?" Shavehead asked.

"Yes," I replied, becoming a little suspicious. The daughter was about seventeen, blond, blue-eyed, rather pretty and incredibly buxom. "Is she our problem?"

"Well, in a word, yes," Shavehead answered.

"What I want to know, Jack, is how she has become *our* problem. If there are any little Arapahoes on their way, I'd say it's more *your* problem."

"*Ahh-h*, but you're wrong, High Eagle," he replied. "You see, I'm just a poor, stupid, uncivilized soul. A savage, if you will, from Wind River. And you've brought me over here, across the Big Water." He laughed. "And here I am, 'midst all of civilization's temptations. How can I be held responsible for succumbing to carnal delights?"

I looked at Shavehead. "Is that what you've told her parents?"

"Of course," he replied innocently. "You're responsible for me."

"But," I countered, "the responsibility is yours."

"A mighty damn fine point that is," he replied.

I brooded uncomfortably for a few moments before giving voice to a perverse thought. "Why don't you stay here, marry the girl, have the kid and spend the rest of your life wearing a bowler hat and swinging a walking stick?"

"It's not exactly my style," Shavehead said, rising from the floor, patting me on the shoulder and adding, "Don't worry, you'll think of something."

Three weeks later, it was time to leave and I had not brought the subject of the impending birth up to Shavehead, believing, rather stupidly, that it might go away by itself.

As we stood on the platform at Victoria Station, waiting to board the train that would take us to Southampton for our return voyage to America, I caught a glimpse of someone familiar in the corner of my eye. It was Shavehead's paramour, the pretty blonde, standing to one side with the man who, if not exactly Shavehead's father-in-law, was about to be the grandfather of Shavehead's kid. The two of them were engaged in what looked to be a potentially ominous conversation with a couple of bobbies.

Frantically, I waved Shavehead over to me and whispered hoarsely, "Over there! Do you see them?"

Jack gave them a quick look and turned back to me. "Do you mean *them?*"

"Of course I mean them!"

"You mean to tell me you didn't take responsibility?" he asked.

I looked at him sharply.

"Just a minute," he said, leaving his satchel, full of sequins and whatever other colorful knickknacks he was taking back to Wind River, souvenirs of seven months in Europe. There was some animated conversation before Shavehead came sauntering back.

"Here, have one," he said, thrusting a large cigar into my coat pocket.

"Well?" I asked, more than a little confused.

"Oh," he replied, lighting up his stogie and puffing away as though he was sitting on top of the world. "No problem, no problem. They just wanted to wish me well and ask what Injun name they should give the tyke."

"And . . . ?"

"I told them I thought Little Covered Wagon would be about right."

When we arrived back in New York in mid-March 1924, Lasky had arranged a press conference, and we were besieged at the gangway by reporters and photographers.

"What was it like being in London?"

"What are your greatest memories?"

"What impressed you the most?"

"What's that old guy's name over there, the one with the two eagle feathers?"

"Say, did you really fight Custer at the Little Big Horn?"

These and other questions were thrown at the Arapahoes, each of whom had a remarkable ability for appearing unflappable. As always I acted as the interpreter.

"It was the same as Wind River," Goes In Lodge replied, surrounded by howling reporters and exploding flash bulbs.

"Wind River!" a reporter yelled above the din. "Whattaya mean, Wind River?"

I watched Goes In Lodge's signs and smiled. "The underground, the subway."

"What has that got to do with an Indian reservation?" a bewildered reporter shouted.

I interpreted the question for Goes In Lodge: "How-go-under-earth-travel-Wind River-same as?"

The old man grinned, nodded regally to the reporters and replied, "All same. Prairie dog go down one hole, come up another."

I discovered that while I had been gone, Jesse Lasky hired a Canadian actor named Richard Traverse to do the prologue with some of the Arapahoes who refused to go to England. Lasky had stationed a stenographer in the audience during one of my performances and from that worked up an act, billing it as "Tim McCoy and the Arapahoes." Unfortunately, Traverse, after an afternoon spent in an unsuccessful contest with a bottle of whiskey, toppled into the orchestra pit and created a gamy reputation for the real Tim McCoy.

I had often hoped that somehow I would find my way back to Hollywood and its considerable glamour. I would, but not yet; for Jesse Lasky was having legal problems and, reasoning I could help him out, gave me an assignment which kept me busy for the rest of 1924. It proved to be so interesting that, had I been even more naïve than I was, I would almost certainly have done it for free.

CHAPTER ELEVEN

Meeting the Messiah

Jesse Lasky's problem was simple enough. He was being sued for libel by the daughter of the old-time frontier scout Jim Bridger. She had taken offense to Bridger's image as portrayed in *The Covered Wagon*. In particular, she was not amused by the impression which the film gave of her father as being a man who drank whiskey and lived with a couple of Indian women. But if the problem was simple, the way out of it for Lasky was, to say the least, complicated.

"You see, Tim, the only way we can get through this thing," Victor Clark explained to me as we sat in his studio office together late in March 1924, "is to be able to prove in court that *The Covered Wagon* portrayed Bridger as he was, historically. Otherwise, this libel action is going to cost us a hell of a lot of dough."

He tapped his pencil against his mahogany desk, looked out his second-story window and frowned. "Mr. Lasky would not like that. Not one damn bit."

"But surely," I said enthusiastically, "there must be lots of people around who remember Bridger and can swear out affidavits supporting Lasky's position."

"That is hardly likely," Clark sniffed. After a heavy sigh he patiently continued. "You see, Tim, Jim Bridger was born in 1804 and died in 1881. Now, just how many guys do you think are still walking around who can remember what the old boy was like in his heyday?"

"I personally know of at least one," I said, trying to be helpful.

I was thinking of a man I had known when I was a cowboy and become well acquainted with during my term as adjutant general. His name was J. D. Woodruff and he was a tall, well-built, flinty-eyed, white-haired old man who had made a fortune in the sheep business. So far as I knew, he was retired and living comfortably near Shoshoni, Wyoming. Woodruff had known Bridger in the 1860s when they spent time together in various places, notably at Woodruff's trapping grounds on Owl Creek. "Yes, Victor, one for sure."

Victor's eyes brightened with hope. "You do?" he asked incredulously.

I nodded and waited as Victor toyed with his pencil, obviously deep in thought. "Would you be interested," he finally asked, "in tracking some of those old birds down and getting their statements?"

"Sure," I replied, knowing there would be more to talk about with some of them than just Jim Bridger.

"Great! I'll call our lawyers in Kansas City now," Victor hooted, picking up his telephone.

"Kansas City? Why Kansas City?"

"Because that's where the suit is taking place. See, the movie really starts in Kansas City, Missouri. So Bridger's daughter reasons that's where we begin picking her old man apart."

"I see," I said, not really comprehending the legal twists and turns involved. "By the way, Victor, how much is Lasky being sued for?"

"Five million," he replied, a decidedly numb tone in his voice.

A couple of days after taking on the assignment from Victor Clark, I checked with Lasky's Kansas City lawyers, the firm of Cooper, Neel & Wright. According to Ellison A. Neel, the patriarch of the firm, the case of *Hahn v. Famous Players-Lasky Corporation* was at once "most interesting" and "most complicated."

"First," he explained to me as we sat in his paneled office and his secretary took notes which would be typed up to serve as my written instructions, "there is the problem of who is and who is not alive. Second, there is the additional problem of the memories of those concerned who may have known Mr. Bridger. Finally, there is a certain difficulty in getting legally admissible depositions if, as I suspect is the case, many of these gentlemen live in out-of-the-way places. We will need to send a notary, or have them brought to a notary. Also, you, of course, will have to do considerable research on Mr. Bridger's life and many of the source books are long out of print. Thus, we will need to deal with rare-book dealers . . ."

He went on for some time. The first thought that came to me was that this was going to be a very expensive experience for Jesse Lasky, what with all the traveling, notaries and rare books involved, to say nothing of the lawyers. And the second thought to hit my mind was how much I was looking forward to getting on the road and tracking down Bridger's old acquaintances.

We discussed the two questions that would face Lasky's lawyers in court: Bridger's alleged cohabitation with Indian women and his alleged drinking. I could not pretend to know what was going on in the mind of Bridger's daughter, but it would probably be a safe guess, I thought, that her righteous indignation with regard to the picture of her father as a drinker had something to do with the fact that the United States was in the midst of an unforgettable experience with Prohibition.

It was clear that Neel felt the central issue in the case was not so much Bridger's boozing, but the matter of his having lived with Indian women. This was a particularly touchy aspect of life on the western frontier. Most of the old-time mountain men, trappers, guides and traders lived with women of various tribes. Naturally, companionship played a role in such arrangements. But life, alas, is not all romance and another reason for such unions was economic. A trapper with an Indian wife skilled in tanning could provide good hides for market. A trapper with two or more "wives" could churn out even more. Boiled down to its essentials, the arrangement was that he fed the women, they worked themselves to the bone and everybody was happy. By present-day standards, not exactly an ideal situation; but by Indian standards, well within the norm. However, to many whites in the East the notion of the vanguards of Manifest Destiny living with "squaws" did not fit too well with the idea that America's westward expansion was a whites-only, God-inspired undertaking.

44. This photograph was used by the Ringling Bros. and Barnum & Bailey poster artists to create billing for the 1935, 1936 and 1937 seasons.

45. A less formal shot taken when "the Greatest Show on Earth" played Syracuse, New York, in 1936.

46. This big Sioux and I were in the Ringling show the same year. We shared the same name, High Eagle. He was one of the last veterans of the Battle of the Little Big Horn and died about twenty years later in an automobile crash.

47. Talking signs in the Ringling show in 1936 with the Sioux chief Sitting Bull's adopted, and mute, son John Sitting Bull.

48. The snake dancers in front of a tent appropriately labeled "Gas House." The tall man standing fourth from left is Iron Eyes Cody.

49. The program for the wild West show I took out on the road in 1938.

50. Tim McCoy's Wild West and Rough Riders of the World in Washington, D.C., on May 4, 1938, the day it closed.

51. The Arapahoes meet the Ghost Dance messiah. Standing behind the seated
Wovoka are, left to right: Charlie Whiteman, Rising Buffalo, Red Pipe, William
Penn, George Shakespear, Night Horse, Painted Wolf, Little Ant and Goes In
Lodge.

52. The messiah told me he
would never die...

53. ...but he did, as this picture
taken some forty years later demonstrates.

54. A last view of my brother, Goes In Lodge.

55. My first television program in Los Angeles. Kneeling at the far left is Iron Eyes, who has since gone on to become perhaps the most knowledgeable and authentic of our modern Indian actors.

56. A telegram from a fan of the program.

```
WUB506 OG492 O.BNA340 CGN PD
BURBANK CALIF 29 404P
TIM MCCOY
KNXT 1313 NORTH VINE ST HOLLYWOOD CALIF
JUST CAME IN FROM NEVADA ALWAYS TUNE IN YOUR GREAT STORIES

WE ENJOY THEM SO MUCH KEEP UP THE GOOD WORK CONGRATULATIONS

YOUR FRIEND

HOOT GIBSON
(08).
(424 PM NOV 29 52).
```

57. Inga, as she appeared when I married her. In spite of having been granted exclusive interviews with Hitler and going on to become a syndicated columnist, and being the most beautiful woman I have ever known, she was completely down to earth and totally devoid of vanity.

58. My favorite photograph from "the Golden Days." More than any other, this captures the spirit I tried to convey during the days when Hollywood produced its Western heroes.

Soon after my meeting with the lawyers in Kansas City I was on the road, living out of a suitcase and thoroughly enjoying myself.

The first man I went to see was J. D. Woodruff. We rendezvoused in a Lander restaurant and before getting down to the matter of Jim Bridger discussed a variety of his experiences. He had moved from his cabin on Owl Creek in the late 1860s because cattle had been brought in about seventy miles away and he'd begun to feel "cramped." His idea of heaven, he explained, sipping on a straight whiskey, was "a little cabin somewhere up around the head of Owl Creek. Just like in the old days. So, if I wanted to eat, all I had to do was look out my window and shoot a big elk or a buck deer. When that got tiresome, I could ride half a day and come upon a buffalo herd. And then, just to keep things from getting too damned monotonous, I'd like an occasional band of marauding Injuns to come round and liven it up."

As for Bridger, Woodruff composed and signed a statement. "I knew Jim Bridger only in the hills," he said, "which, of course, was only one side of him and his life. I could not say whether he was a drinking man or not, for the reason that where I knew him there was nothing to drink.

"At all frontier forts, especially military forts, whiskey was absolutely taboo. So far as possible it was kept away from the soldiers, but, strange as it may seem, the soldiers quite often got a supply when the nearest source was sometimes thousands of miles distant, which goes to show the difficulties of prohibition under the most favorable conditions."

Woodruff snorted as he wrote his next paragraph. "It is safe enough to say, that if Jim Bridger did not drink whiskey and gamble and carouse when the opportunity presented itself, he certainly was an exceptional man of his type in those days."

After proclaiming Jim Bridger a "natural-born guide" who had "the knack for knowing the location and characteristics of the vicinity and whether a wagon or pack train was feasible," who "could take an expedition through where most guides would have been lost," he began warming to his subject. "My remembrance of Jim Bridger," he recalled, "is of an uncouth, ill-mannered, vile-talking man and if he had only one squaw at a time then, he was

extremely moderate and more moral than many others who were
better equipped with education and refinement to withstand the
temptations of a time when there was no law except one's own
sense of the fitness of things."

As I had suspected, this job for Lasky would teach me more
about the old days in the West than just the career of Jim
Bridger. For Woodruff, who was known to the Shoshonis as
White Beaver, told me of the last time he saw his friend the
Shoshoni chief, Washakie.

When Washakie was dying, early in 1900, he sent his son,
Dick, to fetch White Beaver. Woodruff arrived at the old warrior's lodge to find Washakie reclining on a lazy board, his long
white hair falling in sweaty ringlets over his bony shoulders, and
his eyes almost completely shut.

"You don't look so good," Woodruff said in greeting.

Washakie opened his eyes halfway, smiled wanly and replied,
"Washakie don't feel too good, either . . . Washakie's dying."

"Well," Woodruff said, sitting on the ground beside his old
friend, "you can't say you're being cut off in the first flush of
youth. Hell, you must be about ninety-six. You've been chief of
the Sussoni for fifty years. It's been a good, full life, so I imagine
you have no regrets."

"Maybeso," Washakie replied weakly.

"What do you mean, 'maybeso'! Jeezus, you fought all your enemies to a standstill. You fought 'em fair and square and beat the
hell out of 'em all!"

"I remember," Washakie said, a wry grin coming across his
face.

"What about the time you heard the young men saying
Washakie was getting too old to be a chief," Woodruff pressed,
"that it was time for him to step down? Hell's bells, you disappeared for a couple of months and came back with a sackful of
scalps!"

"I remember those things, White Beaver. But, you see," the old
man replied sadly, "I have lost the Trail."

"*Lost the Trail?*"

"When Washakie was a young man," the chief explained, "he
lived like all Indians. But when he got onto this reservation, the

Blackrobes came and said everybody had to believe in this Jesus Christ. Then Dr. Roberts came and built St. Michael's Mission. He is a good man, so Washakie went to Dr. Roberts and followed his Medicine. But now Washakie is old, Washakie is dying, and Washakie doesn't want to go to the white man's heaven. Washakie wants to go where the Indians, buffalo, elk and antelope are. *I want to go to the Great Mystery.* But to get there, I have to follow the Trail of all the Indians who have ever died, follow all those moccasin prints across the sky. But I have lost the way."

Woodruff admitted to me that he was not a psychiatrist but, as he explained, he knew the ways of the Indians. So, silently, he beckoned the old man's son to his side and, putting his mouth to the young man's ear, whispered, "You better go find a Medicine Man. Bring him here with his drum, and be quick about it!"

Dick scurried off into the night in search of the Medicine Man, while Woodruff and Washakie talked about the old days.

Soon, Dick and the Medicine Man, who was wearing a fine bonnet of white ermine tails and shaved buffalo horns painted red, arrived.

Gruffly, the Medicine Man said, "Washakie's a Christian."

"So they tell me," Woodruff answered. "But you and I know what a Christian Injun is: he goes to church on Sunday and acts like a white man, and the rest of the week he's all Injun. So you just find yourself a nice, comfortable place to sit down close to your chief, play your drum and sing the oldest songs you know."

It was a long night. The Medicine Man sang both mournful and joy-filled, high-pitched memories of the bygone days, while Washakie dozed fitfully and Woodruff watched and waited.

Just as the sun rose, the Medicine Man stopped and, gathering up his drum and rattle, walked back to his tipi. Washakie appeared to be sleeping soundly when Woodruff got to his feet and started to walk away.

"White Beaver," the ancient chief called out weakly.

"Yes?" Woodruff answered, turning to face his friend for the last time. Bending down, for Washakie's voice had become even fainter than before, he listened sadly to the Shoshoni, who, with tears in his eyes and his hand clasping Woodruff's firmly, murmured, "Thank you, my friend . . . I have found the Trail."

By the seventh day of May 1924, I found myself in Van Buren County, Michigan, at the farmhouse of William Schoolcraft. When I arrived, he was not at home but out hunting squirrels in a nearby forest. Soon, however, he came in from the woods with several squirrels in hand, a shotgun thrown over his shoulder and a lively twinkle in his ninety-four-year-old eyes. This white-whiskered old man had met Jim Bridger in the spring of 1864 and the statement he gave me for the lawyers provided an interesting insight into times when, as Woodruff wrote, "there was no law except one's own sense of the fitness of things."

"In the spring of 1864," Schoolcraft swore before a notary, "I started West with a group of prospectors. When we reached the North Platte River we hired Jim Bridger to act as our guide. He demanded five hundred dollars for his services, but promised that if this amount were paid him he would take us over a trail that had never been used up to that time, and which I believe afterward became known as the 'Bridger Cutoff,' and would show us a place on the Stink River where we could pan enough gold to load our wagons with. He said that he and another old trapper had panned gold at this place and had secured a large amount of the metal in a very short time, using only the lid of a coffeepot to pan with."

Obviously, Bridger was working a variation of an old con because, Schoolcraft said, "When we reached the point on the Stink River indicated by Bridger, we found not the least showing of gold nor any evidence that gold had ever been deposited in that vicinity. Bridger, of course, had received the five hundred dollars for his service, and realizing that we had been tricked, a meeting was held to determine whether or not we should permit Bridger to live or kill him then and there."

The decision was that if Bridger would guide the party to Virginia City, he could live. Bridger, understandably, was more than willing to do this.

It was another Bridger tidbit and, like so many others, of virtually no use in court. I found during the course of my travels an unwillingness on the part of the old-timers to impugn the reputation of a man perhaps not very unlike themselves. Particularly irksome to them was any mention of the existence of "squaw men."

That, especially for those whose wives were present during my interviews, was going too far. But I did discover one "squaw man" who, to say the least, reveled in the role. And when, shortly after my interview with him in late May 1924, word reached me that the Bridger case had been settled and the old scout's daughter had decided not to press Lasky for the five million but settle for five thousand, it made no difference to me. For this man had put me on the trail of the Indian messiah.

In late May I was on my way to Pine Ridge Reservation, South Dakota, having already sent a letter to the man I wanted to see, a French Canadian named Battiste Pourier. He was known as "Big Bat," to differentiate him from Battiste Garnier, also French Canadian, also a scout, and known up until the time he was killed in a barroom fight at Fort Robinson in the 1890s as "Little Bat."

I traveled by train to Gordon, Nebraska, and rented a car, driving the rest of the way to Pine Ridge Agency headquarters and then another twelve miles to Bat's house on Wounded Knee Creek. I arrived at his two-story square-sawed log cabin in the early afternoon. He had built the house a couple of decades previously, allowing plenty of room for his large and ever increasing family. By the time I made his acquaintance, he and his Oglala Sioux wife had ninety-six descendants on the reservation.

Bat was a tall man, a little over six feet, lean and wiry. His dark eyes twinkled, his nose was long and he sported a white moustache with a thin goatee.

"Ah, Tim McCoy!" he exclaimed, doffing his wide-brim flat hat and revealing a halo of wispy white hair. "Good to see you, good to see you," he said vigorously, slapping me lightly on the back. He appeared to be Pine Ridge's resident old-world gentleman.

Bat escorted me inside his house, with broad, sweeping gestures of hospitality. It was a comfortable place and jammed from floor to ceiling with relics from the buffalo days: red and blue strouding blankets with five-inch-wide beaded strips, buffalo robes, fringed pipe bags, leggings and war shirts trimmed with porcupine quills and scalps, and several brightly painted shields festooned with eagle feathers. Bat's friendship with the Sioux went back a long way, though he frequently found himself on the opposing side during their scrapes with the white men. In his capacity as a scout, he was with General Crook at the Battle of the Rosebud in 1876, facing a couple of thousand warriors led by Crazy Horse. During the Ghost Dance troubles in late 1890, Bat had gone out into the winter snows to help find Big Foot's band and guide them back to warmth, food, shelter and safety. As a result, he had been present at Wounded Knee.

We sat in handmade wooden chairs and during our talk about Bridger—"What? No drink? No frolic? Ridiculous!"—Bat's wife appeared. She was a heavy-set, fiftyish Sioux woman whose round face was crossed by many laughter lines.

She was dressed in a magnificent red strouding dress cut in the old wing-shoulder style, onto which had been carefully sewn at least forty elk's teeth, once an indication of the esteem in which a wealthy and attentive husband held his wife. Around her ample waist was a leather belt, about four inches wide, covered with large, shiny conchos made of German silver. And, somehow, she had managed to save a pair of delicate, white dentalium shell earrings from the old days. Bat had taken good care of his wife and she of him, and it was clear they were very much engaged with each other.

When she brought two pewter mugs, a jar of sugar and a hot pot of coffee, I thanked her, using signs. She beamed a broad, happy grin.

"Ah," Bat chuckled, "you have not forgotten the signs!"

From that point on I was no longer a thirty-three-year-old employee of Famous Players-Lasky, but a contemporary. For example, as the afternoon rolled on, I asked Bat something about the Battle of the Rosebud. "Well," he said, "it was like this: Royall was here, them Shoshoni fellers they was there . . . *but, you remember!*"

At about four o'clock in the afternoon there was a light, almost imperceptible knock on the door. As his wife went to answer, Bat leaned over, tapped my shoulder and whispered in an excited, conspiratorial tone, "I am glad you told me you were coming. These are guests, very special guests. My little present for you!" He laughed and winked. "A bagatelle!"

The door opened and two elderly Sioux warriors, dressed in

white man's clothing, reservation-style hats and moccasins, walked into the cabin. One was tall, husky and, without a doubt, the meanest, orneriest, most powerful-looking Indian I have ever seen. The other had a slight, almost delicate, build and his features were fine. Both had long hair flecked with gray, hanging loose over their shoulders. Neither could have been much under seventy-five or eighty years of age.

Bat and I rose to greet these men, and, for my benefit, Bat spoke in signs as well as Lakota.

"Mato Ciqualla, Kicking Bear," he said, indicating the husky one, "and Ta-tanka Pictilla, Short Bull," pointing to the other, slighter man.

I was excited meeting these men, for I knew that Short Bull and Kicking Bear were veterans of the Custer fight and two of the men who set out in the winter of 1889 to search for the messiah, an enigmatic thirty-one-year-old Paiute in Nevada who was called Wovoka, the Cutter. He was known to the white men of his native Mason Valley as Jack Wilson, so called because in his youth he had lived with and worked for a local family of that name. According to reports the Sioux had received from Wind River Arapahoes, Wovoka possessed strong Medicine which could save the Indians from the disintegration and slow death they were experiencing on their reservations.

The story as told to the Sioux was, briefly, that during an eclipse of the sun, probably on New Year's Day 1889, Wovoka "died" and experienced a vision: God proclaimed him His messiah among the Indians. If the Indians would dance a dance taught to Wovoka by God, and believe with sufficient fervor, a miracle would soon occur. A great cloud would cover the earth, burying the white man forever and bringing relief to the sorrow of the Indians. Dead friends and relatives would be restored to life. The buffalo and all the other animals which had been scared away or killed by the white man would return. In short, Wovoka proclaimed that life in the future would be lived as it had been in the past; the present would disappear and be remembered only as a passing, painful nightmare.

What Wovoka promised the Indians was salvation. In the end, he was a monumental factor in bringing about their destruction.

Sitting in a circle on the floor, the four of us exchanged small talk, drank coffee and smoked from Short Bull's pipe, a fine piece with a well-chiseled catlinite bowl and a stem richly decorated with intricately arranged orange-, yellow-, red- and green-dyed porcupine quills.

When Bat felt enough time had passed, he said to Short Bull, "This man, whom the Arapahoes call High Eagle, is a friend of mine. He is a good man. You can trust him. Do not worry, my brother, for he will never lie about anything you say today."

"*Washtay, lilla-washtay,* good, very good," Short Bull muttered, making the sign by extending his rigid right hand, palm down, across his chest and gesturing outward from his heart.

"You went to see the great Paiute Medicine Man," I began, noticing Short Bull, between puffs on his pipe, looking up from the spot on the floor at which he had been staring intently to glance at me and catch the signs. "What did he say?"

"Long journey," he answered in signs, laying his pipe to one side. "During the winter of 1889 we visited with Yellow Calf and Sage at Wind River. They were the Arapahoes who knew the most about the Ghost Dance, but we wanted to know more."

I made a mental note to talk with Yellow Calf and Sage when I returned to Wind River.

"One day, early in the spring of 1890, Yellow Calf said, 'I've told you all I know, Why don't you Sioux go see this Medicine Man for yourselves?' It seemed like a good idea so we rode west. And that is when we saw the messiah."

"What happened on your journey to Mason Valley?" I asked Kicking Bear.

The big Sioux looked at me suspiciously but Bat said something reassuring in Lakota and he relaxed, but grudgingly, for he appeared to be a man who felt he was giving up some personal, precious ground.

"We went to the messiah," he said. "He had scars on his hands and feet and said he was the same man who had come down to see the white man a long, long time ago. But the white man stuck him on a tree. Those scars were the places where they had nailed him to that tree. Wovoka said he had died and gone back to his father but now he was here on earth to help his children, the Indians."

"And what else did he say?"

"He told us to live in peace, that the white man would be gone after one more year and a spring"—April or May of 1891—"and that pretty soon, the white man would lose his temper and try to kill all the Indians. He said that we should wear Medicine Shirts, painted with thunderbirds, morning stars and other sacred symbols. If we wore these shirts, the white man's bullets would never harm us."

Both the Sioux nodded firmly when Kicking Bear said this.

"He said you could not be killed if you wore these Ghost Shirts?" I asked.

They nodded in unison.

"But I have heard that the Ghost Shirt had nothing to do with bullets or warfare."

Kicking Bear looked at me angrily. Short Bull shrugged his shoulders. "Maybeso," he said, after a long pause, "the Messiah told us something he did not tell the others."

Maybeso, or perhaps Short Bull and Kicking Bear misinterpreted what Wovoka had said. Nobody knows or ever will know for certain. But something that is known is this: it was the idea of the Ghost Shirt, of the bulletproof shield, that sealed the fate of the Sioux, for the Ghost Shirt was directly responsible for the terrible bloodletting at Wounded Knee.

After Short Bull and Kicking Bear departed, Bat suggested I stay the night at his house and promised that the following day he would take me to the battle site. I readily agreed and the next morning we rode horseback to the tragic place.

As we rode toward Wounded Knee Bat explained that while some people chose to call the episode a "massacre," he preferred to term it a "battle." "After all," he said, "both sides were armed, both sides were fighting and both sides suffered casualties."

It was the first time I had been to Wounded Knee, an eerie, quiet place. Not, I thought, unlike the battlefield at the Little Big Horn, another stretch of terrain where there had been swift action, much terror and confusion and then . . . nothing. Perhaps that is nature's way, allowing an impenetrable veil of silence to descend upon a spot, leaving us to wonder what horrible sounds shrieked the place into a timeless void.

"I remember it well," Bat said, slowly shaking his head from side to side as we stood by the trench where most of Big Foot's band is buried. "It was one of the coldest winters I have ever seen. Trees exploded with the frost. Cattle died standing up. And the Sioux who had left their homes after Sitting Bull was killed because they were afraid of the soldiers were dying slowly on the prairie and in the badlands. Soon, it was unclear whether I was guiding Major Whitside's 7th Cavalry looking for my Sioux friends or the Sioux were trying to find us. They were freezing, starving, without strength and, in their miserable condition, losing the will to live.

"When we found them on December 8," Bat continued, the sides of his mouth twitching, "Big Foot, Kicking Bear's father-in-law, was so happy to see us that he leaped out of the wagon in which he had been riding. You see, the old man was very sick, pneumonia I think. But when he came out of that wagon he was smiling and he embraced me. 'Kola,' he said, 'my friend, I have been looking for you. I am so glad to see you!' He told me that he and his people had been as close to lost as an Indian could get but now they were safe and would follow the soldiers back to the agency headquarters."

We paced along the side of the trench, Bat all the while sprinkling tobacco offerings from his leather pouch.

"Then," he said, "the soldiers received orders to disarm the Sioux. Very stupid! What were the Indians going to do? Go against the soldiers' battery of four rapid-fire Hotchkiss cannon? Of course not! But you know how it is with orders . . ."

Bat's voice trailed off. A moment later he composed himself. "That was when the trouble started. The Indians did not want to be searched. There was some scuffling, insults were muttered and then shouted. Finally, a very rash fellow, a Medicine Man named Yellow Bird, told the Sioux they had nothing to fear. After all, he harangued, they were wearing Ghost Shirts. Yellow Bird picked up a handful of dirt and snow, threw it into the air, and there was a shot. I remember only a few things about the fight that followed. There was a great deal of noise, as though one of hell's circles had opened. The Hotchkiss battery cut loose, firing two-pound shells at a rate of almost one a second. Everybody was running, hollering, firing, falling. And in a few minutes, it was over. The tipis were burning, about forty soldiers were dead and probably three hundred Sioux, among them Big Foot.

"You know," he said with tears working down his cheeks, "we found dead women and children about two miles from here, lying in a ravine where the soldiers had chased them."

Bat sadly surveyed the surrounding country. "Soon after the battle a great storm came, the biggest blizzard I ever saw in these parts. Before its full force was upon us I could sometimes see through the whipping clouds of flying snow shadowy figures. They were Sioux, lying on the ground, torn to shreds by the soldiers' bullets. Above the wailing of the wind I heard them singing their death songs. And as they writhed in their final throes, they were tearing at their Ghost Shirts."

"Yes, we found the messiah," Sage said as he, Yellow Calf and I sat in Goes In Lodge's tipi a couple of weeks after my visit with Bat. "It was spring 1889. He was a short, heavy-set, very muscular Paiute who lived in Mason Valley, Nevada, in a little hut made of sagebrush in the desert. He wore white man's clothes, which I thought strange. Around his right arm was a handkerchief and stuck in it were some magpie feathers, his Medicine."

Sage looked at the worn toes of his soft buckskin moccasins, clasped his hands together and sighed, "Somehow, we knew he was the man we were looking for. I don't know how, but we knew."

We were sitting in a circle around the tipi's fire pit, where a rusty kettle bubbled with a stew lean on meat and fat with potatoes. Goes in Lodge's wife, a rotund, ever cheerful, gentle lady, ladled the watery stew into wooden bowls, handed each of us our meal, serving her husband and herself last, and beamed when we made our thanks by grunting and smiling while spooning with pieces of hard, crumbly biscuits. With the redheaded captive, Lizzie Broken Horn, she attended services at St. Stephen's Mission and, as the priest intoned the Rosary in English, translated the words into Arapaho for the benefit of the congregation.

"Yellow Calf, are you sure that the Paiute you saw was the man you were looking for?" I asked.

"Sure," he replied, holding out his bowl for Mrs. Goes In Lodge to refill.

"How do you know?"

As the bowl was returned to him, Yellow Calf crunched a biscuit between two fingers and dropped it into his stew. "Because," he answered, "I saw him die and come back to life."

Yellow Calf had said that with no more emotion than I might have used to describe the saddling of a horse, and it took a few moments for me to grasp the meaning of his words.

"You saw him *die?*"

"Yes," he replied softly. "He talked to us about this dance. He said we should return to our people and live in peace, be good, never lie, believe in the Ghost Dance and everything would soon be fine. Then he told us he was going to die, go up to the Great Mystery and return with a special message for us. And that is what he did."

"He *died?*" I said incredulously.

"That's right. He lay down on the ground, stopped breathing and died. I know he was dead because I tickled him under his nose with a special feather I took from my hair and he didn't twitch."

I looked at Yellow Calf in amazement.

"Oh, yes," he added, almost as an afterthought, "I also put my hand over his heart and it was not beating."

I turned toward Sage and before I could ask him the question, he had answered it.

"Yes, he died. It is harder for me to believe than it is for Yellow Calf. So I kicked him in the ribs."

That sounded about right, what Woodruff would have called "a real Injun touch."

"When I kicked him in the ribs," he continued, "he did not move, so he was dead. Then, pretty soon, his eyes opened, he sat up, stood before us and gave us a message from the Great Mystery."

"And the message?" I asked.

Sage placed his stew bowl to one side and began explaining the message in graphic signs, as though he were painting a picture. "When he was with the Great Mystery, he saw many of our friends and relatives, those who had been killed in fighting and some who had died from the white man's sickness. They told him they wanted to return to their families and wanted all our people to live together again, just as they had done before the white man took everything away. They begged him to tell us to believe this Medicine Man, Wovoka, because he was the messiah, knew what was good, and how to make great things come to pass. They told him to say to us: 'Do as this man says. If he says dance, dance. He will give you some clay paint, white for healing and red for wearing during the dance. Paint yourselves with it. Soon, a Great Cloud will come and on it will be all the Indians who ever lived, mounted on their war ponies; and all the buffalo, elk, antelope and deer. This Great Cloud will cover over the white man and then everything will be as it always had been. *Believe.*' So, since we had seen this man die, we knew he was the messiah and if we followed his directions, we would not rot on this reservation forever."

"Did he say anything else?" I inquired.

"Yes," Yellow Calf said, handing his bowl to Mrs. Goes In Lodge for yet another refill. "He said to live in peace with everybody, including the white man. Not to be too hard on the whites because he was going to send them to some other place."

"When did he say the miracle would happen?"

Sage winced. "The Great Cloud?"

"Yes," I said, "the Great Cloud that would change everything."

Yellow Calf shrugged, "Two years from when we saw him, when the leaves turned."

"Autumn 1891?"

Yellow Calf nodded and turned his face away. His shoulders trembled. He was crying.

In early winter 1924, I began working as technical director on the film *The Thundering Herd*, in which Charlie Whiteman, Rising Buffalo, Red Pipe, William Penn, George Shakespear, Night Horse, Painted Wolf, Little Ant and Goes In Lodge had roles.

We were shooting scenes near Bishop in northern California and were about a day's automobile ride from Wovoka's old stomping grounds. While I felt I might very well be embarking upon a fool's errand, I decided to borrow a company car and drive toward the place to which Yellow Calf and Sage, Short Bull and Kicking Bear had journeyed more than a quarter of a century before. I was going to try and do as they had once done: find the messiah.

It was a long, boring ride through endless miles of uninspiring countryside, but by asking questions in signs and English, I finally arrived at a little hole-in-the-wall place called Yerington, Nevada, and found the house I was looking for on the outskirts of the town. I knocked on the door of the tumble-down shack to which I'd been directed. It was opened by a young Paiute, about twenty or twenty-five years old.

"You speak English?" I asked him.

He nodded.

"I have been told by several of your tribesmen that a man named Wovoka lives here. Is that so?"

The young man glanced furtively to my left and then to my right before nodding once again.

"May I see him?" I inquired.

The door closed abruptly. I started to walk back to the car, the door opened again and a heavy-set, rather grumpy-looking old Paiute came out of the house. He was wearing a wide-brim, dark beaverskin hat, a rumpled dark suit and vest, white shirt and boots. It was the messiah.

His face showed much sadness, though neither then nor later was I able to determine for whom that sadness had been experienced; for the hundreds who had been blasted to smithereens at Wounded Knee or for himself and a dream that had become a nightmare.

I knew he spoke English, for my Arapaho friends had told me —also, he had lived with and worked for the Wilson family in his youth—but he refused to speak in that language and preferred to keep himself removed by at least one step, relying upon his grandson, the young man I had met at the door, to act as his interpreter.

"May I talk with you?" I asked him.

The Paiutes then had, and for all I know may still have, a custom many outsiders found particularly annoying: one man interpreted, the other repeated word for word what he had said, and then the interpreter repeated the initial message. "What do you want to talk about?" Wovoka said to his grandson.

"What do you want to talk about?" the grandson said to Wovoka and then, turning to me, asked, "What do you want to talk about?"

"The Ghost Dance," I said, staring at Wovoka, trying to find some trace of his particular magic; for there had to be something riveting about the man to have caused so many who had seen him to swear upon all that was holy that this was the messiah. I could not see it.

"The Ghost Dance," the grandson said to the old man.

"The Ghost Dance," Wovoka said to his grandson.

"The Ghost Dance," the grandson repeated.

By this time, I was practically climbing the nearby piñon trees, and in the interests of brevity and sanity, will continue this discussion without the third wheel, the interpreter.

"I don't want to talk about that any more," Wovoka grumbled, turning back toward his cabin.

"That's too bad," I said to him, "because I bring you greetings from some of your old friends."

He turned toward me. "What 'friends'?" he asked suspiciously.

"Two men from Wind River: Yellow Calf and Sage. Two men from Pine Ridge: Short Bull and Kicking Bear," I replied.

"I remember them. And what do they say?" he inquired skeptically.

"They say they respect you."

Wovoka, with a sort of that's-more-like-it gesture, drew himself to his full height and said, "They were all good men when I knew them."

"They still are," I countered. "And I know some other good men who would like to see you. They are Arapahoes and were all Ghost Dancers. They believed in you. I think they still do."

"I would like to see the Arapahoes," he said, "but they live so far away. I have never been to their country. It's a long way off."

In fact, Wovoka had hardly been anywhere. All during the Ghost Dance he stayed put in Mason Valley and after Wounded Knee he prudently dropped from sight.

"It is true," I answered, "that the Arapahoes live far away. But these men have come from their country to see *you*." I realized I was starting to lay it on a bit thick but there seemed to be no other way to appeal to this man. As far as he was concerned, he never stopped being the messiah. And one does not treat the messiah like a peasant.

"Where are they?" he asked.

"Just across the state line, in California."

"Impossible!"

"Why?" I inquired.

"Too far!"

"But think of how far they have come just to see you," I beseeched. "They have been told so often by the white man that you are a fraud and yet they continue to believe. It would be the greatest thing in their lives if they could lay their eyes upon you just once before they die."

And that's when I knew I had him.

"All right, I'll go. You send a car for me tomorrow," Wovoka commanded, turning his back on me, walking back into his shack and slamming the door.

"Bring some of your friends," I shouted after him, "there'll be a dance."

If this mortal had been wondering how to behave in the presence of a messiah, Wovoka demonstrated how a messiah might behave toward a mortal. Muttering, I got back into the car and drove to Bishop.

Later that evening, after returning from my encounter with the messiah, I went to Goes In Lodge's tipi and suggested that a dance be held the following afternoon, which was, appropriately, Sunday. If the Arapahoes were in the mood, I explained, I'd be happy to provide the beef, canned fruit, coffee and sugar. I knew from my experience with them that the only thing they enjoyed more than a dance was a dance-feast. Goes In Lodge's response was a hearty "*Ahh-h!*"

Since there was no filming the next day, the Arapahoes spent their time visiting, practicing their songs, tuning up their drums, dusting off their war bonnets and gussying up for the dance.

I arranged with the company for the use of the producer's limousine, hired a driver from among the cameramen and, without telling the Arapahoes anything about the possibility of Wovoka's visit—for to make a promise to someone from the buffalo culture and then not be able to deliver was tantamount to a mortal sin, something harking back to the days when they were nomads and all a man really had was his word—dispatched the driver and fancy car with a map showing how to find Wovoka's shack. Then I waited.

It was a long wait. Sometimes I paced back and forth, and when that became too monotonous, walked over to the Arapahoes dancing by the outdoor fire, eating food, shouting, whooping it up. Then, looking at my watch and figuring it was about time for the car to have returned, I paced around some more. It was a very cold day but fortunately the weather was clear and by keeping my hands in my coat pockets I could keep warm while walking around, listening to the sound of the dance drums and the icy snow giving way under my boots. At about four-thirty the long black limousine, carrying the chauffeur, Wovoka, his grandson and what must have been about five hundred pounds of polished chrome decoration, drew up alongside me. As I directed the driver to keep on going until he reached the dance circle, I noticed that the car was followed by a convoy of five dilapidated jalopies, driven by and filled with Paiutes.

The caravan made its way to the dance circle, where, upon its arrival, the Arapahoes paid it no attention. I took Goes In Lodge by the arm and asked him to call his friends together, because I had something important to say to them.

As the old men grouped around me in a circle, I told them that the messiah had arrived, the man who had started the Ghost Dance. There was no reaction whatsoever from the old men, which was understandable. After all, they might have felt they'd been somewhat taken in a few years back when they had become Ghost Dancers.

But as Wovoka's grandson popped out from one side of the car, trotted over to the other, opened the back door and waited for his grandfather to make an appearance, the Arapahoes began to whisper excitedly among themselves.

Wovoka did not come out.

You smart bird, I thought, you're really riding the maharaja's elephant now, aren't you?

When the whispering stopped, and as the Arapahoes peered hard to see if they could make out the dark figure in the back seat, Wovoka emerged, stood like a rock in front of the car and faced the Arapahoes, who immediately bowed their heads, afraid to look into the great man's eyes. As if on cue, the twenty or more Paiutes who had come with him did the same.

His grandson whispered into my ear, "The messiah would like to say some words to his friends. I'll interpret into English and you interpret into Arapaho."

"Fine, sonny," I whispered in reply, "but I don't speak Arapaho."

"Signs would be okay," he said offhandedly.

It was clear that the messiah's Medicine Show was about to take full control, with me interpreting as a link to the divine.

"My children! Hear me!" Wovoka said in a loud voice. "I wish to speak with you. But first, dance and eat some more!"

While the Paiutes, including the messiah, gorged themselves, the Arapahoes danced, showing off to what they called "the root diggers," but with only half their hearts. They wanted to hear from Wovoka. And Wovoka knew they wanted to hear from him. Unlike the others, who were seated cross-legged upon the ground, he was settled comfortably in a director's chair and staring off into space with a look of utter contentment upon his face. The suspense built.

When the Paiutes were finished eating, they started playing their musical instruments. The sound was not that of the full, resonant Plains Indian drum but the clicking and clattering of little sticks beating against larger sticks.

After about half an hour, Wovoka's grandson tugged at my coat sleeve. "You interpret now, okay?"

The messiah did not stand up, as was the custom while orating on the Plains. Instead, he stayed put in his chair while the Arapahoes and I sat in front of him in a semicircle.

The earth, he explained, is divided into three parts. There is a layer below the one in which we live; then there is the middle part on which we dwell; finally, there is the top place, heaven. And that's exactly what he called it, "hebbin," because if anybody ever got the Indian's beliefs of Medicine jumbled up with the white man's belief in Christianity and mixed them into a fine, confusing brew, it was Wovoka.

It was, he said, to that uppermost layer that he went on New Year's Day, 1889, when both he and the sun died. He met with God, they talked and God told him he was the messiah. Tell my children, the Indians—God directed—always to do the right thing, tell no lies and live in peace with everyone. And that's what he told all the Arapahoes and Sioux who came to him. That and nothing more. But some of them, particularly the Sioux, got carried away and took back this idea about Ghost Shirts, because they wanted to fight the white man. God was not pleased with this and, Wovoka said sadly, the Sioux were killed and the Medicine turned bad. So God decided that the spirits of the dead Indians, and the elk, antelope and buffalo, would not return. At least not now.

The idea, he maintained, was the same as it always had been, and all of his children must try to stick to God's law. And just to keep everything in good order, he was going to give them some of the same batch of paint he had given to Yellow Calf and Sage, Short Bull and Kicking Bear. White paint to cure sickness and red paint to wear during their dances. What's more, he proclaimed, he was going to work a miracle so they would know he was not speaking out of the side of his mouth.

He asked if any of the Arapahoes had been sick. William Penn rose and stood in front of the awed crowd of Arapahoes and tapped his chest. He had tuberculosis and, as he explained, had not been able to dance for a long time. Wovoka directed him to lie down on the ground, painted William's face with white paint, sang some songs over him and, bending down, sucked what Goes In Lodge afterward swore was "the bad Medicine" out of his chest.

But, Wovoka explained, there was still more to come. He was going to teach them a dance to give them good Medicine. They were to take this dance back to Wind River and teach it to their fellow tribesmen.

And I'll be damned if it wasn't the Ghost Dance. So here it was, 1924, and Wovoka, his grandson, twenty-some Paiutes, nine old Arapahoes and I were dancing in a circle, shuffling along, painted with sacred paint, singing the songs. The same old songs, the same old dance.

But whatever he was to the Arapahoes, Wovoka was still a Paiute Medicine Man to me and I could not put out of my head the story that some years before, after prophesying an early winter, he had directed a flunky to dump blocks of ice into the river near his home.

William Penn, the man Wovoka had treated, danced for the first time in several years. He felt great, looked fine and was very happy. At the end of the filming, he returned to Wind River and in three months was dead.

After about an hour of dancing, Wovoka indicated that it was time to go; he had his Father's business to take care of, he said. And with the exception of having their photograph taken with him earlier, not one of the Arapahoes had dared look him square in the eye.

As Wovoka stood in front of the limousine, making his final blessings and, all the while, giving the Arapahoes his whammy-eye, the old buffalo hunters and warriors put their hands into their buckskin pipe bags, drew out five- and ten-dollar bills and marched single-file toward the messiah to present their offerings, which were not refused.

The last words Wovoka said to me were the first he had uttered in English. As he climbed into the limousine and settled into his seat for the long ride back to Yerington, he looked out the window at me. Then he rolled the window down, stuck his unscarred hand out into the air, dropped a cake of red paint into my coat pocket and whispered, "I will never die."

"Is that so?"

He nodded vigorously.

"Never?" I asked.

"No, never," he replied firmly.

But he did, eight years later. His wooden grave marker, standing in a scrub-infested Paiute cemetery at Yerington, notes, with stark simplicity: Jack Wilson. Died Sept. 20, 1932. Age 74.

Perhaps a more fitting epitaph would have been a slow, moody Arapaho Ghost Dance song that has haunted me since Goes In Lodge first sang it to me over sixty years ago:

> Father, have pity on us!
> We are cold, there are no fires to warm us
> Father, have pity on us!
> We are hungry, there is nothing to eat
> Father, have pity on us!
> There is nothing left to believe in

CHAPTER TWELVE

The Golden Years

COME HOLLYWOOD. METRO-GOLDWYN-MAYER INTERESTED
LONG-TERM CONTRACT. NO CAN LOSE.

The telegram was from Victor Clark, formerly Jesse Lasky's Jack-of-all-trades. It had traveled by wire from Hollywood to Cheyenne, thence to Thermopolis, by stage to the Anchor station nine miles below my ranch and, finally, by horse from Anchor station to my ranch, which was now known as the Eagle's Nest.

At the time I received the message, early in 1926, I felt that, re-alistically, I would be spending the rest of my life as a cattleman along Owl Creek. After tracking down Jim Bridger's ac-quaintances and serving as technical adviser on *The Thundering Herd*, I had, in March of 1925, organized and presented a pro-logue to John Ford's *The Iron Horse*. It was almost identical to the one for *The Covered Wagon*. Many of the people involved—Red Pipe, Yellow Horse and Goes in Lodge among others—had been in the first, and the theater, Grauman's, was the same. I figured I was beginning to repeat myself and decided to call it quits.

So I returned to my ranch, expanded it to five thousand owned acres and five thousand leased from the government, built a new, large house out of logs, added a bunkhouse and a barn, con-structed some corrals and settled down with Agnes and our chil-dren, then aged three, five and seven. As the owner of about a thousand head of cattle I was by no means a "baron," but I had nothing to complain about and life seemed pleasant, free from worry and comfortable.

It was at that point that I received Victor Clark's telegram. The next day I rode horseback the forty-five miles into Thermopolis, placed a long-distance call to Victor in Hollywood and, eventually, we had a chat, though the connection could hardly have been worse had he been speaking from a phone booth on the moon.

"What do you mean, Victor, by 'no can lose'?" I asked.

"What I mean," he replied, through the cracks and pops of electricity conducting wildly, "is that I'm now working for M-G-M. Irving Thalberg, who is the head of production at this studio, wants you to do a screen test. Maybe you could be a star!"

"Victor, Hollywood is a long way from Owl Creek. 'Maybe's' just won't get me there any more. Have you got another card somewhere?"

"I do," he replied confidently. "You come out here and whether the test works out or not, we'll guarantee to do at least one picture with you. Okay?"

"I'm on my way."

I had been in Hollywood three days before meeting Irving Thalberg, and had done several screen tests with potential leading women who within six months were forgotten. But that, then, as always, was the nature of the business.

Thalberg, a short, rather sickly-looking and brilliant man who was able to perceive the direction of the public's taste in films as a bloodhound can seek out an escaped chain-ganger, met me at the entrance to one of Metro's sound stages.

"Mr. McCoy," he suggested, "why don't we go see the rushes?"

An hour later, after watching myself on the screen, I sat in stunned silence. Thalberg turned to me when the lights went up in the tiny projection room.

"Well, what do you think?" he asked.

"To tell you the truth," I replied, "I wouldn't walk across the street, let alone pay a dime, to see that fellow."

He smiled, patted my arm and said softly, "Maybe we have other ideas. C'mon, let's go up to my office and talk contract."

Thalberg was not doing this out of human kindness—though he was, in fact, a kind man—but for the same reason everything is done or not done in the picture business: money. What he recognized at that time was that something important and potentially lucrative was happening in the movies: Westerns were hits. As a result, he was searching for Metro-Goldwyn-Mayer's first and, as it would turn out, only Western star. The studios could produce epics and they could pay horrendous sums of money for production and stars, but nothing seemed to be quite as financially successful as Westerns. So, Thalberg reasoned, why shouldn't M-G-M produce Westerns?

Thus, in 1926, I became one of M-G-M's seven "stars," the others being John Gilbert, Lillian Gish, Mae Murray, Ramon Novarro, Lon Chaney and Buster Keaton. Each of us dressed in a separate dressing room and usually paid little attention to one another.

Lon Chaney's dressing room was opposite mine. He was a man who never engaged in the Hollywood social whirl, and where he spent his time, I do not know, though I imagine it was in seclusion at his home. It was from Lon I first learned the importance of make-up.

"To look like this," he said to me one morning when we met in the hallway, pointing to his face, which resembled an oriental death's-head, "is nothing. Some shadow around the eyes, a dark cowl over my head and stretched along the side of the face to create the illusion of sunkenness . . . it's nothing, Tim. But to wear your real face and make it look presentable, now that's a job and a half!"

I was at M-G-M from 1926 to 1929 and during that time made sixteen films, all of them silent. My first film was *War Paint*, like all but a few I starred in, a six-reel, hour-long Western. It was directed by a man who went on to direct another six of mine and eventually become a giant among Hollywood's creative geniuses: W. S. "Woody" Van Dyke. For in addition to being annoyingly arrogant, maddeningly self-opinionated, damned sure of himself and utterly ruthless, Van was a truly great director.

He later filmed *Trader Horn* on location in Africa. After lugging the necessary equipment across that continent and dragging Harry Carey, Duncan Renaldo and their leading lady all over hell and gone and, in the process, exposing cast and crew to the wonders of a myriad of tropical diseases—which Van claimed were all equally susceptible to his cure of gallons upon gallons of gin drunk neat—he returned to Hollywood with several hundred thousand feet of film depicting authentic Africa. This triumph dimmed somewhat when Louis B. Mayer pronounced the results unusable and decreed that a substantial portion of the picture be finished at the Los Angeles County Arboretum because it looked "more like the real jungle."

Fortunately, in *War Paint*, I did not have to undergo the particular and peculiar adventures entailed in the making of *Trader Horn*, though I had been slated for the leading role, only to be replaced by Harry Carey because Mayer felt he looked more rugged. My feeling of rejection was quickly overcome when I saw the gaunt faces of Van Dyke's returnees.

I did, however, have a memorable experience with Van Dyke. It happened shortly after I signed with M-G-M and it was an episode in which he evidenced a degree of concern for my well-being on a par with the level of compassion that might have been exhibited by a nineteenth-century Arab slaver herding a batch of the lately damned across the equator.

Irving Thalberg had asked me to sit in on a story session, and there, in a crowded, bilge-green little office, I took my place around a table at which sat five writers and Van Dyke. As the writers tried out one idea after another, stumbling over the historical and cultural details necessary for a picture which was intended to portray the Indians sympathetically, Van Dyke became bored, tired and, finally, exasperated.

"Do any of you geeks know what the hell you're talking about?" he finally asked.

There was no response.

"That's what I thought," Van said, rising from his chair and striding to the door. "Now, McCoy, you and I are going to write this goddamned thing."

Which is precisely what we did, sitting in Woody's office through the afternoon, on into the evening and finally having the script ready by the next morning. It was not an easy task but not the daring feat it would be today, for the films were silent and dialogue practically non-existent, though actors in pre-talkies did not

simply step before the camera and utter whatever rubbish came to
their minds; lips could be read and tone had to be set. Even
though lines may not have been memorized, they still had to follow the story line. And that is basically what Van Dyke and I
came up with, a story line in response to his question, "Now, tell
me all you know about Indians."

That was impossible, but we managed to put together a tale of
the Indians reacting to white man deception and broken treaties.
War Paint was shot early in the summer of 1926 on location near
Fort Washakie, and many Arapahoes and Shoshonis continued
with the lucrative part-time careers they had embarked upon with
The Covered Wagon by playing bit parts in the film. Contrary to
what some revisionist filmographers might claim, the Indians were
not paid less than white man extras and did, indeed, enjoy themselves immensely. If nothing else, working on a picture was a
break from the monotony of reservation life.

Chase scenes were a great favorite of the Indians', and it was
while filming such an episode that Van Dyke's callousness was
manifested to me. I was supposed to be galloping my horse toward the cameras, pursued by a band of hostiles who were shooting at me. In the excitement of the moment, an old Shoshoni
pulled up alongside me, pointed his rifle at my head and pulled
the trigger. His blank round of .45-.70 Springfield ammunition
was an old one, the powder caked and, as the trigger was pulled
and the shell exploded, hard balls of powder slammed into my
head, neck and shoulders, burned my face, rent my shirt and sent
me flying off my horse and onto the ground.

I lay there for what seemed an aeon, partially conscious of the
commotion surrounding me. The Indians were silent and had
gathered their ponies in a ring around my body, but Van Dyke
was making noise enough for five men.

"Goddamnit!" he roared. "You're not supposed to fall off the
horse. You stupid bastard, you've just ruined a beautiful shot."

Then it was quiet again and I could feel a warm trickle of
blood flowing from my left ear, down across my cheek and onto
the ground. Somebody held me by my left shoulder, causing
excruciating pain to ripple down my arm and along my back. I
moaned.

"Well, at least you're alive. Thalberg will be pleased to hear that," Van Dyke snarled sarcastically.

Strong hands under my arms lifted me to a wobbly stance.

"You ready for another take?" the director spat, turning on his heel and walking away. "And this time, will you try and do it right?"

I collapsed into Goes In Lodge's embrace.

When I came to, I was in a dingy little room in what passed for a hospital at Fort Washakie. There was a bright light shining in my eyes and when I looked to my right, there in a dark corner was Goes In Lodge, sitting cross-legged upon the floor.

"You die?" he asked in signs.

I smiled thinly, shook my head as much as I could and answered, "No."

He did not get up and leave but remained while the doctor removed as much powder as he could from my wounds, bandaged me up and went back to other business. I slept that afternoon and through the night, and early the next morning when I awoke, Goes In Lodge was still sitting in the corner, staring at me. As I opened my eyes, he smiled.

"You're hurt pretty bad," he said.

I nodded.

"We Arapahoes are hard to kill," he laughed.

"But if anybody could do it," I said, "this Van Dyke would be the man."

"A very bad man," he replied, with a scowl.

"It's his job."

"Still, a very bad man," the old Arapaho insisted. "*Niatha,* clever, like a spider," he muttered.

Since then, I have tried to steer clear of cinematic geniuses and other cranks.

After three years at M-G-M, it was time once again to talk contract. Since my pictures were making a tidy sum for Metro, I wanted a raise in salary, which was not likely to happen. I probably would have settled for being paid my long-promised bonus. But after receiving the run-around from Louis B. Mayer, whom one authority of Western films has described as "a man of singular qualities, but friendship wasn't one of them," I departed from M-G-M at Christmastime, 1929.

After six months in London and Paris, where my wife and children were living, I returned to Hollywood and some hard ground: nobody had ever heard of me. I was out of the business. Also, I was, for all practical purposes, separated from my wife. Our marriage was perched atop the roughest of rocks and within two years we would make the arrangement formal and permanent by getting a divorce. So, once again, I retreated to Owl Creek and life as a rancher.

When spring hit the Big Horn Basin I received a telegram from Eddie Small, a producer in Hollywood:

> GO THERMOPOLIS. GIVE ME CALL. URGENT YOU DO SO. THE
> INDIANS ARE COMING. P.S. I AM NOW YOUR AGENT.

I discovered when I made the telephone call that Universal Pictures wanted to make a twelve-part serial, each episode to run for two reels, or twenty minutes. The title for the serial was to be *The Indians Are Coming.*

"A *serial?*" I said, in astonishment. "But it'll hurt me in the business."

"Tim," Eddie replied, using words that ever afterward became a personal motto for me, "nothing ever hurts you in this business except being out of work."

Within a month, I was back in Hollywood and making the serial. It was a real harem-scarem production, with plenty of shooting, burning buildings, trick riding and action. Originally *The Indians are Coming* was to have been a silent, but with the progress being made by members of the new profession of sound engineers, it became the first talkie serial.

The idea had been the brain child of the proprietor of Universal, "Uncle Carl" Laemmle, a diminutive, kindly former buttonhole maker. In the middle of a story discussion with a director, he was inclined to stare at the man's lapel and, when asked what was bothering him, reply in the accent of his native Germany, "Zat is a rotten buttonhole!"

Laemmle was a nut for titles. Once he approached Edward

Sedgwick, one of his directors, and explained he wanted to make a film about a *"mytical* kingdom," something like Graustark or Shangri-La. Sedgwick, who knew Uncle Carl hopped from title to title like a bee moves from flower to flower, replied, "A mythical kingdom, eh?"

Uncle Carl nodded his head earnestly.

"Let's see . . . I've got it! Just picture it, across the marquee, flooded with light, will be enormous letters spelling out the name: H-E-R-N-I-A."

Laemmle loved the idea, but the next morning when he saw Sedgwick crossing the lot, he wagged a finger at him and said in his high voice, "You've been a very naughty boy, Sedgwick."

As for Uncle Carl's infatuation with *The Indians Are Coming,* he was forever badgering his directors about his pet project. "Ve shouldt make a pitcha. Big, little, I don't care. Buhdt, it's gotta be called *Za Indians Are Kommink.*"

Thus, whenever a director wanted to make a film, he would approach Laemmle and say offhandedly that he wanted to make a film entitled *The Indians Are Coming.* When completed, it might be about elephants in India, orphans in New York or the goings-on inside a sheik's harem. But never about Indians.

When Sedgwick finally said that *he* wanted to make a picture with Uncle Carl's cherished title, Laemmle gave him a penetrating look and, with his lower lip protruding with determination, said, "Ja, buhdt zis time, Sedgwick, za Indians gotta kom!"

They did, and for his original investment of slightly over $150,000, Laemmle raked in over a million.

By 1931, I was no longer working for Uncle Carl but a real Hollywood monster, Harry "King" Cohn of Columbia Pictures. He was without doubt the most consistently vulgar human being I ever met, once replying to a cultivated English authoress, who had dared suggest his studio lacked class, "Whattaya mean, we don't have class? Just look at what we got! We got Capra, by Jesus! We got Ronald Colman, by God! Lookit here, we're even gonna do a film about that Tale of Two F—— Cities!" That was Cohn.

I fortunately had little personal contact with Cohn. And it was while at Columbia that I started wearing the outfit that became my trademark: a blue shirt, an orange neckerchief and a white hat, which I later changed to black. The reason for this departure from an accepted "good guy" costume was simple: almost all the other cowboy stars—Tom Mix, Buck Jones, Hoot Gibson, Ken Maynard—wore white and the dark outfit set me apart. Over a period of four years at Columbia I made thirty-two features, with titles such as *The Fighting Fool, Two-Fisted Law, End of the Trail, Man of Action, Silent Men, The Whirlwind, Beyond the Law* and *The Revenge Rider.* The one I would like to see again was a short snip shown to me by Otto Meyer, a master film editor. It proved I was the fastest gun on the screen. There was, in those days, a demand that the Western hero be able to fast-draw, and while the "reel West" differed from the real West in that a fast draw was of little use in a fight, I was able to meet the imaginary mark. From the start of the film—which ran at a rate of twenty-four frames per second—when my hand began to move, until the time smoke spat out of the barrel of my pistol, six frames were exposed.

In the early days of Hollywood, whenever we heard the term "Hollywood cowboy" it was usually meant to imply a fellow wearing a tall white Stetson hat and high-heeled boots who worked in the motion-picture business. That term certainly never referred to an old-time cowhand working on the ranges of Wyoming, Montana or Oregon.

But as the West changed, ranges were cut drastically in size, fences erected, roads built and automobiles brought into the country. When the bottom went out of the cattle market, as it did in the 1920s, there were foreclosures and many cowboys found themselves without a job.

The cowboys had watched Westerns in small-town movie theaters for years. Those cowboys who left the range for a few days to seek whatever escape a small town could offer willingly plunked down their nickels and dimes to watch "moving" pictures, and all they were interested in seeing was Westerns. Each cowboy had his private vision of what it meant to be a Westerner and a cowboy. With few exceptions, that image was shamelessly romantic.

Zane Grey was widely read during the long, dark winter in the scattered bunkhouses throughout the West. Clarence Mulford's *Hopalong Cassidy*, Frank Spearman's *Whispering Smith*, Owen Wister's *The Virginian* all fed the cowboy's vision of himself as the last holdout on the last frontier.

When Bronco Billy Anderson played a good-bad man, a cattle thief who falls in love with a beautiful woman and saves her father's life, in *Bronco Billy's Redemption;* when William S. Hart, he of the steely gaze, robbed stagecoaches in *The Night Stage;* when the Indians went on the rampage and smoke from the ensuing battle filled the screen as though it was billowing from the deepest pit of hell in D. W. Griffith's *Fighting Blood;* and when Dustin Farnum held the dying Indian maiden, Red Wing, in his arms at the conclusion of *The Squaw Man,* the real-life cowboys of the West watched, cheered and wept.

They were the most dedicated Western-watchers Hollywood ever had.

So it was only natural that when jobs became scarce they would pass up the opportunity to become filling station attendants and move to where the range was as yet untamed: Hollywood.

Not all of these cowhands came to escape unemployment. Many were natural wanderers, some were fleeing the hands of the law and a few were leaving wives and children behind them.

These saddle tramps, finding themselves in Southern California, could usually be found hanging around the corner of Sunset Boulevard and Gower Street, where there were some Western clothing stores, a bootmaker's and bars galore. Originally the cowboys called this place "the Watering Hole" but later it was known as Gower Gulch.

Gower Gulch was the only place outside of Wyoming where the true connoisseur of Western Americana could still hear the old cry, *"Whoo-eee! Cowboys in town! Trouble expected!"* And there usually was plenty of trouble. As a matter of fact, I'd be willing to make a small wager that there were nearly as many men killed in Gower Gulch as had been violently dispatched to the old Dodge City cemetery.

Tom Bay, my double in many pictures, cooled a mean hombre named Yakima Jim with a slug from his pistol when Yakima had the gall to pull a knife on him in a Gower Gulch saloon. Later,

Tom didn't fare too well himself, being shot and killed by a jealous girl friend.

Then there was Johnny Tyke, a top hand back in Wyoming and Montana, but a mean drunk. One night in a bar he made the fatal mistake of picking a fight with a character named Black Jack Ward. Black Jack, a Texan, had been associated with Pancho Villa during the Mexican revolution and was, clearly, nobody to tangle with. The upshot was that Tyke was found dead in an alley near the bar from which he had set out in pursuit of Black Jack. His persistence had earned him a .45 slug in the chest.

When the cowboys were not engaged in cutting one another up or busy blowing each other apart, they were acting in films as desperadoes, posse members and townspeople for $7.50 a day. Each fall they took from a horse earned them an additional $7.50, while particularly dangerous stunts might bring them as much as $50 a throw. One of these was the infamous "running W." This was a diabolical stunt routine where a horse was hobbled by his front legs and a thin iron wire was attached to the hobble and looped around an iron stake driven into the ground behind the horse. When the cowboy whipped his mount into a gallop and the horse reached the end of the line and tripped, the result was a bone-shattering fall, for both horse and man. Many of the poor animals had to be shot on the spot and the practice was, fortunately, later outlawed at the insistence of the Society for the Prevention of Cruelty to Animals.

Late one afternoon, I was sitting in a chair for some close-up shots and, during breaks, watching the men from Gower Gulch line up to receive their checks from the assistant director. A New Mexico cowboy named Charlie Huston cut out of line, came over to me and asked, "Say, you don't know where a feller could steal a couple of good horses, do you?"

"Nope," I replied. "But if you look in that line behind you, you'll find some guys who do." For I had spotted an old acquaintance, S. Y. Slim. The last time I had seen Slim was in 1916, when he was riding a beautiful sorrel horse at a gallop, heading out of the Big Horn Basin hell-bent for leather, one jump ahead of the sheriff.

If the horse thieves were in Hollywood, so, too, were the western lawmen. Thus, I was able to meet Wyatt Earp, who served as a consultant on a number of films. He was a balding, white-moustached old man at that time and freely admitted he had never been a United States marshal but had spent most of his days happily engaged in his profession, which was gambling. Unfortunately, I came from Wyoming, where his name then meant nothing, so I did not fully appreciate the role he had played in and around Tombstone, Arizona.

One lawman I became reacquainted with in Hollywood, having previously met him in Wyoming, was Joe La Fors, the man to whom Tom Horn had confessed his hand in the killing of young Willie Nickell. Among the things with which La Fors had been credited was the breaking up of the Wild Bunch, and the subsequent flight of Butch Cassidy and Harry "The Sundance Kid" Longbaugh to Bolivia, where they were eventually gunned down by a horde from the Bolivian army. But at no time when I discussed the matter with Joe in Hollywood did he make such a claim for himself. Instead, he gave full credit to the man to whom it rightfully belonged: Tim Kellerher, chief special agent for the Union Pacific Railroad.

I had known Kellerher slightly while I was adjutant general and spent many fascinating hours with him whenever he visited the West Coast, discussing his colorful career. It was Kellerher who had converted a baggage car into a stable, bunkhouse and armory on rails. With this car and a flying squadron of four skilled gunmen—Joe La Fors among them—he made it impossible for the Wild Bunch to continue operating. Kellerher was about six feet two inches tall and had broad, powerful shoulders. He was clean-shaven and handsome, the epitome of the Gary Cooper-type Westerner. As Frank Spearman, a former Nebraska banker who turned to writing and produced *Whispering Smith*, one of the great Western classics, said to me in Hollywood in the late 1920s, "Tim Kellerher *was* Whispering Smith." Quiet, clever, rugged and deadly, the best of the "good guys."

When it came to stepping on or off a horse, Tom Mix's grace was hard to match. A great showman, he realized the advantage of publicity, and was the first to affect those outlandish Western clothes which were trimmed and piped in various unmatching hues and colors. And it was typical of Mix that he thought nothing of attending a Grauman's premiere dressed in a purple dinner jacket, patent leather boots, a black Stetson hat and a purple cape lined with white satin.

His specially built Rolls-Royce automobiles were trimmed in stamped leather and his brand ꓕꓳ, was stamped into the leather and plastered on every available spot, including the hubcaps. He even had the brand in neon lights atop his house.

When Rod La Rocque and Vilma Banky were married, Sam Goldwyn decided to make it a real Hollywood production. The ceremony was rehearsed like a stage production, the coverage in the newspapers was super-colossal, and to ensure the presence of hordes of screaming fans, the wedding took place one Sunday afternoon.

As each of us entered the church, the cheering from the crowd grew louder, and after the last of the VIP's arrived, there was a lull in the procession of personages to give the bride and groom a dramatic entrance.

Suddenly, from up the street, I could hear cheering, and like everyone else in the church, expected to see the bride and groom. But it was not to be. For Tom Mix had arrived on the scene, upstaging everyone in his own dramatic and inimitable fashion. He was driving a Concord stagecoach drawn by four white horses, and on arrival at the church porch, he threw the reins to a flunky, cocked his big white Stetson at a jaunty angle, buttoned his coat and bowed his way through the fans and assembled guests. With a winning smile on his face he took his seat. The one thing that could never be said about Tom Mix was that he was inconspicuous.

On October 12, 1940, while he was returning to Hollywood from a personal appearance tour, Tom's custom-built Cord skidded on loose gravel, careened off Route 80, about eighteen miles outside of Florence, Arizona, jumped over the edge of the road and into a ravine below. And that was the end of Tom Mix. He was sixty years old.

In the back seat, still in their boxes, were six brand-new, creamy white Stetson hats. He died, as he would undoubtedly have wished, in full dress. And when his body was recovered, there was nary a mark on him, for what killed Tom Mix was the heavy, stamped-leather, metal-lined rifle case he always kept on the seat behind him, which hurtled forward as the Cord left the road, and instantly broke his neck.

The Westerns, as Tom Mix, Hoot Gibson, Ken Maynard, Buck Jones and I knew them, began to change drastically in the late thirties, when the bang-bang-shoot-'em-up-and-get-'em-on-their-horses scripts began to be phased out in favor of the Singing Cowboy. As the ranges had closed, so, too, Gower Gulch began to crumble around the edges, and the transition is perhaps best encapsulated in the following story.

When Bud Osborn, a real-life cowboy, left the 101 Ranch Wild West Show, he migrated to Hollywood and became a well-known heavy in the early serials and subsequent horse operas. His old range pals used to sit in the picture houses of Ardmore, Shawnee and other wide places in the road and watch Bud's performances. Sometime around 1940, one of Bud's old pals decided that if his buddy "Old Bull" could make a go of it, why couldn't he? So he headed for the capital of celluloid and pulchritude.

After batting his brains out trying to ease his foot through the door, he at last found himself in the presence of a casting director. "What can you do?" he was asked.

"I'm a cowboy," he replied.

"Play a banjo?"

"No, mister, can't say as I do."

"A guitar, maybe?"

"Listen," he answered, becoming what the cowboys used to call "a mite bit het-up," "I'm a range man, fresh from the Wild Bunch. I don't play nothin'. I'm just a plain, reg'lar cowboy!"

"Well, you can't be much of a cowboy," the casting director snorted. "You can't even play a harmonica!"

Not all of my films were Westerns. Indeed, some of the early silent pictures I did for M-G-M were period pieces, depicting anything from the Boxer rebellion to the French and Indian War, but each was alike in that I was cast with some of Hollywood's most glamorous leading ladies: Pauline Stark, Claire Windsor, Dorothy Sebastian and a "new face," Joan Crawford. Later, of course, the female leads became less important than the horse a cowboy rode, though I never got a cult going as Mix did for Tony, nor outfitted my mount with a toupee mane as Fred Thompson had to do for Silver King, being content to call each and every horse I rode Pal and leave it at that. Yet the leading ladies sometimes bore a resemblance to the four-legged critters, for some were gentle and others as tough as broncs.

I remember the day Dorothy Sebastian arrived on the set wearing a ring in which was set a diamond seemingly only slightly smaller than a goose egg.

"He asked me to marry him," Dorothy explained before any questions could be posed.

"Will you?" I asked.

"Hell, no!" she laughed and then recounted how her beau had given it to her the previous evening, pressing his case and adding rather gratuitously that even if Dorothy rejected him she need not return the ring. Gazing appreciatively at the glittering stone, she murmured warmly, "You can bet your sweet ass I won't."

To the often asked question of whether on-screen romance can blossom into an off-screen affair, I would have to answer yes. But my love life always has been, and will continue to remain, my own business. During my Hollywood days I was neither monk nor libertine, and never managed to fit the billing uttered by Lionel Barrymore as he, Ernest Torrence and I sat together one evening discussing an actor famous for his roles of high moral standing.

"My God," Barrymore sniffed, "to see that man on the screen, you'd never imagine he's been chasing everything on the M-G-M lot but the goddamned lion!"

I have often, when thinking about my days in Hollywood and recalling the innumerable bits of gossip, been reminded of the story told about a Saginaw schoolboy whose route home from class took him through the Line, where he was beseeched by the whores to come up and spend some time with them. He began to have dreams, not of whores, but of romps with wood nymphs in idyllic, pastoral settings. When questioned as to which he preferred, the girls of his dreams or the painted ladies, he replied, "The ones in my dreams."

"And why is that?" his interrogator asked.

"Because," he replied, "I meet a better class of people."

So many lurid tales have been spun around Hollywood, particularly the Hollywood of the 1920s and 1930s, that the public has come to think of it as a capital of decadent glamour, where everyone in the picture business spent his time getting drunk and copulating into delirium within the confines of a metropolis that was virtually a modern-day Sodom, instead of the Baghdad of the *Arabian Nights* that it really was.

Most of my friends, such as Ernest Torrence, Clive Brook, Ronald Colman, Jimmy Stewart, Warner Baxter, Dick Barthelmess, Fredric March, Jimmy Cagney, Pat O'Brien and Joel McCrea, as well as Frances Dee, Claudette Colbert, Irene Dunne and Loretta Young, never made the scandal sheets, and not much attention was paid to their apparently dull private lives. These people and many other men and women were the backbone of the business, loved it, worked hard and at the end of the day went home to their families to enjoy a normal domestic life.

The crowd I hung out with in the early days consisted most often of Nigel Bruce, Ronald Colman, Richard Barthelmess, William Powell, Aubrey Smith, Warner Baxter, Jack Holt, Cedric Hardwicke, Laurence Olivier when he was in town and, later, a fellow we called, because of his youth, "our bastard child," David Niven.

Ernest Torrence, who had given me some valuable advice about dealing with Jesse Lasky, was the original hub and host for our Friday afternoon-Saturday morning black-tie meetings, dinners and pub crawls. Unfortunately, soon after his richly deserved success in Hollywood he died in New York of cancer of the liver while on a cruise from Los Angeles to London.

After Ernest died, and from about 1931 on, the convener of our sessions was Ronald Colman. He was the gentlest man I have ever known and until his death in 1958 the best white man friend I ever had.

Whenever I think of Ronnie I cannot help but remember an

evening we spent together at a time when neither of our futures looked particularly bright.

"It could be worse," he said in the beautiful, wistfully hopeful voice with which he had been blessed. "After all, old boy, there is always your place over at Garden Court. And if there comes a time when Garden Court is gone, well, I have this place on Summit Drive."

"You never know," I interjected pessimistically.

"Well, should it happen, heaven forbid, that there is someday no Summit Drive, you and I will just have to collect our few remaining belongings together in handkerchiefs, throw the bundles across our shoulders and head on down the road. Mind you, old boy, I don't particularly fancy being a hobo but I think we might manage it together."

Shortly after New Year's Day, 1936, Ronnie and I were walking down Sunset Boulevard on our way home from a long evening together. "Ronnie," I said, grabbing his arm, "I hear Indian drums!"

"Look, old boy," he smiled indulgently, "I know it's been a rough couple of weeks, what with Christmas and New Year's, but, really!"

To humor me, he accompanied me as I prowled through an alley, moving toward what I was certain was the throb of a big Plains Indian drum. Eventually we arrived at the back of a small shop. Ronnie climbed atop an orange crate, peered into a small, lighted window and murmured, "My God, old boy, you're right."

The Indians inside caught sight of Ronnie and beckoned us to join them in their celebration. I will never forget the sight of that most handsome of matinee idols cavorting within the dance circle. As the hero of *The Prisoner of Zenda*, *A Tale of Two Cities* and many other fine films, he was a most unlikely participant.

Later, around 1940, when Ronnie and the vivacious Benita Hume decided, as he said, "to do that thing," in other words, wed, I had the honor to be his best man, and later still, godfather to his daughter Juliet; while Ronnie became godfather and namesake to one of my sons.

It was at Ronnie's house at 10003 Summit Drive that some of my fondest memories occurred. Christmas Eve called for white tie and tails, champagne and caviar, the decorating of a tree and many Dickensian carols. The living room was filled with glitter, both in the form of seasonal ornaments and people. I remember one Christmas Eve in particular. In one corner of Ronnie's living room the great Irish tenor John McCormack was softly singing a song. Scattered throughout the room were Vivien Leigh, Maurice Chevalier, Nigel Bruce, William Powell, Warner Baxter, Loretta Young, Hedy Lamarr and many, many others. On a long couch, two British writers sat discussing the merits of working for Sam Goldwyn.

"Tell me," asked the man who had recently been approached by Goldwyn to write a screenplay, "what is he *really* like?"

The other, who had worked for Goldwyn, thought a moment, wiped the edge of his glass with a finger and replied, "There are, in recognized art, something like thirty-two known representations of Judas Iscariot. And no two of them look alike. But, you know, the funny thing is that they all look like Sam Goldwyn . . ."

Willy Bruce, setting himself down at the piano, proceeded to deliver a flawless impersonation of Maurice Chevalier singing "Louise." Chevalier rose from his chair, smiled and said softly, "You come zee Greek Theatre tomorrow night, you see it done better!"

Later, as the crowd began to thin out shortly after midnight, the quartet was formed. As usual, it consisted of Bill Powell singing lead, Richard Barthelmess, Ronnie and myself backing him up and joining in for the final two lines of the song. Our last number, as always, was "Bill's Song":

> How'd you like to be my little honey,
>   paddling life's canoe a-long?
> How'd you like to be my little darling,
>   singing life's sweet so-ong?
> How'd you like to be my little sweetheart?
> How'd you like to be my little lass?
> How'd you like to share my home, sweet home, dear?
> How'd you like to kiss my ass?

CHAPTER THIRTEEN

Under the Big Top

The popularity of motion pictures during the 1930s affected all other forms of entertainment. The Sells-Floto Circus, controlled by the Bonfils-Tammen empire, which also owned the Denver *Post*, capitalized on the popularity of movies by making a deal with Tom Mix to tour with their show. Sells-Floto had never done as well before and, with success guaranteed by the presence of a Western star, other shows quickly followed suit.

I was working for Columbia when, in the winter of 1934, Samuel Gumperts, a former Coney Island entrepreneur who had taken operational control of Ringling Bros. and Barnum & Bailey Circus in 1932, called me in Hollywood. Would I be interested, he inquired, in touring with the circus? When I replied that I might be, he made me an offer I couldn't, and didn't want to, refuse. Besides, I'd never been in a circus before.

But there was a hitch. Columbia was not prepared to let me off to tour in the summer and make films in the winter, though I explained that the promotion I would be getting across the country could hardly hurt at the box office.

Thus, when my contract came up for renewal in 1935, I signed with Puritan Pictures, an outfit which fully appreciated the lure my tour with the circus would have. Puritan was not one of the more prestigious production companies and the quality of the films I made with them, which were sometimes completed after only three or four days' shooting, left much to be desired. Doubtless, it would have been better for my career had I stayed at Columbia. In fact, immediately after I signed the contract with Puritan, and as a couple of the outfit's executives and I toasted our hopes for future success in my apartment at Garden Court, the telephone rang and a man from Columbia offered to meet the needs imposed upon me by the circus. But I had given my word, and it was too late.

Ringling Bros. and Barnum & Bailey billed itself as "The Greatest Show on Earth," and it was not an idle boast. For while the show, the brain child of five brothers named Rüngeling, who changed their names to Ringling, had made its canvas debut in 1884 as part of Yankee Robinson's Great Show, Ringling Brothers' Carnival of Novelties and De Nair's Museum of Living Wonders, with a menagerie consisting of a single hyena, the road was soon cleared and the way was up. By 1919, the brothers merged with Barnum & Bailey—buying Mrs. Bailey's shares after she had answered the question "Would you rather have half a million dollars in the bank or own a circus?"—and created the largest, most colorful spectacle ever to perform in three rings under canvas.

Winter quarters in Sarasota, Florida, consisted of, in part: hospital, dormitory, wagon building, blacksmith's shop, waterproofing department for canvas, woodworking mill, dining hall, mattress shop, lumber seasoning shed, electrical shop, rigging shop, canvas storage building, paint department, railroad car shop, railroad yard, indoor and outdoor cages for wild animals, bear cage, giraffe house, aviary, ape house, elephant house, rhino pen, workhorse stable, performing horse stable, training barns, practice rings and assorted camels, dromedaries, zebras and llamas.

The big show always opened the season in Madison Square Garden, moved on to the Boston Garden and came back to Brooklyn for the first week's stand under canvas, which is where I joined it in April 1935. I would be with the circus until November, when I returned to the studios in Hollywood to make Westerns. I did this not only in 1935 but through the years of 1936 and 1937.

While the show was in Boston, the wagons, baggage stock, tentage and all other equipment necessary for the road came north from winter quarters, and upon arrival, the new tents—for the show started each season under a bright, new big top—were pitched in Brooklyn. There they were guyed out and the slack gradually taken out of the canvas.

Ringling Bros. and Barnum & Bailey was a railroad show consisting of four trains of twenty-five cars each. Mine was a former observation car with a canopied platform at the back and, inside, a well-appointed living room-lounge, bedroom, bath, guest room, dining room, kitchen and valet's room. The circus rolled into town at the crack of dawn, pitched its tents, fed fourteen hundred people and six hundred animals and gave two complete performances "rain or shine." Then, like the Bedouins, the circus folded its tents and while the audience that attended the evening performance was snugly tucked into bed, slipped out of town without leaving even a single tent stake behind. In order to do this correctly, the show had to be an efficient organization. And the day-to-day operation, while simple enough, was impressive: the horse-drawn show wagons were loaded onto flat-bed railroad cars which were joined where they coupled by a thick iron plate. These wagons were pulled by ropes onto the rear car and guided to the front of the train, where, at unloading time, when the engine was unhooked, the first wagon on became the first wagon off. The German General Staff, which went as far as to send observers to master the technique, found this bit of minutiae utterly fascinating.

Naturally there were difficulties and problems: rain, muddy lots where wagons were buried to the axles, train wrecks, accidents to performers and the constant threat of fire or panic. The circus, any circus, throbs a sensitive pulse, and a sudden change in the tempo of the band—which, in the Ringling show, in the event of a fire was drilled to break into the rousing strains of "The Stars and Stripes Forever"—or the way the clowns run out the back door may convey a message.

Should that message be one of tragedy or danger, everybody from the general manager down to the most junior roustabout becomes a solid unit. Not physically, perhaps, but you can feel it. And if you ask any old trouper what his first thought might have been in times of danger, such as a strong storm or a blowdown, he will invariably say, "The bulls."

Elephants, big and powerful as they are, can sometimes be stampeded by the bark of a small terrier dog. And when they stampede, all hell breaks loose. The young punks take off in any direction with the older ones behind, and it doesn't make any difference to them what is in their line of departure. For once they break from the menagerie tent, they may go through the nearest side wall, knocking cages and wagons out of their path and generally wrecking everything and anyone that's in their way.

I noticed that whenever a thunderstorm broke suddenly, even if it was during the performance, the elephant men quickly unshackled their charges and moved them at a trot into the open, where the animals huddled together in a field with the rain whipping around them and thunder and lightning crackling all around, swaying back and forth and making strange, frightened rumbles in their throats.

Aboard the show train, the elephant cars were specially constructed with partitioned-off sleeping quarters for the keepers, who could quickly get to their charges in the event of an emergency.

When the show played more than one night in a town, the bulls were staked out in a line in the menagerie, each with its own pile of hay in front of it, and the keepers bedded down nearby. This was the setup on our second night in Brooklyn when a policeman came rushing in, searching for the elephant trainer, Larry Davis. Davis was awakened and told that one of his elephants was loose and roaming through the residential section of Brooklyn. His first thought was, *which elephant?* So he went down the line and made a check. "One, two, three . . ." They were all present and accounted for, twenty-two bulky shapes weaving back and forth, tossing hay up on their backs in the dim light of the tent.

"I don't care how many elephants you've got there," said the policeman, "but we've reports coming in from all over Brooklyn and you're the only guys around who've got elephants!"

"I've heard of people seeing pink elephants," Larry joked, "but this is ridiculous. Just what kind of hooch are they selling in this town anyway?"

But the policeman was not to be persuaded, and so Davis accompanied him in his squad car on a drive through Brooklyn in search of the mysterious pachyderm. After driving around in circles for a couple of hours, Davis asked to be taken back to the lot, and to prove his point to the policeman, he was willing to let him count the elephants for himself.

Together they checked the line. "One, two, three . . . twenty, twenty-one, twenty-two . . . *twenty-three* . . . *What the hell!*" muttered Davis. It was Rosie.

A few years before, the Prospect Park Zoo in Brooklyn had wanted an elephant, so the circus, anxious to co-operate, sold them Rosie. Separated from her old friends, relegated to the drab life of a zoo elephant, Rosie fretted away the years. On this particular night, she had broken her bonds, wrecked the small wooden building which served as her staff and, still dragging part of it with her at the end of a chain, took off. Perhaps the sound of the circus band had reached her, or she may have picked up a whiff of the menagerie in the light breeze. At any rate, she had found the lot, crawled under the side wall and was now rubbing shoulders with old Myrtle, dipping into her hay pile and making contented little rumbles in her throat. Myrtle was feeling her over with the finger at the end of her trunk to make sure her old friend was all right, and gurgling and rumbling at a great rate.

When I saw the two of them together, I imagined Myrtle was probably telling Rosie all the latest gossip. How it rained so hard in Paris, Texas, and the mud was so deep they could hardly get off the lot; how she and Modoc had to straighten out those young punks brought over from the Al G. Barnes Show; yes, Mrs. Charlie Ringling was well and traveled with them every summer, just as in the old days. Perhaps she even related that the biggest day's business the previous year had been in Concordia, Kansas, but Jackson, Mississippi, had been lousy; yes, Merle Evans still led the band, Fred Bradna was equestrian director, but there'd been a lot of changes . . . a lot of changes.

Rosie was back home.

Another circus performer who became separated from a show was Shingoo. When Ringling Bros. and Barnum & Bailey traveled through Georgia, shortly after I signed on, it was in the wake of another circus which had been derailed in a train crash. Scores of animals, both large and small, docile and ferocious, were loosed from their chains and cages. A reward had been offered for the return of any of the missing animals and Ringling Bros. and Barnum & Bailey had been asked to receive any returnees and hold them until the wrecked circus got itself together again.

One afternoon, shortly before the matinee, a husky black sharecropper arrived at the paymaster's wagon. He said he had a "striped giraffe" he had acquired after the recent disaster and asked if the circus would really give him fifty dollars for its return. The paymaster assured him that if he brought in his "striped giraffe" he would, indeed, receive the money.

The next morning he returned to the circus lot, "striped giraffe" in tow, and succeeded in causing unprecedented havoc, emptying the midway in record time. For the captive which the sharecropper dragged down the midway with a rope attached to a dog collar around its neck was no ordinary "giraffe" but a snarling, bad-tempered, six-hundred-and-fifty-pound Bengal tiger.

When Shingoo was installed in a cage, one of the Ringling cat men asked the sharecropper how he had managed to keep the tiger from mauling him. "Oh," the sharecropper replied offhandedly, "there wasn't much to it. See, whenever that striped giraffe got uppity, I just kinda slapped him down a few times."

For being allowed to be the small boy who was able to see the circus every day, I rode into the center ring after the Wallendas had finished their chilling high-wire act and, from atop the biggest, dumbest horse I have ever known, promoted the wild West show that would take place after the main performance. I made my exit just before Hugo and Mario Zacchini wheeled their cannon in, climbed inside and were shot from one end of the big top to the other.

Perhaps at this point in my narrative it would be wise to explain my relationship with horses, for I have, above, referred to the seventeen-hand-high palomino horse I rode in the Ringling show as "the biggest, dumbest horse I have ever known." I am not, to put it simply, a great lover of horses. I do not begrudge those people who find in the animals an endless source of inspiration, devotion and affection. However, I personally have never met a horse that really gave a damn about anyone. To me, a horse was never much more than the thing I got on and rode.

The wild West show was a hurly-burly business. The members of the troupe galloped into the big top and, accompanied by rollicking music, formed an impressive line on the track in front of the audience. After various introductions, it was time for me to perform. I tried to vary my routine from time to time, though certain elements of the act were retained always, such as roping six cantering horses with a single loop, and trick shooting—I would have a postage stamp stuck onto a washer and thrown up into the air; a bullet from my rifle, passing through the hole in the washer, would pierce the stamp.

There were other notable performers: Billy Waite, an Australian whipcracker, whose instruments were made of kangaroo hide and who had instructed Douglas Fairbanks, Sr., in the intricacies of the trade, clipped caps off soda bottles and snipped, bit by bit, cigarettes from the mouth of a daring assistant. Steve Clemento, an impalement artist, threw a battle-ax while blindfolded at his two nieces and split the apples on their heads, in an act Ronnie Colman swore, "I never want to see again." Gabril and Maroz, two Kuban Cossacks, galloped down the sawdust track with sabers in their teeth, leaped from their saddles, hit the ground, vaulted over one another, sat facing each other in the same saddle and then repeated their performance, riding out of the tent sitting backward.

And then there were the snake dancers. They were mostly Hopis, but when I couldn't get quite enough to fill the troupe of thirteen, I latched onto Indians from other tribes, including Iron Eyes Cody. A Cherokee from Oklahoma, Iron Eyes is still one of the great, authentic Indian actors. The snake dancers' costumes were authentic and so were the rattlers, which we took in shipments of twelve at a time every month from an outfit called Snake King in Brownsville, Texas. For the price of five dollars apiece we got snakes that the smallest kid sitting in the farthest reaches of the bleachers would be able to see clearly: they were about five feet long. And while their fangs, which we soon learned were regenerative, had been removed in Brownsville, they were still feisty.

Iron Eyes sang the songs and he knew what he was doing. Aside from being an avid student of native American culture he is a most knowledgeable man. With the drums and high-pitched singing for a background, Antelope Priest and Snake Priest began the dance, handing the wriggling serpents to each dancer, gently stroking the reptiles with eagle feathers to calm them down and making their way completely around the arena, holding the snakes in their mouths.

For their finale, the snake dancers let the rattlers loose and watched them streak toward the crowd. The Indians stood motionless, waiting until the serpents were practically crawling up someone's leg before scooping them up and making a dash from the big top.

It should come as no surprise that most of the snake dancers were usually about half plastered. The single exception I can recall was poor Iron Eyes, whose job became the holding together of the troupe. Individually, they were prone to fall off the train in the middle of the night and, still painted from the previous evening's performance, wander into unsuspecting farming communities along the circus' route, terrorizing the inhabitants. On one occasion, a snake dancer was picked up from alongside the tracks, obviously dead, and rather badly messed up from his parting of the ways with the train. His body was taken into town, placed in a coffin, and Ringling's contacted by telegraph to come and pick him up. The mortician received the fright of his life when, about to place the latch on the casket, he observed a bronze hand emerge from under the lid. A moment later a dazed and bewildered snake dancer sat up and started to climb out of the coffin. He was not dead, just dead drunk.

Another problem with the dancers arose when an old Hopi from Arizona arrived backstage in New York. He was in the city en route to Washington, D.C., to plead some case before the government and stopped off to lecture the snake dancers, quite properly, that snake dance was for the reservation village of Oraibi, not a circus. He threatened them with the evil eye, and rather than be subjected to the myriad side effects of a whammy, some of the younger Hopis departed.

The greatest compliment the snake dancers received came during an engagement at Madison Square Garden. New York had enjoyed balmy weather until they arrived, but afterward experienced severe rainstorms. "Will Tim McCoy and his snake dancers," one newspaper editorialized, "please leave our city. We believe their dance can bring rain, but can't they practice their religion elsewhere?"

From when I was a child, from the first time I met Buffalo Bill in 1898, I was mesmerized by the concept of a wild West show. Indeed, Johnny Baker, Buffalo Bill's adopted son, who had co-starred with Annie Oakley and was, incidentally, a better shot than she was, told me, "You're the only man alive who can carry on the colonel's tradition." And so, when I had sufficient funds and some measure of public identification, I attempted to organize such a production.

It was 1938, a year many of us in show business later regarded as probably the worst year of the Depression. The Hagenbeck-Wallace Circus closed down that year when, because of an inability to pay for it, their new canvas was confiscated by a sheriff in Riverside, California. Even Ringling Bros. and Barnum & Bailey, because of insoluble labor disputes, had been forced to cancel out on dates and return to their winter quarters. So, with all the survival instincts of a lemming, I set about putting together America's last wild West show.

It was a hell of a show, designed to play in an arena 150 feet wide and 200 feet long, and, among other items, consisted of thirty-five specially constructed 72-foot long railroad cars; American cowboys, Australian bullwhackers, Argentinian gauchos and Mexican *caballeros*; British Lancers, Bengal Lancers, Italian hussars, Royal Savoy Dragoons, veterans of the U. S. Cavalry and Kuban Cossacks fresh from their diaspora following the Russian civil war; a thirty-two man band; and, of course, Indians: John Sitting Bull, the old man's deaf-mute, adopted son; Ernie Black Elk, son of the now famous Medicine Man; Ernie American Horse, later Keeper of the Cheyenne Sacred Buffalo Hat, and others . . . always, the Indians.

Tim McCoy's Wild West and Rough Riders of the World opened on April 14, 1938, in Chicago, Illinois, at the International Amphitheatre and closed twenty-one days later in Washington, D.C. I lost about $300,000 on that deal and it would be an understatement to say that, aside from being flat broke, I was depressed when the show was placed on the auction block. But I consoled myself with the belief that the end of that particular act did not necessarily signal the ringing down of the curtain to close the entire play.

When the wild West show closed, I returned to Hollywood and began to film a series of eight pictures entitled *The Rough Riders* with Buck Jones and Raymond Hatton. I was rapidly approaching the age of fifty and already starting to do something which I had previously regarded as fatal: I was beginning to look over my shoulder, spending time looking back, reviewing my career. It was time for a change.

In 1942 I returned to Wyoming and ran unsuccessfully for the United States Senate. After selling my cattle, I broke my contract with Buck Jones's company and went off to World War II, feeling that any actor who was physically able to make films could certainly make the war. There were others who felt as I did: Jimmy Stewart, Tyrone Power, Clark Gable and David Niven among them. But a few who were younger were content to do their bit on the back lot of a studio. Ironically, some of them would later become the most rabid of America's super-patriots.

The studio bosses were not pleased at the sudden disappearance of their stars and made it clear to those of us who were preparing to join up that our futures in Hollywood were, to say the least, in peril. There were various reactions to this not so subtle threat. My answer was a brief telegram to my producer which consisted of the words Buck, Ray and I used as a tag line at the end of every *Rough Riders* film:

SO LONG ROUGH RIDERS

For me, World War II was passed viewing the awesome ruin and carnage generated by the then modern war machines, doing staff work, supplying the French air force with planes, photo labs, gasoline—which they had a distressing tendency to burn up in marathon "victory" parades—and the like, while living in everything from rain-drenched tents to only slightly damaged châteaux recently vacated by the retreating Germans, and, when particularly fortunate, drinking the finest "liberated" wines imaginable.

I recall, along that line, one occasion in Germany when, after having hundreds of cases of Liebfraumilch loaded onto U. S. Army trucks, I was presented by the wine master with an astronomical bill. In Germany, it seemed it was always papers, papers and more papers. I took the bill in hand and signed, "J. E. B. Stuart, 4th Mountain Artillery." A Civil War general, Confederate at that, and a non-existent outfit. As my commanding general, Gordon Saville, pointed out afterward, while we savored the fruits of that day's labor, I had actually blown the whole deal by not paying the wine master with Confederate money. To the receiver of that most rubbery of receipts, should he, by chance, be a reader, my apologies. But after all, the exigencies of war . . .

I did not experience any bloodcurdling hardships during the war, for which I am thankful. I was fifty-two years old and make no apologies for not being in the vanguard, yanking hand grenade pins with my teeth and storming with hell-fury the twisted steel dragon's teeth of the German Siegfried Line. I was quite content to view the torn aftermath from the air.

While serving in France and Germany, I was frequently called back to Washington for briefings. One afternoon, we put down in the Azores to refuel and the sergeant in charge of the ground crew came up to me and saluted.

"Excuse me, sir, but aren't you Colonel McCoy?"

"Yes," I replied.

"Well, sir, you don't know it but I've been a great help to you."

"Is that so? Did we serve together? I really don't recall you, Sergeant."

"Oh, no, nothing like that, sir. But I used to live in a small town in Ohio. There was a little picture house in town and during Saturday matinees I used to sit in the front row of the balcony, armed with a slingshot and a pocket full of staples. And any time the bad guys tried to creep up and get the drop on you, I'd shoot the hell out of them."

In the winter of 1944, while stationed in France's Vosges Mountains with the 1st Tactical Air Force, I spent my days drawing plans on enormous operational maps and usually had time in the afternoon to stroll through the lovely countryside and enjoy the scenery. One afternoon, when I was walking along a frozen back road, I came to an old cemetery, surrounded by a decrepit wooden slat fence. The graves were covered with snow but I could still discern, through thin layers of ice, hand-painted lettering on the rotting crosses: *Jean Genet, Mort pour la patrie, 1914* . . . *Pierre Moreau, Mort pour la patrie, 1915* . . . *Jacques LeClerc, Mort, 1916* . . . *Jean Bonnier, pour la patrie, 1917* . . . *Robert Chevalier, 1918.* And there, in a corner of the country cemetery, was a new cross, the whitewash of recent vintage: *Henri Rimbaud, Mort pour la patrie, 1940.*

A more cheerful occurrence during that winter was staying in the Ritz Hotel in Paris. Somehow, over various dinners and evening-long discussions, I struck up a friendship with Ernest Hemingway.

One evening I was sitting with Ernie in his room. He was propped up on top of his bed, wrapped in a bulky sheepskin vest, and writing in longhand in a notebook. It was bitterly cold and the Germans had not seen fit to leave us with fuel for heat. We were, that night, indulging in a primitive but nonetheless effective effort at compensation, belting the contents of the two canteens Hemingway carried with him at all times. One was filled with vile Calvados and the other with martinis which, as Ernie explained, "were no goddamn good" unless mixed at the eye-popping ratio of twelve parts gin to one part vermouth. Water? "Hell's bells, man, I can get water *anywhere!*"

The evening had been rambling on and had reached the point where I had only the vaguest notion which of the two canteens I was quaffing, while, at the same time, I was becoming increasingly doubtful whether I would be able to induce Ernie to leave his cold but cozy warren to attend a party being given that night by the reigning lights of Parisian society, the Prince and Princess de Polignac.

My pleas to Hemingway were greeted by a stony glance. "Look, Tim, after what happened this afternoon . . ."

Ernie had just missed being run over by a Parisian taxi, powered by a charcoal-burning engine, as he was crossing the Place

Vendôme. Being built like a bear, he was able to slap a hamhock hand across the bumper of the machine and vault to safety.

"Jeezus," he had roared. "Wouldn't that be a hell of a thing? After all I've done, to be knocked off by a piss-ant contraption like that?"

Eventually, after an involved conversation in which, if I recall correctly, the subjects of predestination and Vegas-type odds came up, I was able to get him moving by reminding him that the Polignac family made some of the best champagne in France.

After entering the fragile, intricately grilled open-door elevator at the end of the hallway, Ernie leaned against the side and said, "You know, Tim, if you ever want to go back into politics and run for office, just say the word. Hell, I don't know your goddamn politics, but I do know you and you can be sure I'll do whatever I can. After all, I've got some dough and some people seem to think I can write pretty good, too."

As the elevator descended, Ernie placed one of his strong hands on my shoulder, squeezed firmly and said, "It's funny, but whenever I'm with you, I always feel good."

He looked up, surveyed the passage of our little cubicle, bumping and grinding its way down the shaft, wrapped his sheepskin tightly around his barrel chest and grinned through his whiskers. "And that ain't horseshit."

When the war was over, I returned to Hollywood and quickly learned that the market for fifty-four-year-old cowboys was mighty slim. So, traveling from west to east, stopping off in Wyoming to sell the Eagle's Nest, I retired to Bucks County, Pennsylvania. There I bought a pre-Revolutionary estate with a magnificent Georgian home called Dolington Manor, and settled back to enjoy what I perceived as my few remaining years, intent upon living them as a country gentleman. Happily, this was not to be.

CHAPTER FOURTEEN

Moccasin Prints Across the Sky

It is the spring of my eighty-sixth year, my third year of retirement, and I am sitting in the patio of my hacienda near the Mexican border, listening to the fountain. From under the protective roof of an adobe arch, I observe the afternoon drizzle, a steady rain signaling the beginning of humid times in these parts. I have nearly come to the end of my narrative, and as I turn to look back across my span, I cannot help but marvel at the single aspect of existence which is capable of humbling us all: change.

My reasoning powers and memory are in neither worse nor better shape than they ever were—something I regard as good fortune, indeed—though some of my youthful enthusiasms have been replaced by a recognition of certain lessons which my time has taught me. When I was younger, growing up in Saginaw, riding the range, visiting among the Indians or basking in the klieg-lit world of Hollywood, I was certain of many things. Today I am certain of fewer things, though my degree of certitude is more pronounced than it once was. I do not question as much or as often as I used to, except, perhaps, life's points of origin and departure. I have found that the in-between tends to take care of itself.

Like all people in all times, I have experienced my share of sadness, disappointment and grief, without which no life is complete and which no life can escape. I have also been blessed with a great many happy times and might question why it is that way, except I can almost hear Goes In Lodge whispering from beyond the pale, "*It is!*"

Hollywood, with all of its glitter, glamour and, not incidentally, its phenomenal pay scale, was perhaps the most uncertain period of my life. The heights were dizzying, and for many, the inevitable fall, coupled with the steady, grinding passage of the years, was too horrendous, uncomfortable and defeating to bear.

Nothing was guaranteed and one could be a star today only to be washed up tomorrow. This happened: William S. Hart was falsely accused in a sex suit and his career never really recovered; Bill "Hopalong Cassidy" Boyd was identified in a newspaper photograph as having been arrested at a particularly wild party, though, in fact, it was another Bill Boyd, also an actor, who was involved. Comebacks occurred—Boyd was an example—but they were rare. And aside from accusations, false or otherwise, the slightest taint of suspicion could irreparably damage a career: Mary Miles Minter was rumored to have been involved in a particularly mysterious murder, and while a link was never established, Minter's promising career as an actress was kaput. On a more mundane level, one's contract might not be renewed, often for unfathomable reasons.

I remember a story about Basil Rathbone, an outstanding British actor famous for his characterization of Conan Doyle's Sherlock Holmes, when he shared scenes with my friend, the incomparable Nigel Bruce, as Dr. Watson.

"How much are you paid each week?" Rathbone was once asked.

"I am paid five thousand dollars per week," the lean, hawk-nosed actor coolly replied.

"That is a great deal of money!"

"Yes," Rathbone nodded thoughtfully, "it is indeed a great deal of money. And do you know how many weeks I worked last year? *One!*"

During my halcyon days in Hollywood, a period which lasted from 1926 to 1942, I was a most conspicuous consumer. My apartment was maintained year-round, whether I was in or out of town. I employed a Filipino valet named Frank, who cooked meals, mixed martinis, managed household affairs and took good care of me. My cars were always the latest, best and most fashionable models: a long, low, chauffeur-driven Stutz; a series of formidable

Cadillac coupés; and, once, a beautiful, shiny, sleek, convertible-top red Packard which caused Fanny Brice to remark as we left a party together one evening, "Jeez, Tim, that thing's got a longer snout on it than I have!"

I look back on the days of glitter, romance, fame and fine friendships with both joy and sadness, for few of the old crowd remain. But I am satisfied to recall the inscription on an imposing rock I once saw in the great Southwest. It bears the signatures of many early Spanish adventurers who came to the New World seeking their fortune. They traveled far and wide over tortuous trails, following the standards of the vanguards, Coronado and De Anza. Above their name-impressions is chiseled an inscription, carved by some of the earliest. Hollywood should have something of the sort but big business invariably discards all but fiscally profitable memory. Perhaps, though, some of the picture-going public of yesterday feels, still, a certain friendliness for those familiar faces of a Golden Era; retaining in their hearts a faint impression, like the inscription on that rock, which reads, *Pasaron Por Aquí* . . . They Passed By Here.

As I have already explained, World War Two signaled the end of that particular phase of my life, and the end of the war was perceived by me as the beginning of my retirement. And it would have been had it not been for *Inga*. That was her name and the sound of it is much like the way she was: Danish and lyrical.

Aside from her native language, she spoke three others—French, German and English—fluently, though for the last thirty-six of her sixty years she refused to utter a word of German.

She was born in Copenhagen in 1913, into a fairy-tale world where houses were large, grandly ornamented and richly furnished. The parties she eavesdropped on as a child from an upstairs landing were candelabra-lit, Strauss-waltz affairs. This easy ambience is difficult to imagine at this distance, for it retreated from the upheaval of the First World War only to be forever shattered by the calamity and disorientation of the second conflagration.

Her story is a fascinating one and worthy of a book in its own right, for she spent most of her life in the midst of the world's dramatic action, surrounded by its major and colorful figures. But here I will tell only a few of her experiences, intending to give the broadest of brush strokes to outline her experience.

In the early 1930s, when married to a Hungarian anthropologist and film-maker, she spent a couple of years in the Dutch East Indies, now the Indonesian archipelago. She and her husband were there to observe and report on the various and numerous tribes living in the bush, as well as to secure a live Komodo dragon—actually a monitor lizard—for the Copenhagen zoo. For a time she lived in a particularly isolated village, where she was regarded by Stone Age inhabitants as a goddess. The tribesmen erected half-life-sized mud idols, with straw for hair, in her honor. She also, at about the same time, lived for some months in a thatch-roofed hut perched atop stilts in the waters of a shark-infested lagoon.

During a visit to a jungle village she was eating with the headman of the community. Spotting a curious object at the back of his hut, she rose and walked over to make an inspection. It was a smoke-darkened, shrunken but still recognizable head of a red-haired German missionary she had been acquainted with and whom she had seen alive in that same village only two months previously.

"Why?" she asked the chief, her voice trembling with shock.

The chief chewed his food, swallowed, belched and replied, "Bad manners."

April 1936 found her among the small number of guests being treated to luncheon by the Danish ambassador at that country's embassy in Berlin. Gossip seeped into the afternoon's conversation, the main topic being the liaison between Reichsmarschall Hermann Göring and Emmy Sonnemann, a beautiful, Valkyrie-like second-rate actress who somehow managed to get choice roles far above what her talent commanded. The question was whether Göring and the actress were, as rumor had it, planning to wed. It was twenty-one-year-old Inga's suggestion that the answer to the question was simple enough to discover: look up Sonnemann's name in the Berlin telephone directory, pick up a phone, ring her up and get the answer straight from the horse's mouth. The ambassador—whom Inga described as "looking at me with his fishy little blue eyes swimming comfortably in the akvavit he had swallowed by the pony-glass-full"—scoffed, as did the other guests.

Inga's response was to do exactly as she had suggested, and that afternoon, having told Emmy Sonnemann that she represented *Berlingske Tidende*, a Danish newspaper—which she did not— she learned, through an exclusive interview, that the actress and the Reichsmarschall were indeed planning on getting married. When she inquired if she might publish the story, Emmy Sonnemann replied that she would have to ask Hitler's Propaganda Minister, Joseph Goebbels.

Since the story was hardly controversial, let alone political, the Propaganda Ministry offered no objections. Twelve hours later, Inga was in Copenhagen, talking with the editor of *Berlingske Tidende*, and within a few minutes had sold the story. Within a few days, a telegram reached Inga, inviting her to the wedding as "Emmy Sonnemann's private guest."

Returning to Berlin, with an advance from the newspaper, for which she was now a foreign correspondent, she attended the wedding and the small reception afterward. She particularly remembered the gifts given the bride and groom: "Emeralds and rubies the size of quail's eggs were exhibited along with gold dinner sets, sable from Russia, a live nightingale in a gold cage from the Emperor of Japan, choice paintings and pearls."

Adolf Hitler was the best man and presided over the wedding feast. She would later recall him then as being "an unassuming man in a plain S.A. uniform, wearing just the *Hagenkreuz* decoration, and his limp hair falling slightly over one eye."

Through her contact with Goebbels she was granted exclusive interviews with Adolf Hitler in 1935 and 1936. She learned little other than the fact that he expected "the present generation not to live long" and liked carrots. Her degree of political sophistication was such that when asked after the Hitler interviews who the subject of her next "scoop" would be, she breezily replied, "Lenin"—who for a decade had been lying in his marble mausoleum in Moscow's Red Square.

When, soon after her interviews with Hitler, she was sounded out by the German Foreign Minister as to her interest in becoming a spy in Paris, she refused and wisely decided to make a speedy exit from the Third Reich. She fled Germany on a train loaded with Jews and German generals, using as a guarantor of safe passage a silver-framed, autographed picture of Hitler which she placed conspicuously on top of the clothes in her bag.

Hitler had described her as "the perfect Nordic beauty," a remark which opened doors in pre-World War II Germany for the twenty-three-year-old reporter but made life difficult for her when she arrived in America in 1940.

Still, she managed, and became a syndicated, Washington-based columnist, in which capacity she was having luncheon with Vyacheslav Molotov and Andrei Gromyko when news arrived of the Japanese attack on Pearl Harbor. Later, she was a screenwriter for Louis B. Mayer at M-G-M, and, for a time, took over Sheilah Graham's Hollywood column. "That was a pain," she recalled. "I couldn't seem to work up enough bitchiness."

Inga and I first met at a dinner party in Hollywood early in 1946, when she was fashion editor for *Harper's Bazaar*. I had been told by our hostess that I "simply must meet Inga, all the men are crazy about her." While I have not gone into detail regarding my various affections and romances, I should inform the reader that by the time I reached the age of fifty-five I was convinced that anyone "all the men are crazy about" was nobody I wanted to meet. But I did meet her and she literally took my breath away. She was the most beautiful woman I had ever seen, and unlike most who are similarly endowed, was down to earth and utterly devoid of vanity. I seldom left her side afterward.

Shortly after our meeting we were married, an event which caused the Hollywood columnist and wag Harry Crocker to remark that "Inga must've wanted to learn Indian sign language." But if our backgrounds were different, our spirits were akin.

Following our wedding, we retreated to Dolington Manor but within a few months we were forced to leave. I had to go back to working for a living. The birth of our first son and the impending arrival of our second caused us to move West to California, where fortunately I had been offered a television program in Los Angeles.

It was 1950 and television was in its infancy. My first program, at KTLA, consisted of me telling Indian legends and historical stories, and Iron Eyes Cody and a number of other Indians performing dances and re-enacting ceremonies. After two years I moved over to the local CBS affiliate, KNXT, where I performed solo, telling the audience about the real history of the West. Sometimes I was joined unexpectedly by Captain Jet's chimpanzee from the show immediately preceding mine. I can report from far too many experiences with that critter that there is nothing more distracting than trying to give a serious lecture on the Bozeman Trail while a playful, but sometimes snarling, little ape tugs on your trouser leg or starts to climb all over your anatomy.

I enjoyed doing that program, for it gave me a forum to educate people about a portion of American history which is clouded by a great many tall tales. It was one of the most widely watched shows in Los Angeles and in 1952 received an Emmy. That Emmy turned out to be the kiss of death, for several months after the award was given I was without a sponsor.

Again I was faced with the question of how to earn a living. So when I was offered a job on a smaller scale but similar to my act with Ringling Bros. and Barnum & Bailey, I moved to the Kelly, Miller Brothers Circus. A year later I was with Carson and Barnes Circus, where I remained for six years.

The years of the late 1950s and the 1960s were good ones. Inga and the boys would join me in the summer when the kids were out of school and we traveled as a small family within the larger circus family throughout the United States and Canada. The boys loved circus life and seemed to spend the time from September until June waiting in anticipation for summer "vacation." It wasn't always just a holiday, for they had to work—helping put up the big top, cleaning out the wild animal cages, barking into microphones to lure people to see "the blood-sweating hippopotamus" and the "longest snake in captivity." They also had the opportunity to ride and train elephants, perform as clowns and acquire innumerable memories.

In 1962 I decided to move my family from the sprawling and increasingly crowded suburbs of Los Angeles to southern Arizona. Since then, a number of others seem to have latched onto the same idea, and where there were once jack rabbits, hills and open spaces there are now restaurants, telephone wires and highways.

262

Still, the house I constructed then serves the same purpose today: built along Spanish-colonial lines, it centers on an enclosed patio around which the lives of its inhabitants are centered. So it makes little difference how many white men surround me.

Shortly after building the house I signed on with Tommy Scott and his Country Caravan to perform an act in which I did trick shooting and used the Australian whips Billy Waite had taught me how to handle.

Tommy Scott is a one of a kind from Tacoa, Georgia. He started out by selling elixir from the back of a wagon at medicine shows and parlayed that experience into what is nothing less than a one-man entertainment empire: records, traveling shows and gee-gaws are his stock in trade.

It is the nature of his business that most tickets are sold in advance. This arrangement leaves the "advance man," the fellow who maps the routes and takes in the money, frequently in possession of large sums of cash. With so many men scouring the country in search of widespread entertainment oases—for the show played twice a day, seven days a week, ten and a half months of the year—the temptation to abscond with the proceeds is great. This happened once in Phoenix, Arizona. The advance man had several thousand dollars in his briefcase and apparently felt the pull toward some distant horizon. Driving to a trailer sales establishment, he hitched his car to a new trailer conveniently off the blocks, plastered both car and trailer with stickers reading "Jesus Saves" and, claiming to be "a man doing the work of the Lord," took off into the sunset. When I asked Tommy if he was planning to press charges, he smiled and said, "Hell, no, I ain't gonna press no charges. At least *that* thieving bastard has some imagination!"

For thirteen years, three hundred and thirty days a year, I worked for Tommy, crossing the continent many, many times, and what bound us together was not an iron-clad contract but a simple handshake.

Inga died in the winter of 1973. Whenever, during our marriage, there was uncertainty, as there often was, about what I should do next, she never failed to pat me on the shoulder and say, "Cowboy, just pull yourself up by the bootstraps."

And when she would awaken me in the morning, she would invariably smile and laugh, "I just wanted to see if you were still alive, you old Irish bastard!"

Within six months of her death and for the first time in my adult life I stopped working and knew, beyond any doubt, that I would not work again. I felt like a ship which suddenly had its rudder drop off, its bottom rip out and its engine room explode in an oddly quiet but nonetheless devastating holocaust.

It is from her death that I draw the line which separates the time of life during which I was forever looking forward from that during which I am constantly engaged in reflection. In a sense, I now mark my time, and while preparing for the journey west to what my Arapaho friends referred to as the Great Mystery, I have, and continue to enjoy having, the opportunity to remember, evaluate and fit into place the various threads encompassed within the pattern of the weave on the loom that has been my life.

In doing this, it often strikes me that I have been privileged to know, in varying degrees of intimacy, a number of truly remarkable people. Some of them had names which are quickly recognized by many, while others are known little, if at all, outside of a small circle of friends. Almost all of them, sadly, are now gone and so I may be pardoned if I sometimes feel as though I am living partly in a world of shadows.

As I look over my shoulder I realize that another element of the weave of which I write has been a line of life that has taken me to the frontiers, both real and reel; most often when they were closing and always in time to witness their points of termination.

I arrived in Wyoming just in time for the last of the old-type roundups. I became acquainted with, and came to know well, the old-time buffalo-hunting Indians as they were fading back into the place from which they had emerged—some of history's furthest and deepest atavistic recesses.

In Hollywood, I acted in the last of the silent films and started in the first talkie serial. And while movies continue, they have changed dramatically. Heroes are out; good-bad men and bad-good guys occupy the fore to an unprecedented degree. Why this is, I do not know. I cannot condemn the trend, for it is like everything else I have observed, part of ongoing change. But I do mourn the passing of the hero, for we gave the young people someone to look up to, a figure to emulate, and, more often than is generally supposed, imposed upon ourselves an obligation to be true to that image. If people must live their lives cast in various parts, why should the prevailing roles not be dedicated to the highest standards and principles?

Buffalo Bill's image and memory have been much maligned by Hollywood, which, as always, continues to churn out its own mythological version of reality. Wyatt Earp in death becomes a television series and hero, a far cry from the professional gambler he was in life. Butch Cassidy and Harry Longbaugh are heroes in a fine film. Joe La Fors, in the same movie, is their nemesis . . . but where is Tim Kellerher? Tom Horn was "misunderstood," probably the product of a broken home. General Scott, alas, is forgotten. *The Covered Wagon* survives in a severely abbreviated version, only five reels of the original ten having negotiated the tricky passage through time owing to having the images impressed upon nitrate film. And the Indians . . . the poor, damned Indians are still being raked over by the white man.

Now, as I sit under the covered *portales* in my patio, watching the rain as it begins to fall, writing and moving to the close of my story, I think that perhaps it was only natural a telephone call should have come the other day from Father John J. Killoren. Jack Killoren, a Jesuit, a historian, lives and works at St. Stephen's Mission on the Wind River Reservation. Most of his parishioners are Arapahoes, the Shoshonis still sticking close to St. Michael's Mission, founded by the saintly Dr. Roberts.

Jack telephoned, just as this book was being readied for mailing to the publisher. The message he gave me was that Francis Sitting Eagle, two months shy of his ninety-fifth birthday, had died.

Francis was the last of the Indians I took to London in 1923. He had been born in a tipi on Wind River in 1882, four years after the Arapahoes were rounded up and moved to the reservation. When he died, Francis still retained the old-style hairdressing of a braid behind each ear and a thin scalp lock falling down the back of his neck.

He was buried, like so many of the Arapahoes I knew, in the cemetery at St. Stephen's. It is a desolate place.

In death, Francis Sitting Eagle, his face streaked with sacred red paint, was sent off to the accompanying throb of drums played by members of the drum society to which he had belonged. On top of his coffin were his hat and shield drum. When the coffin was lowered into the grave and just before the earth covered that fine old gentleman, two fully packed suitcases were placed in the hole with him. Sitting Eagle, his friends knew, would need them on his journey west to the Great Mystery.

Upon hearing of this I was reminded that Goes In Lodge is also buried in that cemetery at St. Stephen's. At one time there was a wooden marker over his body. Today there is nothing. Most probably he still cradles in his arms the briar pipe given to the Arapahoes by the Honorable Cecil Baring of London, for Goes In Lodge was its custodian. Thinking of this reminds me of the last time I saw that dignified and remarkable old warrior.

It was spring 1931, the time when the buffalo grass begins to grow and the life that has been asleep during winter awakens to a renewed world.

I had ridden over from Owl Creek to visit with Goes In Lodge. It had been a hard winter for him and while he stood erect, and the expression of proud bemusement on his face remained unchanged, he was a sick man. This had been his eighty-eighth snow and it was to be his last.

We sat in his tipi, visited and smoked the holy pipe of friendship. Somehow, I knew we would not meet again and it was clear, as the sadnesses of life often are, that this was a thing he also knew.

As the day was giving way to night and the red glow of the setting sun spread wide over the hills of the Wind River country, we rose and walked outside his lodge. I stood beside him, not knowing what to say, uncertain whether anything could be said. When I looked into his glistening eyes, catching the slight twitching along his broad mouth, I could utter not a word.

"*Natchakaw, banee,* a long time ago, my brother, you must have been an Indian," he said, placing his index fingers together and moving them away from his body, using the sign which means "the same as."

The old man saw my face flush and the tears begin the trickle

that precedes a stream. He held me close, murmuring, "*Ethiti,
ethiti*. It is good. Travel well, Nee-hee-cha-ooth."

As I mounted my horse and prepared to make the journey back
across the mountains, Goes In Lodge held out his arm and
showed the open right hand of friendship.

Riding away from the old buffalo hunter's tipi for the last time,
looking but once over my shoulder, it seemed that this lone man,
his lone tipi and all that he represented would soon vanish from
the land in which he and the eagle had once soared.

I remembered his words in London, as we sat smoking the pipe
in his room and reminiscing of times gone by. I had just made
him a present of a photograph which showed him standing beside
Buffalo Bill. It had been taken in 1913. He stared at the picture
and, obviously moved, said: "When I was a young man, my
brother, I fought in many battles. The bullets went around me
but I was never wounded. I was strong and brave. But now, I am
getting old and my journey is almost over, while yours has just
begun.

"Pretty soon, High Eagle, I am going to die and go way off. I
will leave my moccasin prints across the sky, in what the white
man calls the Milky Way, where they will shine with those of all
the people who have traveled the trail to the Great Mystery.
When I cross that trail, I will be in the Happy Hunting Ground
and then I will sit down.

"You are a young man, my brother, and you are going to stay
here. Maybeso, a long time. And one day you, too, will be an old
man and then you will also cross that trail.

"Do not be afraid, for I will be there, waiting for you.

"All the time, I will be looking down that trail. Then, one day,
way off, I will see you coming. I will smile to myself and say,
'*Ahh-h*, it is my brother, Nee-hee-cha-ooth!'

"You will come closer and I will say, 'My brother is coming!'

"I will get on my horse, go out and hunt. When I find a fat
young buffalo, I will take my arrow and kill him, cut him up and
bring him in. I will make a good fire, take those big buffalo steaks
and put them on the coals. Then I will look up and see you are
there with me.

"We will hug and I shall say, 'Oh, my brother, it has been so lonely. But you are here now. Sit down!' You will sit here, I will sit there. We will take those fine buffalo steaks and eat until we are filled up to our throats.

"Then I will reach down, get my pipe, load it, smoke and give it to you. You will smoke the pipe and then we will put it away. We shall sit there together and have a good visit.

"Our hearts will be big and everything will be *ethiti* . . ."

So I have one more errand left in life, one more journey to take. I must travel back to Wind River, visit that cemetery and decorate with offerings of sweet grass the grave of that old buffalo hunter, my friend and brother to whom I owe so much.

Then my story, having started at the beginning, will be finished and I shall be satisfied, for the circle will have been completed.